Scarf Maven Ties One On

A humorous memoir
by *Terri Kane*

authorHOUSE®

AuthorHouse™
1663 Liberty Drive
Bloomington, IN 47403
www.authorhouse.com
Phone: 1 (800) 839-8640

Published by AuthorHouse   03/04/2015

ISBN: 978-1-4969-7269-9 (sc)
ISBN: 978-1-4969-7267-5 (e)

Print information available on the last page.

This book is printed on acid-free paper.

CONTENTS

RECIPES

ACKNOWLEDGEMENTS

I am sending a heartfelt *thank you* to the men and women of my writing group for your encouragement, suggestions and critiques. Here's a special shout-out to Susan, who has believed in me since our college days.

My husband, Mike, is the greatest order picker, shipping manager, receiving clerk, warehouse manager, export expert and scarf stylist a girl could have. Most of all, Mike is an amazing friend and life partner. We work hard, but we always manage to have fun with everything we do.

This memoir is drawn from my online vintage scarf business, with a sprinkling of other life experiences. The stories are real, though I've taken some liberties to keep the story flowing. The name of the online site where I do my selling has been changed in this story, and all customer names have been changed. Some events have been taken out of sequence. Some places have been changed, and a few storylines are consolidated.

PROLOGUE

I am in my living room watching cable news where political pundits are all talking at the same time. I am wearing a calf-length T-shirt printed with mugs of coffee lattes and frappes. I am ironing on a low-slung ironing board, sitting in my cappuccino-colored damask-covered easy chair. Oftentimes I sing Broadway show tunes while I iron: "There's no business like show business, like no business I know..." if I am feeling bold like Ethel Merman. Or "Where am I going, and what will I find? What's in this grab bag that I call my mind?" channeling Broadway legend Gwen Verdon, if I am melancholic.

Truth is, I am not a washerwoman or a Broadway hoofer, and I really don't mind the ironing. I am pressing a vibrant square silk scarf in mint condition with a design of blue roses by Adrienne Vittadini, vintage 1980's. I love the feel of the fluid fabric and note the crisp colors that only a good silk can hold. I think how, in addition to a beautiful neck scarf, this would make a stylish table topper for an elegant dinner party.

I look around and see dozens of cartons and plastic containers filled with hundreds of scarves, all needing to be sorted into categories: trash, fall, spring, holidays, chiffons, slightly damaged, and ready to be pressed. Ironing is only part of my work. I have built a successful business flipping scarves on VintageCartel.shop. I am a V-Cart Power Seller. I am a V-Cart Top-Rated Seller. I am Scarf Maven.

* 1 *

FRED AND BARNEY MUST GO

"Simplify, simplify." - Henry David Thoreau

It all started with Barbara Walters or, rather, her book *Audition: A Memoir.* I read the whole, long tome in just a few days. Then I put it up on our breakfast bar counter atop a stack of discarded books. I had been on a major reading bender the last few years, and our suburban Baltimore apartment was inundated with books of all stripes -- hardcover best-sellers, paperbacks, fiction, memoirs, thrillers. My husband, Mike, and I bought an extra bookcase for the office (our spare bedroom), but we quickly filled the shelves the same night we assembled the darn thing. I was ordering several books online every week or two, taking great care to make certain I didn't run out of reading material between orders. It wasn't a cheap habit, but a person could do worse.

"Pretty soon, we won't be able to see into the kitchen at all," Mike said, smirking, alluding to the stacks on the counter, most higher than eye level. I typically would reply with a snappy, sardonic comment, but nothing came to mind because I knew he was right. It was getting ridiculous. Was there any reason to keep the books? I very seldom re-read anything, and these weren't exactly reference books I needed to keep at hand.

I decided I would donate the books. It would be a library of contemporary literature, and I would find the perfect home for it. I envisioned a brass plaque affixed to a shelf: "Kane Library." Oh, no, really, I didn't want any attention. No plaque, thank you. But my inner philanthropist took over, and I sat a little taller in my chair while I made some calls to women's shelters and a few community centers. After a couple hours on the phone, I discovered, to my surprise, no one could use the books. I even offered to donate my library to the charity thrift shop but was told that, while they appreciated the offer, they didn't have the space. I couldn't even give the books away.

Perhaps it was time to learn how to sell on VintageCartel.shop. I had wanted to do this for some time. A year earlier, my mother died and my brothers and I had inherited all her china, crystal, silver and various household knick-knacks. We kept what we wanted and sold everything else to a china replacement company. While we walked away with a good-size check, I knew we could have made much more money selling the items one by one on V-Cart. But the technical aspects of setting up a payment account and uploading photos seemed daunting, and I didn't want to start a project that was sure to leave me frustrated and feeling inadequate. V-Cart intimidated me.

Mike was out shopping for a comforter at the Macy's big July 4th sale while hometown parades and heroes were featured on CNN. I picked up the Barbara Walters book, sat at my desk and set out to get this book listed for sale on V-Cart.

Surprisingly, I zipped right through the instructions. I set up V-Cart and Paypal (the banking system of V-Cart) accounts and listed the book in no time flat. Additionally, I learned that V-Cart has a media data-base so the photo of the book cover popped up on the listing automatically, allowing me to postpone the hurdle of learning to upload my own photos. Hallelujah! Barbara Walters was for sale!

I was on a mission. I brought a stack of books to my desk and listed each, researching every title to see what other V-Cart sellers were getting and charging a smidgen below that. My strategy was to sell my books under the "Buy-It-Now" (BIN) category rather than at auction like most of the other best-sellers, so the buyer could get it quicker. I didn't see the point of running an auction for seven days.

I continued listing books, and by the time Mike got home, had several pages of book listings. As I shared my progress with him, I got notice from V-Cart that Barbara's book had sold! The first book listed was the first book sold (it was still on the best-seller lists), and *voila!* We had money in our new Paypal account. It was all very exciting.

Even V-Cart acknowledged my genius with their memo:

Your V-Cart item sold! AUDITION: A MEMOIR by Barbara Walters

You did it! Your item sold. You agreed to ship this item to the buyer within 1 business day(s). Please promptly ship the item and follow the guidelines below to ensure buyer satisfaction.

This was a great incentive to continue the listing streak. And now that Mike was back, we could work faster. He dictated the info as I typed. We worked well together, which was a key to the success of our sales and marketing business that had sustained us for two decades. Next book in hand, he recited the title, author, date of publication, and edition. Mike passed the book to me, and I noted the condition (*bought new, read once, clean hands!*), adding a little blurb from the dust jacket to pique interest.

Sometimes I put in my own two cents: *Well written and quite entertaining. Very enjoyable – couldn't put it down! That Barbara was some femme fatale!* I used large, colorful type for the title and ended all listings with *Enjoy!* Since so many people were selling these books, my listings had to pop.

After the first few, I had developed a template for all book sales, and we were moving quickly. We had a load of fresh vegetables from the farmer's market in the refrigerator and had planned to make a big, healthy dinner. But now, nothing could stop us from our task. We had subs and fries delivered (so much for healthy, though I do get points for intent).

That evening, we sold two more books and marveled at how uncomplicated this really was. We felt like dummies for not tackling it sooner. Even uploading my own photo, when the book was not in the database, had proven to be within my ken. We were fueled by the adrenaline rush of success, and there was no way we could go to sleep anytime soon. We worked late into the night, listing... listing... listing.

When the Diet Mountain Dew and Diet Dr. Pepper (and okay, maybe a few Girl Scout cookies) could keep us alert no longer, we went to bed. I dreamt I was scanning a book cover. The next morning, we slept late and awakened to the notifications of several more sales. It was as if the tooth fairy had visited during the night and left money. Selling things while we were sleeping? Priceless.

We wrapped each book sold in pristine, white dollar-store tissue paper, sealed with a colorful "Thank You" sticker I made on the computer. Mike packed the books in padded envelopes and went to the post office where he got an extended lesson on the rules for getting the discounted Media Mail rate.

After every book in the apartment had been listed -- we kept a few, but no more than could fit on two bookshelves -- we looked around to see what else we could sell. Anything could go. We were addicted, always checking "My V-Cart" (our customized home page) looking over our sales, messages and Feedback. I felt like a stock market day trader constantly watching the big board. At least the stock market offers some relief; it closes daily at 4 PM and is closed on weekends and holidays. But V-Cart is the New York, New York of cyberspace, the site that never sleeps.

————

I subscribed to a half-dozen magazines and every one of them seemed to feature stories about simplifying your life: "Rid Yourself of Excess Clutter!" "Simplify Your Space!" "Ten Steps to De-Cluttering Your Home *(and your mind!)*" – more encouragement to purge anything I didn't love or need.

A woman of a certain age, I read, should lighten her load presumably after learning that *things* aren't really all that important. Losing the clutter in your home can lead to de-cluttering your thoughts, I learned, reducing stress and helping you to focus on the important things in life. Oh, how I wanted to become less stressed and more focused (not to mention more on-trend)! Focusing could allow me to keep my desk clean and well organized, and that could extend to my computer files, too, and perhaps my jewelry box. I wanted to see some blank spaces not only on my bookshelves, but in my closet, drawers and cabinets. I had no recollection of the color of the carpet in the bedroom walk-in closet. Did we even have carpet in there? Simplify my life? Count me in.

My first task: Cancel all my magazine subscriptions.

In *Walden*, Henry David Thoreau said, "I went to the woods because I wished to live deliberately, to front only the essential facts of life, and see if I could not learn what it had to teach, and not, when I came to die, discover that I had not lived."

A worthy sentiment – "to front only the essential facts of life." But really, what was this living in the woods business? I do not like mosquitoes or the heat, and I have a real fear of snakes. I have an affinity for 600-thread-count sheets, strong air conditioning and dinner in a nice restaurant with linen tablecloths and napkins and a waiter with a crumb-sweeper. Yet, I could identify with Thoreau's quest.

Maybe I wouldn't realistically be able to make a commitment to live off the land or take up yoga, as "women who simplified" had done.

I had no plans to wake up at sunrise to clear my head with a long run (or even a walk), and no feng shui for me, either. The de-cluttering of my mind could wait.

—————

Mike and I traveled quite a bit when we started our sales and marketing company. Newlywed business partners, we didn't know (or care) where the line was between work and play, as every trip included business to some extent, and every trip was fun and entertaining. I would sometimes tease Mike that, while I worked hard acting like a sophisticated traveler eschewing the tourist traps and rip-offs as much as possible, my husband seemed to pride himself on the neon light on his forehead flashing "Tourist! Tourist! Tourist!"

When we had business in Toronto, we flew from our then-home, Charlotte, to Buffalo on a super-discount fare of $19 each way on the old People Express Airlines. There we rented a car and drove into Toronto, in just under two hours. The highway goes along the town of Niagara and on our first trip, we had to stop and see Niagara Falls. It was a very hot day, with busloads of tourists picnicking on the grassy banks. We parked and took a quick look at the falls (from the Canadian side).

"Don't even think about it," I said, using my clairvoyance skills.

"What? What are you talking about?"

"I know *you*," I said, "and you're probably thinking you'd like us to get on one of those little blow-up rafts and have a thrill ride."

"Oh, no way! My luck, I'd fall off the side and be gone forever."

Surprised at his response, I was relieved I had put this to rest. I wasn't about to go on any "Maid of the Mist" boat ride or out on the slippery observation bridges wearing a tacky yellow plastic souvenir poncho under the spray of the falls. I could see the show perfectly well from the cheap (and safe) seats.

As an alternative, we had our photo taken through a template that made our heads seem to pop out of the barrel while we careened to our certain death. My husband loves this picture, and we still have it framed in our living room.

After experiencing the hoop-la over the falls, albeit from a distance, my husband said, "Now, let's hit the stores!"

"Do they have a mall here?" He had my attention. Our dollar was very strong then, and visions of upscale shops (and shopping bags) danced in my head.

"No – no mall," Mike said. "I'm talking about the little village."

Hmmmm…. It was clear now. Mike wanted to cruise the tourist shops, and I reluctantly agreed. When we finally found a parking spot (far away from the action), we hiked up one side of the main drag and down the other, my husband insisting on going into every souvenir shop. The places were packed like sardines in a can, and I was huffing and puffing (and pouting).

I had seen these places before – other towns, other names, but the same type tourist joints. Some featured sugar in all its glorious manifests: Salt water taffy, little ice cream balls and low-fat frozen yogurt. Pretty girls on the sidewalk carried trays with samples of Canadian maple candy and ushered spenders into a nearby shop. A heavenly aroma wafted out the door, and through the windows we could see jugs, cans and bottles of real maple syrup in all sizes, from a three inch high Canadiana bottle for just a taste, to a large tin can with spout that probably cost at least a week's pay. The sap was moving in Niagara.

Also moving fast were the delectable maple sugar candies folks had sampled outside, available in several sizes of gift boxes and tins. Most popular were the individual cellophane packages with a two-bite piece in the shape of Canada's maple leaf. People were clamoring for souvenirs, grabbing three of this and five of that.

A store devoted entirely to fudge made on the premises "like your grandma used to make" promised every flavor from the glorious (Kahlua Fudge) to the ridiculous (Watermelon Fudge). I don't remember either of my grandmothers making any kind of fudge at all.

In addition to the fragrant sweet shops, we passed by the requisite wax museum and Ripley's, currency exchanges and game arcades. Stores with every kind of souvenir (most made in China), T-Shirt shops and sunglass shacks were in abundance, all with a *Bienvenue!* maple leaf flag over their thresholds.

In a ceramics and glass shop with mugs, shot glasses and snow globes of the falls, Mike's eyes fell upon something in the corner. "Terri!" Mike said, a bit too loudly. "Do you see who I see?"

"Who, Mike?" I didn't care for the guessing game.

"It's Fred!"

"Fred Berger?" I thought Mike's old friend from Charlotte was in Niagara. I instinctively reached for my lipstick, wanting to look my best when word got back to Charlotte that Fred had seen us. Mike didn't answer and I realized he was already at the far side of the room. I followed.

"Terri, hurry!" Mike was waving me over, but I couldn't move fast because the aisles were crowded.

"Is Fred Berger here?" I asked again, getting nearer.

"No!" Mike said. "What would *he* be doing here?" I didn't know another Fred.

"Look who it is," Mike said, making a grand presentation gesture towards Fred Flintstone. It wasn't the *real* [cartoon] Fred, but a ceramic statuette capturing his essence. Mike was smitten.

"We're getting this," he said. "We need some artwork for our new house."

"You've got to be kidding," but I knew he wasn't.

You'd have thought an eight-year-old Mike had found gold in them thar hills; that's how enthralled he was with this big, hollow, ceramic Fred Flintstone. Mike squeezed and shoved his way through the shoppers to the counter and asked a salesclerk about Barney.

"If there's a Fred," Mike reasoned, "there has to be a Barney Rubble, too." But there was no Barney in stock.

"Usually we do have one," the clerk said. After Mike's interrogation, she couldn't think of any other stores along the strip that would carry Fred and Barney. No, these Flintstones ceramics were exclusive. *Exclusive?* I had just one burning question: What was Fred doing in a Niagara Falls souvenir shop?

I was pondering my next point, but my husband had already picked up the great piece of art and was in line at the cash register. Huh! How many art galleries have their patrons stand in line at a cash register to pay for their masterpiece, I wondered.

Because of all the people milling about, and the "Fred" situation, which had people staring at us, I told Mike I would wait for him outside. He was number twelve in line, so I knew it might be a while. I spied a white bench about a block away and started walking toward it. By the time I got there, though, a party of three with ice cream cones and a half dozen shopping bags had plopped down for a respite. I went back to the store and stood outside, waiting.

"Ma'am, do you need a ride?" a man asked from the window of a car slowed by traffic.

"No, thank you," I said, thinking the Canadians were awfully friendly. But then, I noticed the man was gawking at me, even though the car had moved a half block.

"You're awfully pretty!" he called out before the light changed and the car took off. This was probably the last cat call I ever got, and I wondered if that man thought I was a street-walker. No, I was a street-*stander*, waiting for my husband to exit the store with his new male friend, Fred.

I was studying the day-trippers traipse in and out of the fudge shop across the street, every one of them carrying a wax paper bag of "homemade"-in-a-shop confections. I hoped they didn't purchase watermelon. I felt a hand on my shoulder, and I jerked around.

"I'm here," Mike said.

We toted Fred back to the rental car with us. In my nagging, irritating voice, I asked, "How do you intend to get that on the plane going home?"

"I'll get it on the plane, don't worry." Before 9-11, you could do that. Mike had a proven track record of sweet-talking (and tipping) the sky caps into letting us check extra luggage or cartons at no charge.

During the week of our Toronto stay, Fred stood on the back seat of the rental car, buckled into the seat belt. It gave Mike great joy seeing Fred's constant smile waiting for us after our business meetings. He would ask Fred's opinion on important issues like where we should go to dinner or where to find the best deals on codeine cough syrup and Tylenol with codeine. (Canada has many over-the-counter drugs that are prescriptions here, so we always made a medication stop.)

We got home and Mike put Fred in a place of honor overlooking our office. When we had company, he was sure to introduce our guests to Fred and explain our lack of Barney.

Several months later, Mike was unable to go to Toronto for one of our appointments, so I took my mother along for company. My parents had honeymooned at Niagara Falls, so I included a return visit for her. (The falls endured, though my parents' marriage didn't.) Mike did not mention Barney, and I didn't tell him we were doing any shopping in Niagara. Mama and I took a quick peek at the falls, partially frozen from the early March Arctic blast. The view looked like a picture postcard, a tranquil, twinkling fairytown.

The enchantment wore off as we headed over to the tourist area where Mike had adopted Fred. But I *had* to see if there was a Barney in stock. Sure enough, my eyes went right to it when I walked into the shop. We left Niagara with the big ceramic best friend in tow.

Fred and Barney – together at last. Mike proclaimed it the best gift I ever gave him, and set him right beside his bosom buddy Fred. From then on, guests were told the joyous story of the reunion.

When we moved to Baltimore, we hauled the duo with us, but c'mon…. It's only cute for so long. I cautiously mentioned to Mike that while we were paring down our belongings, we could possibly, perhaps sell Fred and Barney on V-Cart. I was sure we could find a nice home for the pair, maybe in a child's room. To my surprise, Mike agreed. And so it was decided: Fred and Barney must go.

Fred Flintstone & Barney Rubble - Minimum Bid: $15 USD

Up for auction are Fred and Barney ceramic figurines. Each has a coin slit in the back of the head so it can be used as a bank, but you'd have to bust it to get the money out. Sold only as a set. (You wouldn't want to separate these Best Buds.)

Fred is 18" high & 9" at widest point. Barney is 16-1/2" high and 8-3/4" wide.

No chips or fractures. Excellent condition.

Bottom has no imprint, name or etching at all. We put green felt tabs on the bottom to protect our bookshelf.

Freight is $12.99 for domestic USPS. This includes packing material, insurance and delivery receipt.

Smoke-free and pet-free home.

Please send payment through Pay Pal within five days of winning bid.

Sold for $27 plus shipping to the gentleman in Michigan! *Au revoir ma petit* Fred and Barney.

We were on a roll. If it wasn't nailed down, its days in our apartment were numbered. We quickly photographed the items and inserted the pictures into listings. We were no Ansel Adams, but we got the job done. One night, we were relaxing, watching an episode of *Law & Order*. While Detective Benson was interrogating the perp, Mike was plotting to sell our Broadway show posters, souvenirs of the shows we had seen, which were now hanging in the office.

"Sure," I said. "We'll put them up and see what happens." Since we had no idea of the value of the posters, we sold them auction-style. Sales were brisk, with the *Fiddler on the Roof* poster garnering the highest price at auction ("If I Were A Rich Man," indeed!) and *Rent* pulling in the lowest.

And it didn't stop with show posters. While caramelizing onions for our favorite Salisbury steak dinner, Mike was surveying the kitchen cabinets. "What are these things?" he asked, holding up one of a set of four antique Majolica coffee cups. "Can we get rid of them?"

"Absolutely not!"

"Okay, okay, just asking." He put the cup back in the exact top shelf spot where it had been for years, shut the cabinet door and added minced garlic to the onions. But while we were keeping the coffee cups, we had sold several pieces of like-new Cuisinart stainless steel pots from a set we received as a wedding gift. We sold several miscellaneous pieces of Fire King mixing bowls, Jadeite bowls, and a red hobnail glass pitcher. We were constantly on the lookout for things we didn't need.

"What is this, anyway?" Mike asked about a rounded, stainless steel container with a penguin etching and a lid with a knob on top. My grandmother had it in her kitchen and it always had cookies in it. Usually the cookies were homemade, though you might find Oreos or vanilla wafers once in a while. Mama and I thought the penguin signified it was really an old ice bucket, but cookies were fine with us. It was always my intent to have the "penguin" on my counter holding cookies, but I didn't have the room, and we sure didn't need the cookies anyway. No, the penguin wasn't going anywhere.

Everyone who sews has some quantity of fabric stored away, intended for future use, and I was no exception. In my earlier years, I designed and made many of my clothes, including my wedding dress. I also designed and made costumes for local and regional theatre productions. The fact that I had not sewn a garment in at least fifteen years didn't mean that I wouldn't get back to it soon. However, a betting person might note the last time I sewed a replacement button on one of Mike's shirts, I hemmed and hawed and agitated myself. Even with my reading glasses, I couldn't see the hole in the needle to thread.

I would eventually come to terms with my overstock of clothing and list it all on V-Cart, but in the meantime, I had a stack of fabric in plastic bags on the floor of Mike's closet. That burgundy linen would have made a nice unstructured jacket. I can just see a great flowy skirt cut from the slate gray textured cotton. I meant to use the plum cotton as a quilt backing - it's such a pretty color. The sage green cotton would work, too, and I bought it at a great price. Maybe I would make quilts and clothes in my future, and maybe I wouldn't, but I listed the fabric lots on V-Cart and all of them sold immediately. I even unloaded a few bundles of notions like snaps, hem tape, random zippers and buttons, a seam ripper, fabric chalk, ribbons and several packets of assorted pins and needles. I learned that sewers and crafters love scavaging online. Honestly, people will buy anything!

Except our old cassette tapes. We spent hours listing our gems at low prices: Madonna, Kool and the Gang, Blondie, Bruce Springsteen and Billy Joel would be exiting – or so we thought. They were a bust. We didn't sell a single one. Once we started reading the V-Cart discussion boards and learned about others' experiences as sellers, we had a clearer idea of hot items and duds. I was glad we hadn't spent days listing our hundreds of old records; LPs are hard to sell unless they're new and sealed or rare.

"Maybe you'll sell the china from your grandmother," Mike said.

"My Depression glass? That's not china, it's glass. And it's staying."

"Okay, okay, it was just an idea."

I had told Mike the story about Depression glass more than once. But I reminded him again that this tabletop-ware was special to me. My grandparents owned a small grocery store during the Depression, and the vendors used the glassware as sales bonuses. There could have been a dinner plate concealed in a large sack of flour, or a serving bowl could be found in a large container of powdered detergent. (This wouldn't wash with the health department today.) Their little store was a good business until the store was sold when my grandfather died and my father had no interest in taking over. There probably wouldn't have been a profitable future for the little country store, with the proliferation of 7-Eleven and other convenience stores on every corner. But I always loved the pink pieces and enjoyed hearing my grandmother tell me shopkeeper stories.

I remember when my grandmother hosted big family dinners on her large, shaded screen porch. At one end of the porch, nearest the front door, there were wrought-iron chairs, rockers and side tables as well as a porch swing. At the other end, closest to her flower garden, was a long dining table and chairs and her Depression glass would be on the table in all its pink glory. Her dinners, usually once a month or so on Sunday afternoon, were legendary. My aunts, uncles and cousins who lived in town were usually there, and my father was there with his wife and second batch of kids.

We lived next door to my grandmother, and even though my mother was still very close with her former mother-in-law, Mama did not come to the dinners. I always felt bad leaving her home alone, although in retrospect, I imagine she quite enjoyed the time. Grandmama wrapped up a plate of goodies for me to take back home or sometimes, after everyone left, Mama would drop by and graze the leftovers.

Sometimes our distant cousin Becky, who lived in the mountains a couple hours' drive from Charlotte, would come for a day trip with her son, Max, and her mother, my Aunt Edna. I always liked Becky because she danced to her own tune. I never knew what happened to her husband, or if she ever had one, but she was a woman ahead of her time. She grew her own organic vegetables and canned enough to last through a snowy winter. Becky, herself, dug out a root cellar where she kept her bounty. Once or twice a year, Mama and I would take Grandmama and drive "up the mountain" to visit Becky, Edna and Max, who lived in a cozy house with a wood-burning stove. Becky even chopped wood with an axe on a tree stump. Back in the 70's, many families in Appalachia were living in extreme poverty. Becky had first-hand knowledge of this because she was a traveling nurse who visited these forgotten people and attended to basic services. She was instrumental bringing their plight to the attention of whoever-you-bring-these-things-to-the-attention-of, and Appalachia was in the spotlight. People were shocked about this poverty "right here in America." Soon, the Feds were sending in cheese, milk and flour to thousands of families. I admired Becky.

Other relatives and "nearly" relatives joined us from time to time. It seemed to me they just popped in, but I'm sure Grandmama had some clue they were coming. If a small busload of people ended up at her front door, there would always be enough food.

Before we were called to the table, the older children brought around the pink glass platter, stacked high with mini sandwiches of date nut bread and cherry-cream cheese filling or maybe pimento cheese sandwiches on Roman Meal bread. Grandmama would cut off the crusts and then cut the sandwiches into triangles. There was always sweet tea in the pink footed tall glasses, and we sipped and snacked for an hour or so until the ladyfolk brought out the meal.

"What do you put in your pot roast that makes it so good?" someone always asked.

"Oh, just a little bit of this and a little bit of that," Grandmama would answer modestly, never giving away any clues. When she died, most of her specialties died with her, but the dishes on which they were served passed down to me.

I added to my glass collection a piece or two at a time when Mike and I would make sales trips by car all over the South, stopping at antique malls along the way. I found some real bargains on the road, but once people learned the worth of their collectibles, through V-Cart and other emerging websites, it became uncommon to see a real deal.

One of my purchases during our traveling years was a set of old billiard balls, which I bought for $20. One ball was missing, but the set was in the original box and called my name from a higher shelf in an antique mall booth. I had no interest in playing pool, but I thought the old wooden balls in a basket or rustic clay bowl on my coffee table would make an interesting conversation piece. They went straight into the back of the linen closet when we got home, and a few years later when we moved, they went straight into the back of a smaller linen closet in our Baltimore apartment. The pool balls must go, I decided. After doing some research online, I learned these pool balls were not wood, but Bakelite – a highly collectible, early form of plastic. I listed the incomplete set for auction, and unloaded them to the winner – possibly for *her* linen closet – for $92.50. Not bad for a $20 investment and years of closet space.

I sold my dozen or so pieces of McCoy pottery – little cachepot planters in green, ivory, and peach, which collected dust on my living room shelves. I never planted anything in them -- I didn't want to get them dirty. Oh, and I didn't do houseplants anyway because I got too frustrated carrying dead plants out to the garbage. I didn't even particularly like the planters (too folksy), but Martha Stewart was gung-ho on McCoy. I was the happy young housewife and if Martha collected it, I collected it, too. The planters all sold fairly quickly at auction.

But one day, I got a nasty note from a woman whose V-Cart name was Tabithaa722. She had just received her ivory McCoy planter and accused me of selling a reproduction and calling it "authentic." She said I should be ashamed of myself. I quickly refunded Tabithaa722's money and wrote a note back to her apologizing and proclaiming my innocence. She responded nicely, with some pointers on how to spot fakes, and I took this to heart, along with my own research, and determined that my other McCoy pieces for sale were in fact real. Tabithaa722 praised me for my quick action as a seller, and left good Feedback.

Years ago, my mother-in-law gave me several large Fitz & Floyd bunny figurines and a bunny cookie jar. She had redecorated her breakfast nook and apparently it was no longer a bunny-friendly environment. She said the white, pink and blue pieces would look great in *my* white, peach and green kitchen, so she magnanimously insisted I have them. This was not something I would have acquired for myself. I have an acute allergic reaction to "cute" and further, I do not care for *tchotchkes* just sitting around. It's different with my Depression glass, not merely decorative and not even on display. It's *working* tableware, as it mixes and matches with my wedding china. But the bunnies were something else. As a dutiful daughter-in-law, I felt I couldn't refuse her gift, so I kept the stupid bunnies on the shelf of a kitchen étagère. But when Mike's mom passed away, I decided it was time to pass away those bunnies, too.

I couldn't find any pricing info on the Fitz & Floyd bunnies, so I put the four pieces up for auction. At the end of the 7-day auction period, only one sold. I had started the bidding at $15 (including shipping) and after 8 bids, the 12" long bunny with a butterfly on its back went for $34.50. Mike and I packed it carefully, with nearly a whole box of bubble wrap, lots of tissue paper and miles of packing tape. We double-boxed it, just like the experts recommend, leaving a few inches space between boxes, filled with peanuts and marked it FRAGILE on all four sides of the carton. There was no way that comely cottontail was going to break in shipment.

It broke in shipment. We had to refund the money to the customer; meanwhile, we were out nearly $12 in postage. Buying postal insurance for a fragile item is tricky. Proving the package was packed the correct way isn't an easy task; you have to get full cooperation from the package recipient, because it's their responsibility to fill out forms and file the claim with the post office. The insurance isn't cheap, and since most of our items are low-ticket, we decided we could be self-insured.

I let the bunny cookie jar listing renew for another week. It was large, with a mama bunny and several babies on the top and ceramic ribbons cascading down the sides, and it sold at auction for $68. The woman who bought it, Miss Dottie, wrote a long note to me when she paid, saying she was very happy to find this piece. She hailed from Eufala, Oklahoma, and still lived in the same house where she was born. Miss Dottie told me this bunny filled a gap in her cookie jar collection. "I have most every other kind of animal," she wrote, "but not a bunny rabbit." Her late husband had built a high shelf in her kitchen, living room and dining room to house her three hundred cookie jars, lined up, side-by-side. Oh, Miss Dottie thought this bunny was so pretty and told me her grandchildren would love it. She would bake cookies to put in it and leave it on the counter for a while, until she found a permanent spot on the shelf for it. She reminded me to double-box and wrap it thoroughly to prevent breakage. We knew the drill. Oklahoma, OK.

I felt her message begged for a chatty response. I wrote and told her I understood her love of cookie jars, and my assortment of Depression glass included a cookie jar -- my one and only-ever cookie jar (since the Penguin was officially an ice bucket). I told her I bet her collection looked beautiful on the high shelf lining her rooms and how fortunate that her late husband had taken an interest in showcasing her collection. Truth was, I thought this décor sounded absolutely hideous and anyone with over three hundred cookie jars needs to have her bread box examined. I was thinking she should've given the cookie jars to needy children (those without a grandma), perhaps filling them first with thumbprint and icebox cookies, but I kept my righteous opinion to myself. I cheerily suggested she make carrot cake cookies to put in the bunny cookie jar for the grandkids and told her I would send my Grandmama's recipe with the package. (This was one recipe I managed to snag.)

GRANDMAMA'S DIVINE CARROT CAKE COOKIES

Ingredients
- 6 tablespoons butter, softened (please use real butter)
- 3/4 cup packed brown sugar
- 1 egg
- 1/2 teaspoon vanilla extract
- 1-1/2 cups all-purpose flour
- 1 teaspoon baking powder
- 1/4 teaspoon each baking soda
- 1/4 teaspoon salt
- 1/4 teaspoon ground cinnamon
- 1 cup grated carrots
- 1 tablespoon finely-grated fresh ginger (my secret ingredient – I'm quite sure my grandmother never put fresh ginger in anything she cooked) - *optional*
- 1/2 cup raisins
- 1/2 cup chopped pecans (or walnuts)

Directions
- In a bowl, cream butter and brown sugar with an electric mixer. Add egg and vanilla, mix well. In another bowl, combine the flour, baking powder, baking soda, salt and cinnamon.
- Add the dry ingredients to the creamed mixture a little at a time until blended. Hand stir in carrots, raisins, pecans and ginger (if you choose to add it).
- Drop a rounded tablespoonful on a baking sheet lightly sprayed with Pam or rubbed with butter.
- Bake at 325° for 12-15 minutes or until edges are lightly browned. Cool for 2 minutes on pan, then with a spatula, move from pan to wire rack for complete cooling.
- Yield: About 24 cookies.

NOTE: *These are excellent as sandwich cookies filled with either ice cream or cream cheese frosting!*

We probably used ten pounds of packing material on that cookie jar. We tissue-papered every ribbon, bunny ear and protrusions, and used enough bubble wrap for the bunny to do the moon bounce. Packed in styrofoam peanuts and double-boxed in a large carton, we mailed it out to the tune of $19. We felt sure this one wasn't going to break – but it did. Miss Dottie wrote us an aggravated message saying the mama bunny ears were both broken off, as were most of the ribbon pieces.

"Really, it's just all in pieces," she wrote, "so much so that I can't even glue it back together." Her message elaborated on how she had looked forward to receiving it and then how disappointing it was to open the package and see the casualty. Dottie felt bad for the bunny, she said, tragically losing parts (hope she scheduled that head exam). She didn't even acknowledge the recipe; guess there is no point in making carrot cake cookies if one doesn't have a bunny cookie jar to put them in. I refunded her money, and Mike and I vowed not to sell anything breakable ever again. Meanwhile, I was down two bunnies, with two still left on my étagère.

Our stuff was flying out the door and we were starting to see some blank spaces around the apartment, in our closet, in the kitchen cabinets and on the bookshelves. Of course, a few things came *in* the door from time to time. I had discovered V-Cart's bounty! The selling site was originally meant for vintage items but had evolved into a global marketplace for both old and new items. Most anything you can imagine resides there and can reside *here* for a song and some quick fingers. I imagined many things, and they arrived at my door in three to five days.

Selling books was taking time away from reading books. But I was buying all my books on V-Cart, too -- used when possible -- with new releases usually discounted greater than the online booksellers. My plan was to read the book and then immediately list it for sale. It became a game to see how fast I could flip it -- and whether I could recover my initial investment. I probably broke even.

It wasn't just the books on V-Cart that grabbed my attention. My favorite cosmetics were discounted, and so were my shampoo, body wash and moisturizing cream. I bought a brand new pair of Hush Puppies at a super discount. An online clothing store I favored worked with small businesses that auctioned overstocks and customer returns on V-Cart at big discounts. I bought a couple of things. Mike discovered "unauthorized" toner cartridges for our laser printer. He also found out that using these refilled cartridges voided the printer's warranty. But we were saving quite a bit of money (as long as we could avoid the need for tech support from the manufacturer for the life of the printer).

I was a tourist in a new world, and there was plenty of sightseeing: I discovered Pinheiro pottery from Portugal and bought a vintage set of peach-colored salad plates. A month or so later, I found the same plates in a medium green and I bought a few. Someday, I intend to go to the Rafael Bordallo Pinheiro museum and factory in Lisbon (though I bet V-Cart has the pottery for less).

VintageCartel.shop was great entertainment, too, even when I didn't buy. I found a stunning vintage pair of Judith Ripka 18K gold and sapphire earrings for $19,200 "or best offer" (Mike suggested we offer $100). I loved perusing the Hermés Birkin handbags, some selling for upwards of $60,000, and a plain black leather Birkin bag could be had for only $24,000. (If you were really strapped for money, there was a gently used Birkin for $7,200.) But these were the places where you know not to touch the merchandise and just enjoy the views. With a little browsing (okay, hours and hours and hours of early morning surfing), I found the side street, hole-in-the-wall vendors with interesting items at prices I could afford, minus the Ripka or Birkin labels.

I discovered a V-Cart store with very inexpensive sterling silver and gemstone jewelry. I bought earrings and bracelets directly from V-Cart shops in China, Thailand and India and couldn't believe it arrived in my mailbox just a few weeks later. My jewelry cache quickly overflowed.

This was a land of exotic riches; the weather was always comfortable, the natives were (usually) friendly, and if we didn't understand the language, the message was automatically translated. One vendor from Zhejiang Yiwu sent out a notice advising when businesses in China would close for New Year's:

Dear every reverent and great buyers,

As our Spring Festival Holiday in China, we will have a rest during Jan.24-Feb. 10, but you still can bid and purchase our cute and wonderful items,Maybe we are delay respond your message, and only be able to send your items after Feb. 15, so sorry about any inconvenience and hope you can be so kindly to comprise us.Thank you SO SO SO much^_^

Warmest regards to Northern Hemisphere, coolest regards to Southern Hemisphere!

Best wishes from China.

The sellers in China I dealt with were always accommodating. After a purchase from another vendor, I received this message:

Welcome the store that you arrive at me!I sell a picture up this beautiful item now, your seeing it is such special with beauty, if you like it, don't miss it, biding to own it now!I will promise after provide the service of the superior quality with sell for you, is the shopping store that you have a satisfaction!

Probable translation: They were happy to have me as a customer.

It was the summer of love, adventure, travel, and delight. It was the summer of V-Cart.

* 2 *

BLACK IS SO SLIMMING

"Inside some of us is a thin person struggling to get out, but they can usually be sedated with a few pieces of chocolate cake." -- Author Unknown

I've always lived in denial, at least about certain things. Actually, "certain things" is not accurate, because it's just one *particular* thing. My weight – rather, my *over*-weight-ness. My heft. My amplitude. My problem.

Denial is a homey, comfortable place, and there's nowhere else I'd rather be most of the time. In my mind's eye, I can look like Nigella or maybe Barbie and be happy and content. It's fitting that when I was a young child, my favorite game was *pretend like* (which I thought for years was called "tin-like") and *Oh! Doo-dah-daze!* I could be anyone or go anywhere I wanted.

There was a large part of lightening my load that needed to be done (other than the obvious); Mike and I had the "simplify" momentum in full swing, and there was no reason for further procrastination. It was time to put both feet on the ground, or at least the carpeted floor, and face the facts. I was ready to tackle selling some of my clothes.

Since that first book sale on V-Cart, I had been thinking that perhaps, possibly, I could get rid of some of my clothes. Several years ago, I gave a trunk-full (that's a *car* trunk) of career-wear to a charity to clothe women re-entering the work force, but it didn't make a dent in my closet. And it was heavenly when, several years ago, I lost a substantial amount of weight and on the way down the scale revisited favorite outfits from the past. As my basic items became too big, I bought more clothes; they were sure to take up less room in the new smaller sizes. I bought mostly inexpensive tops and pants and referred to them as *disposable*, getting what I loved in two or three sizes, so it would always fit. I've been able to justify hanging on to this wardrobe for the same reason as so many women: I would lose and gain over the years, and I'd never have "nothing to wear."

Since I worked from home, I didn't need much, but seasons and styles don't always cooperate. I couldn't very well wear a suede coat in the spring or a gauze skirt in January. I will admit to wearing a lightweight white linen blouse I loved on a cold November evening when we went out to dinner. I wore it defiantly, *because I could*. I had lost the weight, and it fit. Rules be damned, I loved it, and it wasn't nearly as negligent as wearing white shoes after Labor Day or wearing matching lipstick and nail polish. That night, I fell on the way out of the restaurant and found myself face down on the sidewalk. I was checking limbs and digits (and my face!) to see if there were any real injuries. It felt like ten minutes went by, but I know it was only seconds when a stranger came up to me and asked if I needed any help. *Who, me? No, I didn't need any help, thank you.* Then, I realized Mike was just standing at attention, like a zombie.

"Mike? Mike! Can you help me?"

"Oh, yes, of course. What do you want me to do?" I think I mumbled something sarcastic, and then stood up with my husband's help. I noticed a little blood on the sidewalk and blood on the arm of my rebellious blouse. I would be forced to toss it (even though it fit!).

On the way back to the car, I was tending to my bloody elbow with a small Kleenex, while giving Mike hell for not rushing to help me.

"I was sort of stunned. I didn't know what to do," he said.

"Well, I'll tell you: In case it ever happens again, rush over to see if I am dead or alive, okay?"

Mike was feeling truly embarrassed some stranger had come to my aid. He reached for my hand and mumbled, "Now I know."

"Now you know."

My (probably) well-meaning mother-in-law once said to me, "When you stay the same size year-in and year-out, you never have to buy new clothes." Did she think *not buying* new clothes was a big attraction? She had been a size 4 petite all her adult life and proudly mentioned a classic Burberry raincoat she still wore after forty years. Good for *her*. However, I had been in the family for over a decade and had yet to see the Burberry.

So on that rainy Sunday, I decided it was time for a merciless pruning of my wardrobe. Mike insisted tackling the armoire would be an easy start. True: It wasn't as much of a mystery to me as the closet, because I rummaged in it several times a week. First, we designated areas on the bed: Keeping, listing, and tossing. Then we opened the first of two small drawers toward the bottom of the stately antique.

Swimsuits and cover-ups were covered up in the bottom drawer that had not been opened in ages (but I knew where they were if we needed them). The suits had not seen the light of day since we were on the beach in Venezuela (back when it was safe to go to Venezuela), and I pointed out the topless sunbathers to Mike. But unfortunately, he left his glasses behind in our hotel room and was unable to see any action.

I fought for keeping the beachwear. Who knew when we might go to Cannes or the Seychelles or even Myrtle Beach? We might need these things someday soon, I said, though I knew the truth was, even if I found myself going to one of those beaches, I wouldn't find myself in a swimsuit. That's where my stylish cover-ups would be handy (if they happened to fit at the time), and Mike's trunks and cover-up shirts were timeless. Besides, I couldn't cozy up to a store that would allow me to sell used swimsuits, even though V-Cart allows it. That holds for other semi-unsavory items like used makeup and skincare products -- hard to imagine ordering a half-used bottle of lavender-scented body soap. (V-Cart's official policy is that used cosmetics are allowed only if the applicator has not come in contact with the body.)

We left the swimwear drawer intact.

I opened and slammed shut the next drawer. No, I couldn't face this right now. Workout clothes – sports bras, yoga pants and long tanks. I knew that if I'd opened this drawer more often, I might be able to wear the stuff in the first drawer!

The folded items on the shelves were nice and neat, and as Mike pulled out things one-by-one, I nixed getting rid of almost everything.

"Please put it right back where it was," I said firmly.

"When was the last time you wore this?" Mike asked.

"I'm going to wear it as soon as it fits," I said, as if it were imminent. My kind and wonderful husband didn't ask me exactly when (or how) that might happen.

We moved on to Mike's sweaters, which sat in several stacks on the top shelf. Many had not been worn since Alexander Julian was a major men's designer. Gray, blue, red and even mauve (yes, mauve! Julian's line *was* called "Colours" after all and mauve was sure a color) were in Mike's stack. As long as we've been married, I have been the one picking out Mike's wardrobe. My husband says he doesn't care about clothes or how he looks, but he did enjoy the compliments he received when we were working trade shows in our jewelry showroom. He was fashion-forward while the rest of the salesmen wore boring (often *polyester*) suits. I taught Mike to accept the comments graciously and not always point to me, with a "she did it" –like accusatory point of the finger.

Mike began tossing his sweaters onto the bed into a fresh stack. "We'll list all these for sale."

"Are you planning on never wearing a sweater again?" I asked, as many of his discards were in the current fall/winter outfit rotation.

"Okay, let's go through here, and if I wore it last winter, we'll keep it. If I haven't worn it in a year, we'll sell it." While it sounded reasonable, I knew we would be keeping most of the sweaters. Mike doesn't wear wool (allergic), so it's hard to find warm sweaters for him, and when we do, they tend to be expensive. But as a quick concession and to show support for his plan, I magnanimously agreed we should sell the mauve silk-blend polo with matching cardigan. Mike had aged out of that look, anyway.

I tried to push listing the bulky red cotton Mister Rogers sweater with patch pockets and a tie belt, but it was Mike's all-time favorite and was not going anywhere. Into the LIST stack went a yellow cotton crew-neck pullover with the tags still on it. I don't know what possessed me to choose a yellow sweater for him; just holding it up in front of Mike gave him a sickly pall. We could let go of a Kelly green cotton cable knit; with Mike's (premature) salt and pepper hair, Kelly green was no longer a good choice. I liked him in shades of blue, olive, wine and occasionally red. An old favorite brick-colored pullover had been stretched so much east/west that it was too short north/south. Mike was heavier now, and it was my fault. When I lost weight, Mike lost weight. When I gained weight, he gained.

The olive crewneck and the khaki cable-knit were staples. My favorite was his black and gray argyle V-neck. Definite keepers. All of the zip-neck fleece "wooly-bullies" as we called them, would stay. He had the same style cotton pullover in several colors and these were everyday sweaters that take the chill off. My husband slept in a long-sleeve crew neck sweatshirt and sweatpants, summer and winter, and when he saw the better fleece he liked on sale (the ones that don't shrink), he would buy a half dozen pieces or more. (The sweatpants were in the chest of drawers, which we agreed would not be touched yet.) The armoire held extra sweatshirt stock, not yet in rotation. All to keep.

And just like that, we were finished with Mike's sweaters. The tally was: Six on stand-by for a swift exit and eleven folded, plus the sweats, back on the shelves. I suggested taking a break to watch a rerun of "House Hunters." But Mike was operating in one of his stubborn streaks and started pulling out my sweaters and knitwear. I knew this would not be as easy a task as Mike's sweaters.

"Do you want this?" he asked as he flashed up a rib-knit wrap tunic.

"Yes! Put it right back – it's staying."

"Have you worn it lately?"

"No, but I might. I was just thinking about this top last week," I said, trying not to laugh.

Unfazed, Mike was putting things into the LIST stack without waiting for my response. I wasn't inclined to laugh anymore. "Hey! Cut it out. These are all keepers."

The stack of my sweaters on the bed was falling over, and I was re-folding each one, trying to get things back in order – and back on the shelf where the sweaters should be in case I needed them.

"Everything's black!" Mike said. "You don't need more than one black sweater." Oh, that silly husband of mine. Maybe they were *mostly* black, but they were all quite different and each served a specific purpose. There was a three-quarter sleeve, nubby sweater and a slinky-knit tunic with long sleeves and a flattering V-neck. From my days of being in love with the cardigan-and-tank sweater set look, I had two black sets (one with long sleeves, one with three-quarter sleeves). There was a dark gray duo, and a dark purple sweater set that Mike lumped in with the black knits. He's truly color blind. But those could be listed along with a few other sweaters I could part with. I typically ignored the fashion stylists who insisted on brighter colors next to the face.

I wasn't nostalgic over my red hand-knit sweater (a female version of the Mr. Rogers sweater) that I wore to Thanksgiving with the relatives several years ago. We packed according to the unseasonably cold weather forecast for our trip down south, but it was a surprise (surprise!) 86 degrees in Charlotte. My outfit sure looked good -- until my face started glowing and glistening like a nuclear reactor, matching the red of the sweater. Unless I got a job as Santa's helper at the North Pole, I didn't need it.

A light blue cashmere sweater set worn only once gave me hives. I was scratching myself silly the night I wore it with a colorful scarf and plain black pants to a cocktail party, but I loved the outfit and got compliments. Keeper. I loved the classy charcoal gray cashmere sweater set with the beaded trim, worn with a tea-length flow-y black skirt to a formal wedding during one of our many trips to Charlotte. We had such a good time, reconnecting with people we hadn't seen in years. Several old friends didn't recognize me at first because of my dramatic weight loss. It felt good. *I* felt good. I was wearing one of the most fabulous outfits I had ever owned.

Those special sweaters were packed in plastic zipper cases to keep the moths away – where they would stay. I found comfort knowing they were there, yet the knots in my stomach were starting to tighten.

"You'll have to find a place to put them," Mike said, "because we don't have any room."

"Put them back exactly where they came from – there was room before."

Mike huffed. "You said you wanted to get rid of things, and now you don't."

"Mike, most of the things I need to get rid of are in the closet." I seemed to be safe from his nagging for the moment. It was a good thing, because my eyes were welling up over the cashmere. How I dreaded opening that closet door!

To even get to the vicinity of the walk-in closet, we had to move the vacuum cleaner and a laundry basket full of miscellaneous clothes that were not necessarily intended for the washing machine. Mike wanted to know what was in that basket.

"I have no idea, but I'm not going through it now." I moved it over to the side.

A hook on the outside of the closet door held several hangers with new and laundered blouses: A French blue wrinkle-resistant button-down, a khaki linen shirt-tunic, a black and white pinstripe blouse and two classic solid white blouses in different sizes. I hadn't really noticed them lately, even though they had been there in plain sight for years. My "thin" wardrobe plan at one point had been to wear a tailored blouse, jeans and loafers or boots all the time. "Tailored." I liked that style. Heavy people can't do tailored very well, since nothing ever really fits.

"I'll sell all these shirts," I said, not wanting to burst into tears. And that darned closet wasn't even open yet.

Mike laid the blouses across the bed in the last remaining free spot and opened the closet door. He flipped on the switch for the fluorescent lights; they blinked and buzzed and then the closet was lit. Showtime!

I'd forgotten how nice the built-ins were; folded clothes, handbags, shoe boxes and hats covered everything, an errant sleeve or two hung over the sides of the shelves. My handbags were on one long shelf, many in drawstring dust bags, one after the other, two and three deep in some places. Mike pulled them all down and piled them in a mess on the bed. (I made a mental note to remember to change the linens after this project was over.)

Some of the bags were twenty years old, but all were in good shape. The small navy Coach shoulder bag would go. Who does small bags anymore? Even though I usually only carried a wallet, keys, lipstick, a pen and some tissues, I liked the idea of a large bag that could hold a book, a legal pad, and any meeting notes. A light blue bag went into the LIST stack, and I decided to part with a chic red authentic Fendi clutch, purchased on deep discount and carried maybe once. Where does one place a clutch, say, at a dinner? The table? The floor? A clutch was too complicated for my new, pared-down life, and I knew it would fetch a good price at auction.

Somehow over the years, I had accumulated four beaded evening bags and though they were all beautiful, on the rare occasion I needed an evening bag, I chose a small solid black bag. The beaded bags could be listed. Despite my fondness for totes, several straw, canvas and leather ones could go. I didn't have to pause to consider whether to list a black backpack. A backpack? Why on earth I bought this, I'll never know. I also didn't care for the unstructured hobo-type or drawstring bags I favored in years past. I green-lighted listing about half of my black leather bags. Wearing the 'woman-of-a-certain age' badge of pride, I decided to stick with larger, tailored leather bags with short handles.

That wasn't too painful, I realized, as we moved to the shoe department. All the shoe cubbies on the far end of the closet were full, and dozens of shoe boxes were stacked in several columns on top of the cubby case. The gold tapestry high heels I wore to my wedding rehearsal dinner were safely stored in their shoebox. I had kept them because a girl never knows when she might be in need of such a shoe, though I remember they hurt my feet something awful. Some day, I thought, I might want to wear those pumps to a formal function. A very short one, where I was seated. I hadn't even worn heels of *any* color since the last time big shoulder pads were in vogue. Alright, the gold tapestry heels could go and so could my ivory lace wedding pumps. I remember taking them off halfway through our reception and dancing in my stocking feet.

I was surprised how many pairs of heels I still had in boxes on the shelf: Cobalt blue pumps I had worn with a matching blouse and a full, float-y floral skirt I made myself; pinky-beige, ultra-soft, low-heeled slingbacks with a fabric bow had been favorites, matching a shirtdress in a coordinating color; a pair of orange wedge-heeled espadrilles – still fashionable, but the wedge was entirely too high now. Navy pumps, classic black patent pumps, red pumps. I was well-endowed in the sandal department too, with many pairs of casual thong-style flats, most never worn: Silver metallic, chain-adorned slip-ons, multi-colored strappy (code word for painful) slides, turquoise nubuck fancy flip-flops, bronze huaraches. All of these could go, I told Mike, and he took them out of the closet and made a tall stack on the floor.

"Oh, wait," I said, opening a box of eggplant-colored suede pumps. "I have to keep these."

"Are you going to wear them?"

"No, but I want them. They are so beautiful." These were the most expensive shoes I had ever worn. I'd bought them to go with a similar-colored coat dress I had designed and whipped up back when I was dressing for success. That was a classy outfit. I must have given away the dress years ago. (Big shoulder pads.) As I was wrapping the eggplant shoes in the tissue and neatly putting them back into the box, I noticed Mike was tossing shoes from the cubbies into a large paper bag.

"Just a minute! I have to examine each pair," I said taking the shoes out of the bag as fast as he was putting them in. I stopped when I pulled out a pair of black suede casual shoes with a small wedge heel. "I never saw these before. Where did they come from?"

"Very funny. You're not going to keep them are you?"

"Well, I don't know." I sat on the corner of the bed and tried them on. New shoes! They fit. Shoes (almost) always fit. I loved them. "They're keepers." Mike reluctantly put them back into a cubbie.

I found some new footwear that day shopping in my own closet (if you don't remember it, it's new!) -- mostly flats and loafers: Black patent leather driving mocs, black suede, black leather and good brown, updated loafers with silver trim, and classic brown top-siders. I hadn't worn brown shoes in ages, but I might need them in the future. I vowed to wear the saved shoes soon. Going were the kitten heels, sling-back shoes and pumps. Someone else would love the cumbersome clogs in burgundy, brown and black (it was a phase) that I would walk out of every time. I felt proud that I cleared out at least two-thirds of my stock.

Three large drawers stuffed with scarves took me back years. I had silk scarves, cotton scarves, square scarves, rectangular scarves, scarves with fringe and Hermès scarves (well, maybe just one *real* one, and it was in its original orange box, not laying naked in a drawer). I picked out over half of the scarves to put in the LIST stack, and the remainder fit in one small drawer. What I didn't know then was that the sales of those scarves on V-Cart would provide great research for my new business the following year.

Belts! One drawer held nothing but a few leather belts and several jingly chain belts: A silver concha belt, another silver concha belt with red leather trim, a gold-tone chain belt with a coin medallion on the end, and a matte gold-tone draping charm belt that was very expensive and worn only once (but it sure looked good -- or so I thought at the time). Truth is, I hadn't worn a belt since I was a newlywed, but I kept thinking that maybe someday I would be able to wear those belts again. It might be in a future life, but I kept the faith – and all the belts.

I finally turned my attention to the main event, the clothes hanging on the rod.

The dust was in the same place it had been for years, and I don't think I had moved anything on the left side of the closet since Thursday night meant "must-see TV." Apparently, the walk-in closet was where my clothes went to die. Working from home didn't require much in the way of wardrobe pieces. My daily uniforms, my calf-length T-shirts (nouveau career-wear), were folded in the chest of drawers along the other wall. In the wintertime, I sometimes wore a pair of slouchy socks with the tee, but most of the time, I walked around barefoot. (I'm not a slippers kind of person, but my husband sure is. Every year during the post-Father's Day sales, Mike's ritual is to buy three or four pairs of slippers to last until the following year. He likes the corduroy or heavy felt types and would gladly wear them out to the grocery store if I let him. But "no slippers out the front door" is one of our maxims.)

Every trip to visit our families down south, I needed a special outfit to help me feel good about the weight loss. We were visiting often, dealing with ill and aging parents. My mother-in-law didn't live to see my *big* weight loss, and for some reason, I found that childishly gratifying, as surely she would have tried to take credit for it somehow. Maybe it was punishment for those thoughts, but I soon found myself feeding my anxiety, and the weight piled back on.

Dr. Phil preaches that when one loses weight, one must get rid of the larger clothes, as an incentive not to gain back the weight. I didn't listen (but I doubt it would be much of an incentive for me). As I packed on every pound, I had clothes for all sizes along the way up. I kept thinking I would be "back" on a losing streak soon, so I had been unwilling to move anything out of the closet permanently.

Unable to face failure, I stayed in denial. But life became easier with a less-cluttered closet.

The bed was overflowing with items to list, so I suggested we sit at the dining room table to sort through my clothes. This wasn't an easy task, so we fortified with my Diet Cherry Dr. Pepper and his Diet Dew. Mike brought in an armful of items on hangers and slapped them down on the table. He wiped his upper lip, plopped himself down in a chair and quickly downed a half can of the Dew. "Ahhhhhh!"

"Tired?" I was hoping he might suggest we stop now and finish up the next day or the next year.

"No, but this didn't even make a dent in the left side," he said, taking the hangers off and handing me the items one at a time, "and they're all the same thing."

"They are not all the same, Mike, just let me take a look." In fact, all the clothes in the first few batches he brought in were black and might look the same to an untrained eye. But noting the detail, one would see there were pants with tapered legs, boot-cut legs and wide legs. Pockets are important details. I had pants with two pockets on side seams; pants with one pocket on the side seam; pants with two J-pockets in front; pants with two back pockets; pants with flaps on the two back pockets; and pants with *buttons* on the flaps on the back pockets!

It really began to look like a store. Going were the black knit pants with a drawstring waist (four pairs in three sizes, including two pairs with tags), black Capris with a drawstring waist (I never did well with Capris) and several pairs of black woven cotton trousers with a touch of spandex in the assorted sizes. These had been my favorites. The thinner, better me wore them several times in rotation, though they still looked new. Also about to hit the road were dressy black, lined rayon/silk blend straight-leg pants that I never quite got around to wearing. My special-occasion outfit ideas apparently didn't pop up during the time I fit into silk pants. Sometimes life happens that way.

And those were just the pants. It was a sea of black, black, and more black. Not ebony, deep slate, midnight, ink, carbon or jet – just plain black.

I didn't realize I had so many clothes. But looks were deceiving, because my actual wardrobe wasn't really that extensive. Most of the clothes didn't fit, and many pieces were duplicates in various sizes.

"Is that all?" I asked Mike.

"No, we've only pulled out half of what's on the left side rack."

I felt more than a little embarrassed. I had forgotten about so many of the pants and tops. "I don't know how these got here, I've never seen them before," I insisted, examining yet another pair of Capris with tags – these in black linen. But I knew my argument didn't have legs, so I started talking about how much money we would rake in by selling all this online. I didn't know whether to laugh or cry. I think I did a little of both.

The black tops had to be sorted. Again, I was trying to explain to Mike why I had so many black tops to add to the stack from the armoire. There was the black knit shirt with a sweetheart neckline, a black knit top with a U-neck and a black knit top with a flattering wide portrait neckline. I had several black knit tops with three-quarter sleeves and several with long sleeves. I had one with cap sleeves and several black tank tops, to wear under jackets and big shirts. I agreed to sell most of the black tops. When I had been on my big loser shopping sprees and jokingly called these weight-loss clothes "disposable," I surely hadn't meant it literally. While I was not optimistic that I could lose the weight again, I felt sure I could recoup some of my money with sales on V-Cart.

As we completed the foraging for clothes to sell, it was hard to distinguish where one overflowing stack of black items ended and another began. Was this mess better than the mess we just fixed in the closet? I thought surely Mike would want to stop for the day, but he said it was time to go through *his* walk-in closet in the guest bedroom/office.

Mike's closet held a couple of jackets and dressy pants, six or eight pairs of Chinos in all colors from stone to khaki (please don't call them 'beige'– we don't use that word in our home). A random navy and olive were nestled in at the end of the rack. On the other side were about a dozen button-down dress shirts (long sleeves only), and at least twenty-five polo shirts that he preferred to hang rather than fold.

"Make sure the collar is folded down when you take it out of the dryer and put it on a hanger," he had taught me after we were married, "and make sure the hem is straight and button all but the top button." Lessons for the washerwoman, the wife. Lightly starched button-down dress shirts were put on a suit hanger the minute they came home from the dry cleaners. No wire hangers' for us (even though the dry cleaners told us they heart-ed us right on the paper hanger sleeve). Mike preferred wooden hangers for his favorite shirts and jackets, many of them collected as a child from annual Florida trips with his family: Souvenirs from the Fontainebleau Hotel and Resort, Montmartre Hotel and the Princess Resort. Added to that were lower-brow plastic hangers from the likes of Hampton Inn, Courtyard and Holiday Inn Express. You might expect those from a former traveling salesman, collected in the days before hangers were permanently attached to the rod.

Mike taught me about maintenance mechanics and procedures, wooden hangers and buttoning tabs, but I taught him about fashion. Even before we were married, I got rid of all his polyester and introduced him to natural fabrics – or at least favorable blends. (I so did not agree with the theory that you don't try and change a person.) Out went the polyester polo shirts and in came the brushed or pique cotton polos. Jeans or cotton Chinos (flat-front, no cuffs) became the uniform for casual days. In some parts of the country, this is considered strictly golf-wear, but in the South, it is standard preppy-wear.

I introduced Mike to top-siders and loafers for pairing with casual outfits. He has a narrow foot and always wore Bally Italian shoes because they came in AA width. While the Bally's were very nice, I helped him find other shoes that were less expensive and more appropriate for daily wear. We saved the Bally's for dressier occasions.

Other guidelines (rules, of course) for Mike's wardrobe included no rayon -- think sturdy, not slinky. No corduroy pants, unless they were the finest pinwale, and only on cold days. All socks are dark gray, navy or black (eventually we went with all dark gray to make it easier, since Mike couldn't always distinguish between those colors). Black shoes, black belt. Brown shoes, brown belt. No shirts without collars (except his sweatshirts to wear at home only). Button-down shirts buttoned-up to the button second from the top (no man-cleavage). White dress shirts are nice, but no off-white – ever. And never pair that white shirt with black pants, unless a waiter's job is in the works. That was basic fashion theory for men. Other details were made up as we went along.

In honor of our wardrobe purge, several of Mike's polos needed to be tossed, as we discovered a few small holes or stains. Some of the older ones had shrunk so we put them in the LIST stack (we would include measurements so no one would be deceived by the 'tad-smaller-than-large' description). Mike claimed many of the newer ones had shrunk, too, and I went along with it – though we both knew they were plain ol' too small. Anything not wearable would be put up for auction.

Still not ready to take a break, Mike started vacuuming the closet and called for me to come and look. "See how nice and new this carpet is?" he said. "You can tell we haven't been in here much." It was exhilarating to see that much open – available! – storage space.

We were both anxious to get all the clothes listed and out of our simpler, pared-down lives - not to mention off the dining room table. Mike had brought in all the bed-stacks and put them on the dining room chairs. There they would sit until they were not only listed, but sold, packed and shipped.

"Let's just take a small, manageable stack of my tops and list them right now," I suggested, and Mike was hot on the trail to help me. I logged ten items on a spreadsheet so I could easily transfer the info to the V-Cart listing template, taking measurements, noting the condition and including comments about the style. Mike and I worked well together; he would shake off the dust (remind me to vacuum later, I always said), then hold the shirt while I measured. I typed up the details and Mike put each shirt on a hanger to be photographed.

"Mike, that shirt is backwards!"

"How would I know that?"

"The tag always goes in the back."

"Oh, okay," he said. Did he not know that?

Mike was perplexed when he got to my shirts with the wide portrait neckline. I had three alike in different sizes. "This won't stay on the hanger, the neckline is too big," he said. "Let's just skip it."

I stopped my logging and asked him to give the shirt and hanger to me. I took a few little pieces of tape and the shirt was attached to the hanger. It looked fine.

"Here are the other two," Mike said.

"We can use one photo for all three sizes," I told him. Clearly, Mike could use some training as a fashion stylist.

"Does that look right to you?" I asked when I saw that Mike had put a shirt with a collar over a hanger all lopsided, leaving the back to drape much longer than the front.

"You fix it, then," he said. "I guess I don't know how." I could see this was going to take a long time.

It could be said that our photography studio wasn't the most ideal. Items were staged on the back of the *en suite* bathroom door about six feet in front of my desk. We had an over-the-door hook and put each piece on a hanger. Sometimes we used tape to set the sleeves or legs just so. I took pictures with my trusty Kodak point-and-shoot digital camera right from my cushy, rolling office chair. I could roll a bit to the left or right as needed to get the best shot, camera pointing up over my monitor. My fashion stylist husband would be called on to flatten this or fluff that.

I barked instructions. "Balance it on the hanger, Mike, it's listing to the left!"

"Make sure the tag is nice and neat!"

"Drape it over the doorknob!" The nickel-toned doorknob was always a thorn. When it could be covered by the garment, it was fine. Sometimes I could merely crop it out before uploading the photo. Often there was no choice but to leave the doorknob showing in the photo when the listing went live on V-Cart.

NOTE: Doorknob not included.

Neither of us knew a thing about photography, except that lighting was the key to everything. I did a little research, but when I started reading about hard lights and soft lights, they lost me. Mike called the photography shop around the corner from us, hoping they could suggest an easy, inexpensive solution. He was asked, "Do you have a bounce umbrella?"

"Uhmmm… I don't think so," Mike said as he determined that conversation finished.

We *did* have a 20-watt bulb in our ceiling fan, and a pole lamp which held three "spotlight" fixtures —sixty watts each. It was pretty dark in the studio. The two large windows had mini-blinds kept closed to ward off the heat from the afternoon sun. We learned that opening the blinds made no discernible difference anyway. The flash of the camera often yellowed our photos, but at least all was illuminated. And, fortunately, when an item is black, the one-word color description pretty much takes care of it. For a blue shirt or a pink skirt, we had to make sure the monitor's color resembled the in-person version.

I took close-up shots of details like buttons, collars and pockets; this was the best way to proceed, and I barked out instructions.

"Move it to the left."

"It's crooked!"

"Is that *lint* on the arm?"

When I uploaded the pictures, the colorful blouses were showing nicely. But the black items had black circles and dots that looked like big stains on the clothes. I shot them again and again before realizing the spots were from the poor lighting. I expanded my descriptions to include an apology for the photos, adding another note to explain the spots were on the photos only, not on the actual garment. These weren't the clean and concise listings I liked, but it was the best we could do.

Listing each item was tedious. I put the first ten pieces of clothing up for a seven-day auction (the standard), rather than a "Buy-It-Now" (BIN) flat price. I offered free shipping but started the bidding at $5.95, to cover postage. By then, we had learned people love free shipping, even though they surely knew they were paying for it one way or another. We didn't have a clue what to expect with these auctions; we would test the market and see if these clothes would sell. As soon as the photos were taken, the items were put back on the dining room table, in a new stack, LISTED.

By morning, all ten items had bids and several watchers. VintageCartel.shop tells the seller how many people have clicked the WATCH option to show the particular listing on their "My V-Cart" page. Seeing this activity motivated us to list more items right away. I would list several black items, then toss in a colorful blouse or two, just to break up the monotony. The New-With-Tags (NWT) blouses were set to Buy-It-Now rather than auction, and I asked $14.99 each -- less than I paid for the blouses, and not a good return for my investment. (Do not try this at home.)

Our procedures were precise. When something sold, I would take care of the paperwork and my order picker (Mike) would get the item and bring it to me at the order-packing table (my desk to the side of my computer table). I would carefully wrap it in white tissue paper, seal it with my THANK YOU sticker, and tie on a complimentary-color ribbon. The shipping clerk (Mike) would take this to the carton-packing area (kitchen counter) and put it in a small carton or mail pouch, affix the shipping label, and then toss it into the US POSTAL SERVICE regulation mail bin that he carried back and forth to the post office every day. Often, the bin filled right up -- you'd think we were operating a store.

Our procedure sounded simple enough, but it was rarely easy, and sometimes tempers flared. "Mike, I need the slinky black top with the ruching on the side."

"Huh?"

"The ruching! The gathers."

"I'll look, but I don't have any idea what you're talking about," Mike said. Those picking clerks really should have some fashion training, I was thinking, as Mike added, "Which stack is it in?"

"I don't know," I said while I was typing the packing list and label. "Look for a V-neck."

Mike rummaged through the stacks and pulled out a shirt, holding it up so I could see. "Is this it?"

"No, Mike, that is a black slit-neck tunic with soutache trim," I explained, as if that meant something to him.

"How about this?" he asked, flashing up a black cowl-neck top.

"No, Mike."

"Well, I thought this had gathers," he said in earnest, pointing to the cowl.

"The gathers are on the sides."

After a couple more attempts, when I sensed Mike was on the verge of exasperation, I would typically get up and find the item myself. I knew I was being unreasonable, but I couldn't help feeling like it wasn't my job to do that. Ironically, one thing I always preached to employees at companies I worked with is that in a small business, though you will have a job description, the bottom line is that your job is to do *whatever needs done*. I knew I should have been more patient with Mike, but he was the photo stylist, though truly, I appointed that task to him knowing he hadn't a lick of experience to his name. Later on when we started selling a real inventory of jewelry and scarves in our real online V-Cart store, we bagged and numbered every piece so it would be easy for the clerk to locate an item. (You'd be surprised.)

Every day, we had orders and, mercifully, our stock was dwindling while our Paypal account went up. This online selling thing seemed to be working out.

* 3 *

THE WHITE PICKET FENCE

"Never lick icing off a sharp knife." – Author Unknown

Once upon a time, when we were young newlyweds in Charlotte, Mike and I had a charming storybook yellow wood and brick house. We had a fireplace, gardenias and rose bushes we planted ourselves, and at the end of the driveway was a mailbox with an adjustable red flag. From spring through fall, a basket of lavender geraniums hung from the front landing, and red geraniums in terra cotta planters lined the three brick steps. On early summer evenings, perhaps after a pesto pasta dinner made with herbs from our garden, we would hear the tinkling chimes from the ice cream truck. Sometimes Mike would run out, line up with the other kids and get a Popsicle or two. We didn't always respond to the call, but we liked the idea of it.

We lived in a condo until we bought our little house about a year after we married, and that first year was filled with high-highs and low-lows. From our engagement day on, Mike's parents insisted I call them Mom and Dad. It was awkward then, and it never got easier. I would much rather have called them by their first names, but they made their expectations clear ("if you love us, you will…").

When we visited with them, the four of us sat in the den, or occasionally the breakfast nook. The living room was closed to family, and I didn't see it with the lights on for years. But my mother got the rare treat of sitting in there when she was invited – or *summoned* -- over to meet the future in-laws. Mike and I were not included, and we were worried sick about their interrogation of my mother. I called Mama's house every three minutes or so until she got home around nine. I had to know what happened.

Finally, she answered. Mike's parents were nice, she said, but the first hour, all they talked about was how hurtful their other son's wife had been to them. Mike's older brother, Martin, had moved his family to Texas several years earlier for a big job offer. Mama said the Kane's went on and on about how Martin's wife never invited them over for dinner. Martin's wife wouldn't bring the baby over to visit (I later found out it was because she was concerned about their nervous dog). Martin's wife wore dresses that were matronly. Martin's wife was never available to go shopping. Martin's wife didn't know how to decorate the baby's room. I think that was all my mother could remember, but that was enough. I very clearly understood it was a veiled warning for me.

The way Mama described the second hour of the visit, it sounded like a game of Twenty Questions (and Comments). And my mother wasn't offered so much as a glass of water the whole evening. (I believe this is an interview technique used by the CIA and police operatives everywhere.) Further, she had to bite her lip so she wouldn't say anything about the disgusting dog jumping up on her, shedding and slobbering, and no one saying a word. (I had made my mother swear she would ignore the dog and not take offense at anything said to or about her.) Mama survived, and I survived, too.

My future father-in-law made it known that he didn't want Mike and me working for a "wage" from a business we didn't own. "You'll always be at someone else's mercy for your livelihood," he pounded into our heads.

"Pensioners!" Mom said. "You don't want to be a common pensioner."

"I'd love to know I'd be getting a pension," Mike said, baiting her while I cringed.

"Michael," Mom started up.

"Michael!" Dad echoed. "Listen to your mother!"

"But, Dad…"

"Michael, forget it." Apparently Dad didn't accept the bait.

"Michael," his mother fell for it hook, line and sinker. "When you have money, you don't need a pension."

"Dad gets a pension," Mike threw out. Oh, boy, was I waiting for the fireworks.

"Daddy gets a pension," Mom said, her voice getting louder and louder. "But he was an owner, Michael, not someone who waits all their lives to get a little monthly check."

"What's wrong with a little monthly check?" Mike wouldn't let up.

"Michael…" Mom was really loud now.

"Oh, for god's sakes, forget it!" Dad has spoken.

I was so nervous, sitting in the straight chair, I started perspiring and then I giggled just a bit.

"What's funny?" Mom asked me. Crap! I was in trouble now, I thought, as a drop of sweat dripped on the chintz, and I reached for my pocketbook to grab a Kleenex. "Wait a minute! We're trying to help and Terri thinks this is funny!"

"No, I don't think it's funny. I'm just nervous, I guess."

"Sheesh, why would you be nervous?" Dad asked. All eyes were on me.

"I don't know. I'm sorry." When did I get so meek?

After a little bit of a pause, the business conversation resumed. After a few weeks' worth of conversations and debates, we (meaning Mike, his parents and I) decided to start our own jewelry and accessories business. It was an exciting time, as visions of earrings danced in my head.

Mike left his job as a sales rep for a popular line of fashion jewelry. The timing was good for me; I enjoyed my job as editor of the local city magazine, but because of the instability created by a constant change of publishers, I was starting to realize it was time to move on. Besides, the long hours kept me away from my new husband and working together sounded ideal. I had some fashion expertise, too; I was a young woman who never left the house without earrings, and I loved the scarves that this new woman named Oprah wore on TV.

Mike's father helped develop our business by giving us some start-up money and later on by financing our growth. He suggested I would run things while Mike was out selling. Dad taught me some business basics about spread-sheets, profit and loss statements and inventory control. At the same time, he made sure to get his hooks into me by constant comments like, "Sheesh, Terri! When you said you had no business experience, I didn't know you *really* didn't have any."

I always felt we had assigned seats in the den when Mike and I made our three-to-four times a week visits. Mom ruled the long sofa where she sat with the nervous little yapper, sharing her nightly ice cream. Mike sat at the end of the sofa, as far away from the dog as possible. Before we made our appearance, I reminded him to *please* sit there so I wouldn't have to. I sat on the uncomfortable straight chair and Dad was always in his easy chair. The TV was constantly blaring the Weather Channel, though no one was watching except when there was a hurricane brewing. We weren't allowed to talk while the hurricane report was on. Dogs, decorating and hurricanes were Mom's interests. Dad didn't seem interested in anything but business.

"Michael!" Dad would stand and gesture with his head to Mike to come to the kitchen. I later learned he wanted company while he made a mixed drink to calm his stomach. They hid in there while Dad sipped his "medicine" because Mom didn't approve.

"Uh-oh," Mom often said. "Your father-in-law must be having words with Michael over something or other." This always gave me a nervous stomach, and I felt I needed some sips of Dad's medicine.

Not wanting to waste a minute, Mom used this time alone with me to give "lessons" on what it's like to have money. It was hard not to laugh, because Mike and I had no money. Yet when I pointed this out to her, she would say either "everyone knows the family does," or "you will have money soon enough." *Exactly when would this be?* I wondered.

The first lesson was about giving to charity ("never let them put your name on a plaque or in a program") and the high expectations the community would have for Mike and me ("you'll be invited to many affairs"). I listened, wondering if this conversation could possibly be happening and noting the social invites hadn't yet begun to arrive. If I was marrying Mr. Gotrocks himself, I surely wasn't aware of it.

Mom shared wardrobe guidelines. She also shared some information: "We never had a fat person in the family before." My first thought was to counter with "Well, now you do!" but I feared she might think that was smart-aleck-y. My second thought was to apologize, but that didn't seem quite right. I just didn't know what to say, so I remained silent.

While seemingly acknowledging my fashion sense (for a fat girl), Mom had a few things to say about Mike: "When he's with his father, out to dinner, it's coat and tie." Mike always wore a button-down shirt with his Chinos, and a sweater if it was cool. "A tie is expected."

"But no other men wear ties in the restaurant!" I countered, knowing this would be Mike's first line of defense (yet also knowing what "other people" do was totally irrelevant in Mom's world). We usually went to a steakhouse on Sundays, the same family-owned place they had been patronizing for years, and our reservation was for 5 PM, because Mom said she would fall ill if she ate later.

"I'd like the petit filet," she would say to the server in her petit voice, "and it has to be rare with absolutely nothing on it!"

"Yes, ma'am," I was certain the waiter remembered us from previous visits.

"I mean it, now! Absolutely nothing – no salt, no pepper, no marinade, or -- what's that... sooey sauce." Mom had difficulty recalling the name (and proper pronunciation) of the exotic soy sauce. "Did you write that down?"

"Yes, ma'am, I've got it."

"And tell them to make sure the grill is clean." I thought I was going to die, (but I didn't).

"I'd also like a plain baked potato, done inside, with absolutely nothing on it." The server furiously scribbled, trying to keep up.

Before the server was out of earshot, Mom always said, "In New York, a waiter wouldn't have to write it down, he'd memorize it, but down here...."

"Oh, for god's sakes..." Dad said.

"Well, it's true! They don't know any better in the South."

"Mom!" Mike had to chime in, and I shuddered to think what he might say next. Sometimes a discreet little kick under the table from me worked beautifully.

"Michael, drop it," Dad warned.

Occasionally we went to a large chain steakhouse, but Mom insisted the steaks came frozen from the home office and already had marinades and spices on them. "That's how people like their steaks down here, because the meat's not good to begin with."

I took issue with Mom's constant reminders of how backwards (or even stupid) people in the South were, compared with her home-townies in New York City. (At some point, I realized she hadn't been back to New York, even for a visit, in thirty years.) I couldn't change her mind, though Mom occasionally told me I was an exception to the common rednecks because I went to school in the North (*un*common redneck, I guess). But more likely, she probably thought I came from the same neighborhood as Elly May Clampett – before her family got rich and became the Beverly Hillbillies. At least a debate about Mike's wardrobe was less frustrating than my having to defend the entire southeastern United States.

And as a little P.S. to one of the wardrobe discussions, Mom told me I had to stop Mike from wearing flip-flops in public.

Another lesson was about saving money. "We're not spenders," she insisted. I tried not to take anything personally, but the implication was surely that she thought *I* was a spender (or would be one day).

We did get an occasional taste of the family treasure trove. One day, Mike's parents announced they wanted to give us a computer with word processing and accounting software for a wedding gift. Personal computers were starting to take off, and we all went to the computer store to find out how this newfangled tool could help our business. I could hear my future mother-in-law huffing, showing her impatience; she was in a rush to get next door to Talbot's. We were with the salesperson for over an hour, hearing the merits of a computer, and debating whether to buy IBM or Apple, definitely leaning toward Apple. But Dad obediently heeded Mom's signals and ended the discussion by telling the salesman, "We'll take the IBM."

I went with Mom to Talbot's while Mike and Dad sat in the car. It was crowded because there was a big sale in progress. It looked like it was the tail-end of the sale, because there wasn't much selection left, but Mom was looking for a navy print skirt. Of course, anything she bought had to go to the tailor's, because Mom didn't wear her skirts down the calf. "Just a few inches below the knee, or it's swimming on me," she always said. I helped by pointing out a few nice skirts, but they were the wrong shade of navy. After a few minutes, with the salesclerk there trying to help us, Mom recoiled and said to me in disgust, "They only have the *huge* sizes – the 10's, the 12's, the 14's." Several other shoppers took a pause and stared. The salesclerk looked at me and winked; she was well over a size 14 too. I was pretty tough, but it was still embarrassing.

I found myself sobbing when we all went to our condo to ceremoniously unpack the new computer. When my mother-in-law asked what was wrong, I blurted out, "This is such a nice gift!" The computer came with several thick loose-leaf instruction notebooks, and I read at least the first couple of pages of volume one. This began my long love affair with the personal computer.

We were very grateful. Maybe I had misread them, I thought. Maybe they weren't really evil people. I was too naïve to realize by taking Dad's money we were totally at his mercy and soon learned his generosity came with more strings attached than a paper kite.

———— ·····———

Like both my parents, I was born and reared in town, and Mike's family moved to Charlotte from Boston when he was a young child.

We were Charlotte fixtures, active in several organizations, and I was chairing a mayor's committee. It was an idyllic setting for our new life together. Or, you might have thought so, had you read the blurbs from the paper, seen us on TV or peeped into the large windows when the blinds were open.

The thing was, my in-laws lived just two miles away. They hand-picked the house for us, most likely to ensure we stayed nearby. Mom and Dad toured open houses for weekend entertainment, and they discovered a development of Patio Homes in-progress. The first of its type in our area, all homes had sold out shortly after the initial offering. Still, Mom and Dad visited the model home one Sunday afternoon and that very day, the developer learned a sale fell through. We were out of town, but my in-laws put down a deposit for us, and we got the house. Mom left a message on our answering machine, and when we checked it and heard about the house, we both felt sick because we weren't familiar with the project. When we got back in town and saw the model, we were relieved and delighted. We loved it! Ours would be built on a corner lot with a large side patio enclosed with a white privacy fence and plenty of space for a garden. The Homeowner's Association would take care of all outside maintenance, such as grass-cutting and painting. We had three bedrooms, a garage, spacious closets and a large eat-in kitchen as well as a dining room. We were grateful for their help. All was well....

... for maybe a week. Having thanked my in-laws profusely for their help, I thought our indebtedness was paid. But, then, Mom insisted on going with me to the builder's showroom for the meeting where she would "help" me make decisions about finishes and upgrades. Mom considered herself an expert interior designer and, indeed, her museum-quality home was picture-perfect every time she redecorated, opening up a new exhibit. My in-laws never did any real entertaining, but "exquisite taste" was the consensus of the few lucky individuals allowed beyond the velvet ropes. I wasn't excited about her offer to accompany me but *she* sure was, and I thought taking her with me was the least I could do since she was marginally invested in the house.

We met with Ruthie, the new home coordinator, and right away I told her that I wanted the kitchen cabinets painted white. I love a clean and crisp white kitchen, and I hoped to find some antique glass knobs for the cabinet doors. Ruthie held a clipboard with a form where she wrote notes.

"Oh, no, no," Mom said. "The oak is much too nice to be painted." Ruthie erased my comments about paint before I had a chance to get a word in edgewise. My neck was getting damp and I'm sure my blood pressure soared. Apparently Ruthie assumed Mom wore the pants at this meeting.

I picked out the floor tiles for the kitchen and bathrooms without incident. The bathroom lighting fixtures I liked would cast shadows, Mom said, so she pushed me to order more expensive fixtures similar to those in her powder room. (Cha-ching!) But I didn't mind that too much, and we moved on.

Ruthie showed us paint chips and Mom didn't say a word until I chose a medium blue color for the master bedroom. She reared her head back and gave me a quizzical look.

"That color's way too dark – you have to go several shades lighter."

"But…"

"Does Michael know what you have in mind?" she asked. She knew as well as I that her son wouldn't notice - or care – if the walls were hot pink or brown stripes, which was precisely why he wasn't there with me for the decorating confab. I went with the much lighter blue Mom suggested.

The standard white paint was fine for the office, but I studied the paint chips to find a color for the guest bedroom.

"Here…," my mother-in-law pulled a fabric swatch out of her small navy leather Ferragamo handbag and magnanimously said she had decided to let me use the custom-made draperies, like the swatch, from her guest room.

"You've seen these. It's time for me to re-decorate anyway – I've had those drapes for so long." We needed to match the paint to the swatch, and she already knew the name of the peach paint color that would best coordinate, because she had used the same color. I liked the Waverly peach floral chintz fabric and was grateful for the drapes, though I thought she might have discussed this with me in advance.

I found my footing and stood my ground on choosing white countertops and white appliances, while my mother-in-law insisted I would tire of white and urged me to go with beige. But I was not (then or now) a beige kind of person. Further, I did not want wallpaper or even a border in the kitchen or bathrooms -- I wanted the white to be a blank canvas. To my surprise, there was no further dissention on this subject.

Mom said we should have our closets expertly outfitted with built-in shelves, cubbies and organizers. I thought it was a great idea and was glad she suggested it. She was on a roll and insisted I order custom-made window blinds. I compromised; I would like that for the living room and dining room, but the kitchen and bedrooms would be fine with plain ol' mini-blinds. She reluctantly agreed.

Happily spending our mortgage money on upgrades, Mom kept pushing me to get pricey fixtures in the bathrooms and kitchen. After a half hour of looking at books and samples of expensive knobs, racks and faucets, I told the decorator we would go with basic fixtures from the standard offerings. I couldn't see paying an extra eight hundred dollars for deluxe medicine cabinets or six hundred dollars for each faucet with a slightly different shade of silver-tone than the ones we could get at no additional charge. As long as it could spout hot or cold water, it was fine with me. Mom backed down on this topic, but one eyebrow remained raised and her chair was pushed a little farther back from the worktable.

The standard landscaping included shrubs in the front, but I wanted to order additional plants to go around the side of the white fence.

"You can't pay interest on shrubbery!" Mom said, acting horrified, (I believe it was in retaliation for the faucet decisions), effectively ending the discussion. She went on to insist we order storm doors and windows. I guess she thought that was an interest-paying-worthy investment, yet she balked when I wanted the automatic garage opener. "You don't need that," she said. "You'll never use it – you'll park in the driveway and use the garage for storage." I sucked it in.

We were near the end of Ruthie's work order form, and I was relieved I made it through that stress-fest, (mostly) pleasing my new mother-in-law. I kept in mind that the new house was the prize. I was still in the enchantment phase of my fairy tale and hadn't yet realized the gravity of the villain to the storyline. I was still learning my new role.

Four months later, we moved into the new house, furnished with pieces each of us had – an eclectic mix of antiques and contemporary. My mother-in-law gave us some of her cast-offs, and we bought a few new items. The decorator from the furniture store came over to help us arrange it all.

Just a few weeks after we were settled, Mike's brother, Martin, his wife and two daughters were in town for their annual pilgrimage to visit the gramps. We invited everyone over for a cookout and a look-see. Mike sweated over hamburgers on the patio built-in gas grill, while I gave tours of the mini-manse. I set out large, artistically-arranged platters with salads and sides on the large dining room table. An antique quilt served as a tablecloth and it was lovely.

"These are delicious!" said my sister-in-law, and Martin nodded in agreement. "What do you put in your hamburgers?"

"Chopped onions, egg, a dash of Worcestershire and crushed saltines." I recited the standard meatloaf recipe.

"Saltines?" she confirmed.

"Filler! Filler!" said Mom in a sing-song voice. "You don't need to put in fillers anymore. You really don't have to stretch out a pound of hamburger to make it last a week," the implication being that before I married into her upper-crust family, I had to do things like that. I was too busy stewing and seething to explain to the woman who rarely cooked more than a baked potato and whose favorite food was ketchup, that the saltines kept the very lean meat moist. Besides, Mom didn't eat the hamburgers of the riff-raff. Due to her many allergies, she required a very rare, plain sirloin hamburger, ordered from me like she ordered her steak from a restaurant: "Absolutely nothing on it – not even salt or pepper -- cooked in a frying pan. A clean one!". We had to slice a tomato for her and put it on a separate plate. She said she couldn't take a slice off the serving platter since there was a chance it had touched mozzarella and red onion, with the sprinkling of cracked pepper and basil chiffonade.

After dinner, my nieces were watching a video in the living room, and the adults were lingering around the table talking about business, which was always the topic whenever the family was together. At one point, Martin excused himself to go to the bathroom, and he came back with a peculiar grin on his face.

"First casualty of the new house!" he said, holding up the hot water faucet knob like a trophy. He claimed it had come off when he turned it, but I felt certain there was a conspiracy proving Mom's point that we should have sprung for better faucets.

This triggered a conversation where my mother-in-law took credit for the entire home décor (minus the faucets).

"Didn't we do a good job on the decorating?" Mom asked everyone. She laughed when she told the story about the "dark blue" paint I had wanted, and how I mentioned painting the kitchen cabinets. No one was laughing with her.

"You can live here forever, since it will be just the two of you," was Mom's concluding jab. (Sadly, we knew at that time we would not be able to have children.) As if I wasn't agitated enough, this further irked me because I always envisioned us eventually living in a larger house with a garage door opener, a medium blue master bedroom and white kitchen cabinets.

Nevertheless, we enjoyed entertaining and strived to be the host and hostess with the mostest. We raised money for charity at a ladies' luncheon in our home, we frequently hosted Friday night Sabbath dinners and our patio saw many cookouts with luminaria and just-picked salad. We invited family for Passover Seder dinners typically serving roasted leg of lamb and brisket for those who did not like lamb. In the summer, we filled our house with vases of my pink and yellow roses or white gardenias in a rose bowl. One winter, I bought a flat of purple pansies, planted them in a rectangular wooden box and covered the soil with green moss for an elegant centerpiece. Another time, I made a small hole in the top of an egg, drained the egg out and used the eggshell in an egg cup as a vase for a few daisies. I had seen Martha do this very thing, and after several dozen or so tries with the eggshell, I was able to salvage enough to have one at each place setting. I think my biggest fete was a wedding shower for my brother's fiancée when I crafted heart-shaped real ivy topiaries and served four types of homemade pies. It was all a massive amount of work to make it appear so easy and effortless.

MY MAMA'S SWEET POTATO BOURBON PIE

Ingredients
- One pie shell (unbaked)
- 2 cups cooked sweet potatoes
- ¼ cup butter
- 1 cup milk
- ¾ cup regular sugar
- ¾ cup brown sugar Splenda

- 1 teaspoon vanilla extract
- Dash of salt
- Dash of nutmeg
- ¼ cup bourbon (or maybe a small splash more!)

Directions
- Boil, bake or microwave the sweet potatoes until done. Let cool and peel. In a bowl, mash potatoes until there are no lumps. (You could use a food mill or a ricer.)
- Combine all ingredients and mix until smooth with a wooden spoon or an electric mixer on light.
- Pour into unbaked pie shell.
- Bake at 425 degrees for 15 minutes; turn down heat to 350 and cook for 1 hour, 20 minutes.

Often our soirees received mentions in the daily newspaper's "society section" written by a venerable woman named Grace who had the last word on what and who was in or out. It was a well-read column and people took note of those "mentioned in Grace." It was good to be "mentioned in Grace." I knew a reporter from a local TV news station (from my former newspaper days), and when she needed a Hanukkah piece at the last minute, she called me. Mike and I were on TV lighting the menorah and saying the blessing, and the news crew stayed for latkes and applesauce. The tape ran for several Hanukkahs after that. It was good to be on TV.

Meanwhile, our jewelry sales and marketing business was growing; we had two showrooms and big expectations for our future. But life in the proverbial house with the white picket fence began to erode in small ways, and I tried not to acknowledge it. That meant when something happened to puncture our façade, we felt totally surprised.

After a while, even the ice cream truck wasn't the All-American suburban experience it seemed. We had been the first to move onto our street, and when our next door neighbors moved in, an older couple, we greeted them with a cake fresh from the oven. We had hoped the people moving in would be a young couple we could befriend. But he was a retired sheriff (or so a decal on his car stated) with a pronounced hunchback, and his wife always wore a housedress and slippers (and sometimes curlers) while walking the dog. Mr. Sheriff was a charter member on the board of the Homeowner's Association and apparently since he was out of the sheriffing business, his mission in life was to enforce the rules of the Homeowner's Association. He never failed to appear on the street while we were ordering from the ice cream truck, a Firecracker Bullet Pop for Mike and maybe a Creamsicle for me. Mr. Sheriff never ordered anything, not even a Nutty Buddy. He was there to inform the ice cream man that our community had a posted 'No Soliciting' policy, so the driver should choose another route in the future. We never learned what this man had against ice cream; who shoos off the ice cream truck? By the middle of the summer, the exchange between the elderly ex-sheriff and the cute, young ice cream man got louder and meaner.

"Can you read?" Mr. Sheriff approached the truck just as Mike had ordered a strawberry shortcake bar.

"What say, sir?" the ice cream man said as he counted change. He looked like a young Brad Pitt with a scruffy beard, before scruffy was popular, and wore a white cap and apron.

"I represent the Homeowners Association," the enforcer said, "and we don't allow strangers selling things on these private streets." He pointed to the little 'No Soliciting' sign planted in between the bushes and flowers (underneath the large sign welcoming folks to our neighborhood). "I want you off the property *now!*"

"Chill out, man, I'm just selling some Good Humor here," said the dairy man.

"Hey, hey, hey!" Mike said, standing between the window of the truck and Mr. Sheriff of the Homeowner's Association, as though a brawl was imminent. "First of all, he's not a stranger, he's our ice cream man!"

"You can get your ice cream right down the road a piece at the grocery store…" Mr. Sheriff was pointing.

"And second, my wife and I are members of the Homeowner's Association, too, and we have a God-given right to a Popsicle every now and then." I wished Mike had left me out of this. "It's in the Constitution."

"What Constitution?" asked the enforcer, irritated and probably insulted to hear a lofty subject being brought up in the presence of a Popsicle. But it *was* a good point. Was Mike referring to the Constitution (with by-laws) of the Homeowner's Association or to the *real* Constitution where ice cream trucks have rights. "And we have a posted rule…."

"Relax! Relax! Can I treat you to a Creamsicle?" Mike asked.

"What flavor can I get you, sir?" asked the dairy man.

But the enforcer stomped his foot, stuttered a bit and waved his hands, as if to rid himself of the dirty criminals afore him. And with that, he was off to his house, no doubt to make some calls and rally-up a case.

I guess the ice cream man eventually decided he didn't need the hassle because we never heard the tell-tale carny music in our neighborhood again.

Mike and I thought we might go to an association meeting and complain about the needless cessation of our ice cream privileges. We were also having some street-parking issues when we had company and "the enforcer" would log license plate numbers and times, threatening a fine. We never made it to a meeting, but we heard they were well-attended because the notices promised refreshments. (We wondered if they served ice cream.)

Our butt-in-sky neighbor was a distraction, but our cardinal problem hailed back to the in-laws. Over the five years we lived in the Patio Home, every time they visited our house there was a covert battle over the room temperature. Call us weird, but we liked our air conditioning during the hot, sticky Charlotte summers, and we also had a ceiling fan we ran most of the time. When Mom and Dad walked in the door, the minute my back was turned, Dad snapped his fingers, pointed to the fan, and Mike would turn it off. A little later, usually after Mom whispered something to him, Dad would say, "Geez, Michael! Make it warmer in here," but, again, only when he thought I was out of earshot. And being a good little doobie, Mike went right to the thermostat. We urged them to bring sweaters when they visited, but of course they never did. The night of one big family dinner, by the time the meal was in full swing, all of us "under 70s" were perspiring. I remember putting a box of Kleenex on the dining room table so we could mop up.

Mom had given us spare furniture pieces – true -- and I was grateful even though she never *asked* if we wanted the piece. She seemed to sport an attitude that we would be fortunate to get anything she was discarding. And it was always made clear the furniture wasn't a gift, it was really more *on loan,* subject to being recalled at any time. One day

I was out for some appointments and called Mike from our showroom. After we discussed everything and then some, he casually said he needed to tip me off that his mother had sent her handyman over to exchange kitchen tables with us. She sent us a square oak table and four ladderback chairs and retrieved her round, white wrought iron glass top table and matching chairs, which we had been using since we moved in. I bought a round tablecloth and rounded placemats to dress it up a bit, and I loved the chairs. After the recall, I offered the accessories to Mom since I had no use for them any longer, but she looked appalled, like I had offered up doo-doo and quickly declined. The stealthy swap happened again later with a comfy living room chair I loved, exchanged for a small, uncomfortable museum chair I didn't love.

Mike and I went on a working vacation to Seattle and Vancouver, and when we came back, exhausted and irritable from a sleepless red-eye flight, we saw that our rose bushes were gone (the ones we sweated and strained over) and shrubs had been planted in their place.

"Someone stole our rose bushes!" Mike said as we pulled into the driveway. I had dozed off, but was wide awake in seconds.

"This has to be the handiwork of your mother," I told Mike.

As soon as we got inside, rather than go straight to bed, which was not a possibility now that we both were over-stimulated, Mike called his mother. He told her we were home, the flight was good, the trip successful....

"Did you see anything outside the house?" she finally asked him. Uh-huh, I was right! Mike's mother was the mastermind behind the whole prank. She asked for me to get on the phone, too, and proudly announced that for our anniversary gift, she sent over her gardener to plant shrubs that had been dug up in her courtyard. (She didn't want them anymore -- even the shrubbery was a cast-off.) Mom reminded me that I had wanted extended shrubs when we bought the house. *Yes, yes, that was true, but it was a year ago, before we planted the rose garden against the fence.* I was heartsick even as we were prostrating ourselves in gratitude for their "lovely" surprise.

Mom and Dad thought they were doing a wonderful (even charitable) thing for us, and I tried to see it from their point of view, but I just couldn't.

The friction continued to escalate. We had a birthday dinner for Mom in our home, with all the local cousins in attendance. Mom had recently redecorated her porch by the garden, so I sponge-painted a large clay pot to match her teal and pink chair cushions and made an English garden in the pot, using several varieties of plants and flowers. I patterned this after one of Martha's English gardens, naturally, and I was rather proud of the result. It was our gift to her, and that night we used it as a centerpiece on our dinner table. Everyone oohed and ahhhed over the English garden while digesting the roast beef. When they left, Mike loaded the planter into Dad's Lincoln while Mom warned not to get dirt in the car. But it was a lovely, elegant evening and a good time was had by all (we surely thought so!), but the next day, Dad ordered Mike to his office and blasted him.

"Look what all we've done for you, Michael," Dad told him.

"What did I do wrong?"

"You know, Michael…"

"No, Dad, I don't know. Tell me."

"I don't have to tell you," Dad insisted. "You know what I'm talking about!"

"Dad! *Tell me!*"

"Oh, for god's sakes, Michael," Dad said, and after a pause, "you can't even get your mother a proper gift!"

"We gave her the big planter!" Mike told me he pleaded the case.

"Michael… I really thought Terri would know better."

"Dad?"

"Michael, that centerpiece was an afterthought. You only gave it to Mom after you realized everyone else brought gifts."

"That's not true! We made it just for her…"

"Don't give me that…"

"We used the colors on your porch!"

"Yeah, right." Dad would acknowledge nothing.

"Dad, it was a nice gift and Terri custom-made it." Mike said he thought invoking my name might end the argument.

"*Ingrates!*" Dad called us.

Mike said he calmly walked out the door and said, "See you later." Then he went to the car and cried.

Dad didn't even listen, Mike said. We didn't have a present wrapped up with a bow on top (like he *expected*), so we were forever "ingrates." Forever.

The next time we visited their place, my mother-in-law said she put the planter by the door and wanted us to take it. "I have no use for it," she said. "The plants all died anyway." We took it home, cleaned out the pot and sold it for $40, minus the little garden.

My relationship with the in-laws was complicated, fraught with constant angst. *What did they want from me? Why couldn't I please them?* My confidence was draining and my ego was deflating. Mom and Dad never apologized, and they never forgave anything – they held grudges and every little incident was subject to being brought up any time.

It was impossible to anticipate their reactions, because there were a few occasions when I would be overwhelmed with their kindness. On one visit, I was sitting in the austere straight chair in the den when Mom casually passed to me an article from one of her magazines. It was about a conference for women entrepreneurs, coming up in Chicago and several big names were listed as speakers and workshop leaders.

"Would you like to go to the conference?"

I thought it might be a test. By saying I would like to go, she could harken back to the "spender" allegation. Yet, if I said I wasn't interested, she could say I was a know-it-all, unwilling to learn. It was hard trying to read her mind and react accordingly. (Oh, boy, was I young!)

"Well, yeah, it sounds great," I finally said.

"Good. I'd like to pay for you to go."

"Really?" My head was spinning, anticipating some kind of blowback.

"It sounds like something I would've liked to do," Mom said. "And by the way, this is coming out of *my* savings, not your father-in-law's bank account."

I instinctively started thinking of clues in what she said (and didn't say). *Why was she doing this? Why did she make a point to say it was coming from her account?* And most perplexing, *Why would she ever have wanted to go to a conference for entrepreneurs?*

"Thank you! I'd love to go."

I couldn't help but wonder if Mom was offering a cloaked apology.

The conference was wonderful, and I met many smart women, a few of whom I am still in touch with today. The very evening I got home, I made a point to call and tell Mom all about the high points and thank her once again. She seemed pleased.

The goodwill didn't last long, and the friction in our personal relationships carried over into our business talks. Eventually, it all became one big quagmire. Dad got frustrated when I didn't understand things right away. "If you don't understand, you're stupid, and I know you're not stupid…," was a common dagger. It took me months to get the gist of what "living off our inventory" meant, except I knew it was something we surely didn't want to do. And we weren't, Dad assured us, but he seemed to want to keep that anxiety kicking deep within our souls.

Completing our taxes at the end of our first year in business was a very worrisome task. The family's CPA at a "Big Eight" accounting firm was handling it, but Dad kept asking me questions about our return and said, "You always have to know more than they do, so you can watch and make sure they're doing it right."

"How can I know everything about doing taxes without going back to school?"

"You have to know, Terri," he said. "Maybe you should take a class."

I did not want to tell Dad I had no intention of taking a class on taxes, now or ever.

"Aren't there times when you can trust someone to help you with the business?" I tried hard to make certain this was asked innocently, without a smart mouth.

"Sheesh…."

I never quite got an answer to my question. I was admittedly math-challenged, always one who was proud simply when I remembered to record all checks and ATM withdrawals. Dad felt the same way about attorneys. "You need to be smarter than they are," was a frequent battle-cry over the years. Dad had a Harvard education, and perhaps because of that, he fancied himself both a lawyer and a CPA as well as a businessman. "You have to know more," he would say. "You just do."

Occasionally, my father-in-law seemed to have a little reticence working with a woman. He would seldom yell at *me*, but he would take it out on Mike. One Sunday when we all went out to dinner, we were talking about the dogwood trees in bloom and how all politicians were idiots. It wasn't unusual for two (or sometimes three) conversations to be carried on simultaneously, and while my left ear heard Mom talking about the Westminster Dog Show, my right ear heard Dad ask Mike, "What were your net sales last month?"

"I don't know off the top of my head."

"Michael, what do you mean, you don't know?" Dad asked, and Mom and I both fell silent.

"I'll call you with the figure as soon as we get home."

"Oh, for god's sakes, Michael. When I was starting my business, I had my sales figures in my head at all times. Not once would I dare tell *my* father I didn't know. *Not once!* You have to know what your sales are."

"Who is going to need my sales figures at the Longhorn Steakhouse?"

"Michael, don't be smart with me."

"Michael, don't be smart with your father," my mother-in-law had to chime in.

"I'm not, Dad, I just don't know what the exact figure is, and I don't want to give you wrong information."

As soon as we got home, Mike called his father to report our sales figures for the last month, but Mom said he was too busy to come to the phone. We figured he was still angry, and we didn't hear anything more about this.

There were several jewelry-buying semi-annual trade shows, both in Providence, RI and New York City. Mike and I would make mini-vacations around the shows, taking a few days in Cape Cod or seeing a Broadway show and visiting some old friends on a long weekend in NYC. One day, I think Dad was in a particularly bad mood when we were talking about an upcoming show and reviewing our jewelry-buying budget.

"Terri, are you going?" Dad asked.

"Yes, we're both going."

"Only one of you needs to go," he said, and I knew then and there our mini vacations were over. "Terri, you're not afraid of going to New York by yourself, are you?"

"No, of course not."

"But Dad…" Mike said.

"Michael, you will stay home and work on sales. That's your job, and Terri will go and do the buying."

"Dad…"

"That's it, and that's it. Terri will go by herself," said Dad. "You don't need to spend *my* money for both of you to go on vacation when you're building up a business."

Dad called Mike one day and summoned both of us to take them to the mall that evening. Dad usually drove, but this time he said his eyes were tired and we were to pick them up at 6:30. We went to Belk's and Dad and Mike made a B-line to the leather sofas and large-screen TVs in the rest area of the mall, while we ladies shopped. Fortunately, Mom was a one-store kind of person, so I knew we would not be traipsing all over the mall. We went to the home department, and she pulled out her pocket-size tape measure and got to work. She was measuring pillows, lamps and candlesticks. I didn't ask any questions.

When she was finished and the tape measure was back in the Longchamps bag, Mom wanted to go to the perfume counter. The Estee Lauder lady came over to help, and Mom said she wanted to buy some perfume. I feigned interest in the new seasonal eye shadow colors while they chatted.

"I want to get a bottle of perfume for my daughter-in-law," Mom told the stylish lady with smoky eyes and burgundy lips. Gesturing to me, she said, "What's good this season for a young, beautiful girl?"

Moi? What I *didn't* say is that I am not a fragrance person. Getting within ten feet of a fragranced person will make my eyes burn, and possibly cause an outbreak of hives. Like a coward, I chose not to say anything (though surely she would've understood because of her many allergies). One large, expensive bottle of "Beautiful" perfume in a little shopping bag came home with me. Mom was pleased as punch ("beauty for beauty," she told me), while I was merely bewildered.

Just when I thought I knew my mother-in-law, she surprised me. It was a nice gesture, but I couldn't help thinking that now she controlled how I smelled.

Admittedly, I didn't know Dad very well when we all got in bed together (so to speak), and in our early days, Mike seemed daunted his father was so controlling. We enjoyed what we were doing, we worked hard, and we were making a profit. While we were grateful for the help, the bullying became worse in direct proportion to how much profit we were making. I believe it was a grand ploy to keep us close to him.

Dad repeatedly said I had a lot to learn, but when he became consumed with his own company's growth, we were on our own. No longer were we his chief concern in life, and things were calm and peaceful for a while, though we were still under his thumb. We volunteered regular reports on spread sheets, but there was rarely any discussion about our progress. Occasionally, Dad would start a high and mighty argument to make a point. The more frustrated he became with his own business, dealing with the brokers, attorneys and shareholders, the more he tyrannized us.

We had sold our soul and could not find a civil way out. He refused to let us pay him back, and we even had a letter from his attorney saying the money was a gift. "It will mess up my taxes if you pay me back," he said. Yet he constantly ended conversations with, "I wouldn't have given you the money if I had known...."

They expected us to be totally available to them at all times. Mom needs a ride to two grocery stores. Dad needs someone to go with him to his doctor's appointment. Mom wants Terri to return some things to Talbot's. Dad has to take the dog to the vet and needs help from Michael. Mom needs to go to the paint store. Dad needs Michael to take a bag of soil from the car to the patio. We also had to visit frequently; it wasn't unusual for one of them to point out that we hadn't seen them in a few days (they had been counting), and heaven help us if the visit was less than two to three hours. With Martin and his family making only one annual trip to town, Mike and I were their sole entertainment, companionship and personal servants.

One evening when we were in their den watching the clock to determine when it was safe to leave, Mom pointed out that I was wearing a new outfit. Shortly thereafter, Dad called Mike into the kitchen to ask where we got the money to buy new clothes. "If you can buy new clothes, then you can finance your own business." God knows, I wish we had.

I was enraged that the in-laws lorded over our home. (Never let someone put their draperies in your house because apparently it marks some native territorial right.) I did something I'd never done before nor since: I picked up a small plant in the kitchen that Mom had given us ("because it has bugs in it") and threw it hard against the white wall. It was in a plastic container, so there were no pottery shards to contend with, but the black dirt splattered all over and left a stain on the wall. It felt good.

Every day, I wondered, *how could they treat us this way?* When I would discuss an in-law incident with my mother, she insisted I must have misunderstood -- surely they didn't mean what they said. "They meant it alright," I would retort, and inevitably, I ended up in an argument with my mother because she took their side most of the time.

In retrospect, after 450 miles of distance and years of TV psychotherapy with Dr. Phil, I learned the proper phraseology is *we allowed them* to treat us this way. But at the time, we were so downtrodden, we felt helpless to change our relationship. We did the next best thing -- we ran away from home. We didn't pack a bag and abscond in the middle of the night; we found a Realtor who put a FOR SALE sign in our yard. In just six days, our house sold after a bidding war and the new owners wanted to close in just three weeks.

It was a good thing we left quickly because we had become neighborhood pariahs: The Homeowner's Association sent us daily missives with the rules for signs, insisting they be very small and in a front window – no yard signs allowed. We boldly ignored the rules, even when they stole the sign and threatened to sue. Mike put out a replacement sign every morning. By the time we left Charlotte, we were outlaws with in-law problems. We hit the highway driving a large rental truck and towing our car. Destination: Baltimore. We didn't look back once.

Our friends and relatives were shocked we moved. Neither of us had really talked about the possibility of a move. The in-laws were thunderstruck and immediately jumped to the conclusion we were moving to get away from them. We never confirmed or denied their claim. Mom and Dad decided we were selfish and ungrateful, and a cold war began that would last seven years.

"We're free!" Mike said repeatedly on the long drive north. "I can't believe we actually did this." The farther we got from Charlotte, the more the euphoria began to wear off. Somewhere near Raleigh, Mike quietly murmured, "We'll be okay... *won't we?*" I was already feeling shaky, and he scared me so much I started crying and by South Hill, Virginia, Mike was crying, too. We both felt weights lifted off our backs, but at the same time, the sacrifices we were making weighed heavily on our minds. Our sales and marketing company could move with us, but in many ways, we were truly starting over.

* 4 *

EFFECTIVE IMMEDIATELY

"It's how you handle adversity, not how it affects you. The main thing is never quit, never quit, never quit." -- Bill Clinton

Your contract with us is terminated, effective immediately.
Best,
Arnie

The email was from the owner of our premier client, a small candy company my husband and I nurtured for two years and grew to be a viable competitive force in the national marketplace. That's what we did – we helped grow small businesses, and somehow we landed a sweet niche in candy. Once referred to as "guerilla marketers," Mike and I could put a candy line on the map (and in the stores) while staying on a shoestring budget.

It was around six on this Monday morning, and I was heading to our home office preparing to start another busy, in-season week for confectionary matters. In my peach nightshirt with the cupcakes print, I was barefoot, and my sinuses hadn't even settled yet. I sat down at the computer to check the fax and email and see if we had received any purchase orders overnight.

"Mike!! Mike, wake up!" I called into the bedroom. "You need to come in here." I really think I could have handled this more delicately; I could have gone back to the bedroom and jostled him awake gently and then when he was fully alert, maybe give him the chance to go to the bathroom and have a swig of Diet Mountain Dew. I even thought about calling him on his cell phone, which is usually by the bed, but I noticed it was on his desk recharging. I rarely woke Mike up, so I didn't have a ready protocol. Poor Mike.

"I'm coming, I'm coming," Mike said in a daze as he ambled in looking for his glasses, his hair sticking straight up, and his sweatpants askew, hanging around his hips like a teenage boy heading to the cellular store. "What? What's going on?"

I relayed the message: *Terminated.* I think that's the word that got his attention. We've never been *terminated* before, and it sounded like Arnie had put out a contract for us both, and we should immediately plan a big spaghetti and meatballs last supper.

Mike lunged for the phone immediately.

"Wait, let's make some notes," I said, but he didn't miss a beat dialing Arnie.

"No, I'm calling now." I followed my husband to his second desk in the dining room.

Not surprisingly, there was no answer. The secretary and crew weren't due in until seven. We felt sure Arnie was there because he just sent the email, and he was not tech-savvy enough to do it from home or from a phone. Ducking and ignoring problems was his M.O., but he had to know sending this email would get a reaction.

Mike called constantly, alternating between Arnie's cell phone and the main office number. He hung up when he got voice mail and immediately tried again.

"Yo," answered Arnie, on the seventh call.

"Hi, how are you?" Mike chirped, as though the termination message never hit our inbox. I rolled my eyes and went to my desk, but the conversation was loud and clear on speaker phone. Why were they were exchanging pleasantries and talking about their weekends? (My husband is a weird kid.)

"Now, the email?" Mike asked.

Right at that exact moment, I decided to parlay our recent online selling of household junk and clothes into a new sideline business to generate some fast income. Clearly, there was nothing that could salvage the situation with Arnie; he was a very stubborn person and would never change his mind, even if he wanted to. And besides, how could we go back into a relationship with someone who treated us this way? Sure, we had a contract with him, but we learned years ago that a lawsuit is just too costly, and the company you sue may be out of business altogether by the time a court date rolls around. With our stellar reputation in the candy business, I knew we would find a suitable replacement line, but that would take some time.

"No hard feelings, I just can't afford to pay you anymore."

"You just decided this over the weekend?" Mike asked.

Several months earlier, I had discovered a V-Cart store of inexpensive sterling silver and gemstone jewelry. New, not vintage. I was skeptical about the stones being real, but after communication with the company and some online research, I felt confident. My first purchase was a dressy pair of silver and garnet drop earrings that I loved. I went on to extend my jewelry wardrobe with several more pieces, but it was frustrating that the listings didn't give much description and the photos were often difficult to decipher. Sometimes it felt like a crap-shoot when ordering, as I was never quite sure what I would get, what size it would be or an exact color. But the prices were right, and the designs beautiful. As a marketing professional, I was usually sizing up selling points of everything I see to some extent or another. For instance, I knew this company's sales would be much better, and they could command higher prices, if a little more time was spent writing the listings.

Here was my opportunity: I would buy jewelry and other accessories from this jewelry vendor and others, and then re-sell it under our Terri*art* name, with good photos and details… lots of details. I would give measurements so there were no surprises. Often, the earrings in the listing photo looked big enough to choke a horse, and when they arrived in the mail, they were tiny studs. When these Asian jewelry makers gave any measurements at all, it was in metric. Who knows metric? Well, I do now, with the help of a metric ruler. But I ordered several pieces pre-ruler and just guessed the size.

One big selling point to push is that ordering from Terri*art*, the jewelry would be shipped from within the US. I would acknowledge that it was made in China, Thailand or India, but the customer would get it fast and from a trustworthy source. Oh, yes… I would employ lots of *spin*.

Mike was still on the phone. "What do you mean, you are going to handle all sales in-house from now on?" Mike asked Arnie.

"The customers will just call in their orders, and we really don't need salespeople."

Citrine dangle earrings… Blue Lapis pendant… Spider Turquoise drop earrings… I could envision each piece, one of a kind, probably made by artisans in a remote village.

"You really think our sales came from just answering the phone?" Mike asked.

"No, you guys have done a great job," Arnie said, non-chalantly, "but I just can't afford it anymore."

I could give fashion tips with the listings and suggestions on how to wear each piece. I would make it fun for women to buy jewelry for themselves, and informative for a man buying jewelry for the women in his life. And I would do it all with a wink and a smile; the low price point made it a whimsical purchase.

"Well, Arnie, what about the sales kits and the newsletters that the customers love?"

"I never thought that worked, to tell you the truth."

"How do you think we expanded the business so much?" Mike was getting frustrated.

"But we should be doing even *more* sales by now."

"There's a recession on, you know. But still, we've increased every month - you've always said you are happy with our sales, and we've never heard a word otherwise," Mike said, still trying to reason with Arnie.

I was in a buying mode, going to favorite sources where I was now ordering inventory. Beautiful Rose Quartz earrings, one pair with the stone set inside a wire heart and another pair, very long dangles. Mint Green Jade discs… earrings with Black Onyx stones set in filigree… a large Mosaic Jasper pendant, violet-colored with all-natural blue designs embedded in the stone. Most were one-of-a-kind designs. I was back in the wholesale jewelry business where we wouldn't have to operate at the whim of a wishy-washy client. (Just at the whim of a wishy-washy customer, every now and then.)

"Mike, you know we had originally made some projections…." Arnie was still defending his decision.

"That was before the economy tanked!" Mike tried to reason with him. "And besides, you didn't hold up *your* end – you said we could grow the line with holiday and boutique items."

"You and Terri had to know I had no intention of putting one dime into expanding the line until your sales were much higher."

"Arnie, the sales increases we projected were based on a larger and updated line."

Pastel Blue Topaz bracelet… deep London Blue Topaz ring (size 6 only, so I'd have to remember to push it as a pinkie ring)… all of this inventory would be here in about two weeks.

I was excited about the items I was choosing and my minutes-old selling plans, but my stomach was doing flip-flops listening to that conversation. Why was he trying to convince Arnie he was making a mistake by "terminating" us? I wrote a note and handed it to Mike: END THE CONVERSATION!! Mike's response was to take the call off speaker and move with the phone into the living room.

I didn't care. I had already moved on and ordered several dozen silk scarves from China I knew would sell. My initial orders totaled about $1,000. About the time I finished the transaction, Mike walked back into the office, off the phone now, looking exhausted and defeated. I knew he was preparing to repeat every word of the conversation (and then some) to me.

"I don't want to hear anything about that call," I said, right as his mouth was opening. "We just started a new business and our merchandise is on the way."

Mike perked up a little bit, though he had a confused look on his face. I sent him to Staples to get card stock, bubble wrap and a new cyan toner cartridge (in anticipation of increased usage due to the turquoise Terri*art* logo). Within the next few hours, I designed a jewelry hang tag, which I could print on card stock, and I ordered ribbon to tie through it. I also ordered black and gray velvet jewelry display forms for my photos.

There are mystical and mythical properties associated with gemstones. Over the next several days I designed a keepsake information card for each stone, telling some of the legends and stories: Garnet (fire, faith and fidelity), Turquoise (wards off disease), Amethyst (encourages sobriety), Chalcedony (helps prevents drowning), Onyx (enhances communication skills) and several other stones. A card would ship with each gem piece.

I decided that an info card detailing the history and care of silk scarves would accompany every scarf purchase. *TIP: Remove a lipstick stain by placing a piece of tape over the stain, press it down and then yank the tape off. Sprinkle talcum or baby powder on any remaining color and pat it gently with a clean cloth.*

Thus began my research, and I still refused to talk with Mike about Arnie. He was onboard with me for the new V-Cart business venture, and we had just two weeks to re-launch our Terri*art* accessories line to a new market.

Elegant and *sophisticated*, I don't know which word conjures up a better description of the way I fancy myself. I have the foresight to know these days it's only in my mind's eye that I live up to this image; my high-falutin' dress-for-success days in the fashion business ended long ago at about the same time big frizzy hair became passé (though, unfortunately, now I battle my big frizzy hair).

Mike and I had had a good run with our first scarf and jewelry business (way before online selling), with two office/showrooms in Charlotte – one at the gift market and one at the apparel market. We had a booming business and were leaders of the independents in our field. We were constantly on extended sales trips and we worked many of the apparel trade shows throughout the South, where store buyers and owners would come and order their clothes and accessories for a season. The shows were killers. They officially began at nine or ten AM, but we found if we opened early at seven, there were many buyers milling around, walking the halls and looking for something to do. We served cappuccino and fruit breads and had some good sales in those hours before the buyers were spent out, both physically and financially.

We hired a showroom model to give scarf-tying demos, and I schooled buyers on the latest trends (toned down and appropriate for the diaspora beyond Seventh Avenue and the greater tri-state area). When someone from Terri*art* spoke, people listened. It was grand fun, and my years of studying fashion magazines from *Seventeen* to *Self* finally came in handy (though for the most part, I was only repeating info about new trends gleaned from the factory trade shows we ourselves attended as buyers several times a year).

The shows usually ended at five, but we rarely left the showroom until seven or later, often until ten or eleven. When we closed early, it was because we took our best customers out to dinner. Typically from small towns, the customers were excited to be in the big city of Charlotte, raring to go out at night and get a cocktail, since many of their hometowns were dry.

Mike was a great salesperson, beloved by our customers. He kept track of their birthdays, children's names, upcoming weddings, surgeries and vacation cruises, and he always followed-up. Everyone knew Mike truly cared about them.

There was Bunny B. Baker in Fuquay-Varina, NC who ran a dress shop. Her adult brother, who was mentally challenged, always sat behind the counter and he took a mighty shine to Mike, following him around the store and laying his head on Mike's shoulder. And in a military town in eastern North Carolina when it was nearly 100 degrees one July afternoon, Patsy (of Patsy's Dress Shop) was debating whether or not to turn on the air conditioning, wondering if it might help business if the store was cool. She sent her sales clerk out a few blocks to the drugstore on Main Street to get cups of shaved ice for Mike and me so we wouldn't pass out from the heat, while she looked through our samples of holiday jewelry and accessories.

I traveled with Mike to Plains, Georgia, where we sold Terri*art* earrings to a little general store that catered to busloads of tourists, coming to town just to drive by Jimmy and Rosalynn Carter's home and visit the "quaint" shops. They would peruse "ol' timey" things like reproduction Depression glass referred to as antiques, and reproductions of Carter campaign memorabilia. Naturally, there were bags of peanuts for sale everywhere. And there was always a jewelry nook; the sales clerk would point out a pair of earrings and say that Miss Lillian, the president's mother, had bought a similar pair for herself (decades earlier) to wear to church. Souvenir-hunters bought this tale --- and the jewelry, too.

After a while, as our business grew, Mike traveled alone while I watched over the warehouse and office employees. He came to know more of the customers than I did. Apparently, he talked about me when he was in the stores, because quite often during a trade show, Mike would usher a buyer into the showroom saying, "Here she is... here's Terri." I was mortified, feeling like a Miss America on display. But there was the time one woman gave me a big hug and said, "Your husband loooooooves you!" The grand presentation didn't seem quite so bad after that.

From our first road trip with the jewelry samples, making sales calls on independent dress shops, drugstores and hospital gift shops, Mike would always survey the buyer, asking if there was anything she needed that she couldn't find. Mike was always looking for a hot new line to carry along with our own Terri*art* jewelry. We had a good business brewing; this was in the days before big box stores took over retail and forced Main Street out of business.

One shop owner said she wanted a fabulous (but very inexpensive) handbag line, and another suggested finding a line of belts a bit larger than small/medium and medium/large. Big and colorful Origami-type paper earrings were in vogue (hey, it was the '80s, remember?) and we had calls for them. We chose not to carry that trend, because a sample order we placed came in broken and crimped. No paper dangles for us – way too fragile to fool with.

The number one request surprised us, as it was (way) outside of the accessories field. Many buyers were looking for a low to medium priced boxed chocolate line – something different that wasn't in all the national chains.

We found a great chocolate line in Michigan, a regionally-known family business that was hungry for growth, and we sold ourselves as the ones who could spearhead that growth. It took many visits to Detroit, working with the company to design sales tools and promotions and to get the plant prepared for sales increases. We were off and running the week after July 4th, the traditional start of booking candy orders through the holidays. This dove-tailed nicely with the accessories, as the bulk of our seasonal candy-selling was over before the dress shops ordered for the holidays. It was a great fit with our first candy company. We increased sales significantly, and word in the industry spread like wildfire. The following year, we got a call from a non-competing candy company specializing in novelties and kiddie candies. The owner asked if we would work with them, too and – just like that – we were off to New Jersey for another opportunity.

———— ∿•᎙ᕱᏋᎷᏜᎶᎧ᎙•∿ ————

Five years later, several things happened all at once. We began losing our jewelry and scarf customers when Walmart took over small-town America and shops fell like dominoes. Mike and I were tired of traveling and schlepping the samples all over the South. We couldn't possibly keep up this pace much longer, even though we were (relatively) young and (relatively) healthy at the time (and why not throw in beautiful and wealthy, too). We didn't stock inventory on the candy – it was all sent out directly from the makers. Taking orders and collecting commissions and fees for marketing and consulting was becoming far more lucrative than wholesaling jewelry and scarves, so when we got an offer from a competitor to buy us out, we jumped at the opportunity. Basically, they would pay us to exit the jewelry business and shepherd our customers their way. We negotiated to stay away from accessory sales for ten years, but we would keep the Terri*art* name. It was a sweet deal.

Another major change took place. Mike and I left our families in Charlotte and moved to an apartment in Baltimore. Errr… rather, the suburbs of Baltimore; clearly, we were not the elevator-building, street-parking types populating the trendy renovated areas of the inner city. We felt light and free as we traded our apparel market jewelry showrooms and our warehouse for a home office. We swapped tax deductible lunches with customers and vendors in trendy bistros for microwaved leftovers on paper plates at home.

The benefits of our new epoch quickly outweighed the sacrifices. We worked with entrepreneurs to make their small businesses more efficient. Mike and I emphasized customer service, sales tools and presentations, public relations and marketing. It was liberating not to fret over inventory and constant travel; we just had to worry about moody, stressed and often financially-strapped proprietors, most mired in a "this is the way I do business" mind-set.

When we swapped dressy casual outfits for nightshirts and sweatsuits, Mike and I became full-on fashion frumps. Being of a certain age with attendant wear and tear comes with benefits however: Comfortable shoes with padding and rubber soles, elastic in the waistbands and for me, a pass on using hot curlers every day.

Now that his hair is a bit more salt than pepper, this casualness (slovenliness?) appeals to my husband just fine, but I cringe when I think of my now out-of-style (and out-of-fit) outfits from Saks and Neiman's. Occasionally, I make a valiant effort (or at least pretend I could if I wanted to), though lately, dressing for events from a tony wedding to a business tête-à-tête in New York City to a casual dinner with friends coming through town has been known to send me into full-fledged panic mode.

Often feeling as though I had moved from grief to acceptance of the atrophied fashion sense, I still enjoyed fashion magazines and websites. I watched programs on cable TV; a makeover show was a guilty pleasure even though it reminded me I personally would need more than a makeover – I would need a complete renovation.

One day during busy season, I was taking a short lunch break in the kitchen eating leftover ratatouille. Mike had been to the post office and tossed our stack of mail on the counter. I spotted a silver glow from halfway across the room; it radiated like a bright and shiny quarter bathed in a spotlight, calling out to me. I reached over to pull the intriguing catalog out of the stack of mail, behind the gas bill and on top of my husband's *Chain Store Review* trade tabloid. As far as I was concerned, the phones ceased ringing, my email didn't ding, and I told my husband I was off-duty indefinitely. I took the thick look-book over to our most comfortable chair where I could browse in peace and quiet.

Before e-commerce became popular and "Project Runway" took over TV, you knew when the seasons were about to change because the catalogs started coming in the mail. I received many of them, mostly fashion compendiums. When we were in Charlotte, my mother-in-law gave me stacks of catalogs she received from big-name American stores as well as British standards. Every time we got together, she would give me a stack to take home: "These came today," she would say, but would only pass them along after the yapper-dog had slobbered all over them and ice cream was spilt on the covers.

My mother-in-law ordered from catalogs all the time, often getting into long conversations with the customer service person on the other end of the phone: "Thank goodness for catalogs," she would begin the chit-chat. "We can't get nice things here." After the chatfest, usually coinciding with her soap opera starting on TV, she would hand the phone to my father-in-law so he could give the credit card number and shipping address. It wasn't unusual for her to get a half dozen packages in a day. I would order something occasionally, but did not have the patience to wait four to six weeks, which is what many catalogs promised at the time.

I was loving this new spring catalog, realizing I hadn't seen a catalog from Lord & Taylor in some time. This was back when Lord & Taylor was *Lord & Taylor*, before their grand expansion that watered down the brand. I had not even stepped into the venerable New York City grande dame of a department store since my fashion days. Most catalogs went the way of dial-up Internet service about the same time I stopped mall shopping as a hobby and started ordering whatever I need exclusively online – at high speed.

I grabbed the catalog, fluffed up some pillows, folded the afghan neatly across the arm and made myself comfy-cozy in the chair, ripe with anticipation. It occurred to me I should have a cup of tea standing by – perhaps a full-bodied Earl Grey blend in a good china cup with saucer - but I had my Diet Cherry Dr. Pepper. In a can. *A can!* How elegant and sophisticated was that? I shook my head in silence, wondering if I deserved to order from this glossy catalog.

I hadn't even opened to page one before I found something I had to have. There on the front cover was a pair of beautiful silk scarves, the design "exclusively ours," the copy said. Really works of art, the scarves had a background of white with a black border around the edges. Inside the borders was an explosion of yellow roses, from buds to full cabbage heads. (Colors really come alive in silk.) I remembered a yellow jean-style jacket I bought the previous year and had never worn. *This scarf would be perfect with the jacket.* It would tie the yellow jacket to black pants or a black skirt, meaning I would have a new outfit. I'd be crazy not to get the scarf. The roses looked so real and inviting, all I could think of was whether I should order the square or the oblong.

My husband joined me, sitting on the sofa, turning the television on and taking a break. This was one of those times when I yearned for a sitting area in the master suite, furnished with a luxurious tapestry-covered chaise lounge next to a sunny window and small table with a reading lamp, priceless trinkets and a vase, perhaps holding fresh yellow roses.

I studied the photos and read every word on every page, still giddy over a genuine catalog. I was daydreaming: *If* I were a lady of leisure, I would wear this dress to high tea. *If* money were no object, I would get this cashmere sweater set in every color. More than once, I had a reality check, like when I realized I *did* have a light blue cashmere twin set in my armoire and had only worn it a few times because, really, it was not necessary to wear something like that while I typed up proposals and marketing plans at home. (And would I wear it *over* or *under* my nightshirt?) *If* I had someplace to wear these shoes, and *if* I felt comfortable wearing high heels, I would definitely want the featured black patent leather sling-backs. I ordered the oblong scarf.

A couple of weeks later when my L & T package arrived, my heart started beating a little faster, and I took the carton into the bedroom so I could better savor the moment. It wasn't easy opening it, because my nail file couldn't crack the seam. I had to fetch the kitchen shears, which could easily cut through a chicken carcass (should I ever have the need), so packing tape and corrugated cardboard was no challenge at all.

Inside a nest of white tissue paper was another brown carton. As I struggled with the over-abundance of brown tape, I felt I was opening Russian nesting dolls packed one inside the other, graduating down in size to a nubby thimble-size doll.

Inside this second carton was a signature gift box tied with a pretty white satin ribbon and a gift card attached. Gift? This was for me; a gift *to* me, *from* me, you could say. But I could use the ribbon for another gift at some point, so I carefully untied the bow, rolled it up and put it in my bureau drawer.

Mike came into the room right about the time I was opening the box. "What's that?" he asked.

"It's just a little surprise," I told him, frankly irritated I wasn't left alone with my spoils.

He saw the gift box and said, "I got it for your anniversary gift. I knew you would like it." I had to laugh, in spite of myself, at these words coming from a man who is a wonderful husband, but a man who doesn't "do" gifts. Whatever I want, I buy and he's fine with that, just don't send him out to purchase a gift for his wife (or anyone else). He'd be paralyzed with fear and wouldn't have a clue where to go or what to get.

Fortunately, the phone rang and Mike rushed back into the office to catch it. Alone again. I pulled the lid off the box and found more tissue paper with a beautiful sticker on top sporting the store logo. It was so inviting, I didn't want to rip into it (but really, why would I save a sticker?). I carefully unraveled sheet after sheet after sheet, thinking this wasn't exactly "green" packaging. Underneath the first layer, I found a pouch of free samples: Tiny perfume vials clipped to postcards advertising the scent, a small tube of eye repair serum (man, did I need that!), and lipstick in a color called Lusty Beige. I vowed that Lusty Beige would be my new signature color on those few occasions when I even bothered to wear lipstick at all.

Voila! Folded in the box, the scarf looked pristine and perfect. I marveled that the prettiest rose was showcased by the fold. I carefully put it around my neck and looked in the mirror. Women know as hard as it sometimes is to look into a full-length mirror, there is an outside chance there will be a pleasant surprise when checking out one's façade. Granted, it's not terribly likely, but the possibility *does exist* that the Queen of Sheba will nod at you from the mirror and make you feel just swell.

No doubt about it, the scarf was gorgeous. Me? Well, the reality was that this fine foulard folded over my faded fuchsia knee-length nightshirt with flowers of an unknown variety was just *wrong*. The mirror seemed to show a noose made from yellow roses about to choke me senseless. I looked less like, say, a regal brunette Grace Kelly-type and more like Roseanne Barr, Domestic Goddess and wearer of polyester.

I'll look better when I am dressed up, I told myself. I practiced saying this as I continued tying the scarf over and over. I went into the closet and pulled out my yellow jacket thinking it might help improve the overall picture, but when I noticed it had a little dust on the shoulders, I felt like a housekeeping failure as well as a fashion flop. Maybe if I could just find that large black handbag with the white stitching... or did I sell it?

Finally, I realized that by ignoring the contrasting print hanging out below the jacket and squinting at just the right angle into the mirror, it was possible to believe this might, perhaps, make a nice outfit (with a black skirt or pants).

"You goin' somewhere?" Mike asked as he sauntered back in and plopped on the bed.

"No, Mike, I'm just trying on some things." *And then I might go to Walmart to stock up on paper towels and a bag of chocolate peanuts whilst wearing my nightshirt with this yellow jacket and scarf.*

"You look beautiful, as usual," he said. "I need you to type up an order – the customer's waiting for it."

Jarred back into reality, I hastily pulled off the scarf and threw it on the bed. As I was taking off the jacket, I got a cuff button caught in my mess of a leftover hairdo.

"There's no big rush," Mike said, oblivious to my struggle to get unhooked from the death grip the yellow jacket had on my hair. *No, other than you just said the customer is waiting for it.* Then the phone rang again, and Mike ran back into the office. Finally free, I put a small wad of torn hair in the trashcan, hung the jacket and put it back in the closet to collect a little more dust.

I sat on the bed for a final fantasy moment and carefully folded the scarf. I followed the existing crease lines and somehow managed to get it back in the box. I derived some measure of satisfaction doing do, because this is not unlike putting toothpaste back in the tube or refolding a map (in the old days, when we used real maps). I wrapped the ribbon around the box, enveloped it in tissue paper, pressed down the sticker and what was left of the stickiness held just fine.

Eventually I would get rid of the trappings, steam the creases and put the scarf in my armoire with all the others. But I wanted to savor the luxurious feeling and at another point, open the box one more time.

—⟶⦙⦙⦙·◦·❀◦❀◦❀◦·⦙⦙⦙—

Several years later, when our V-Cart scarf business was starting, I remembered how I felt while opening the box with the gift to myself, the luxurious silk scarf. I wanted my customers to be able to savor a similar experience, whether they were ordering a used polyester scarf with an overcast edge, or a rare, vintage Vera mod print silk scarf. I wrapped each scarf in white tissue paper and sealed it with a Terri*art* sticker and a satin ribbon tied in a bow. This made my scarves memorable to the buyers, and I received as many comments on the packaging as I did on the fast service and beautiful merchandise. Terri*art* Scarves were a hit!

* 5 *

BREAKFAST WITH MY TIFFANY

"A shocking crime was committed on the unscrupulous initiative of few individuals, with the blessing of more, and amid the passive acquiescence of all." – Tacitus

When I was in my twenties, if anyone had told me I would marry a traveling salesman, I would have rolled my eyes and argued tooth and nail. No way, I would say. My husband will be very sophisticated. His name will be Ethan or Allen and he will be tall, dark and handsome. He will wear a bespoke suit to work at his own company and move mountains with one soft comment to his staff. He will propose to me with a Cartier ring of his own design, perchance a fiery canary diamond centerpiece set in platinum. He will own a tuxedo, a silk in midnight navy with a white pin-tucked shirt, a black cummerbund, onyx studs and monogrammed platinum cuff links that I have given to him. He will love the symphony, charity fundraisers and silent auctions, and we will dance at the Rainbow Room on theatre trips to New York while discussing our plans to have five children. I was always on the lookout for this man.

On the trail of establishing my career as a journalist covering the arts and entertainment, I was at a bar gathering information for a story about nightlife for *Charlotte* magazine. It was Golden Oldies Night, and Mike the DJ was playing songs like "Under the Boardwalk" and "Stay." The dance floor was filled with men wearing loafers without socks and the women who like that type. As the booze flowed, the dancing became increasingly provocative, and I think someone staggered into the ladies room to throw up. This was not my scene. My mission was to take the notes I needed and get home sooner, rather than later.

But sometimes fate just whips around the corner and surprises us with a smack on the head, and this was one of those times. During a break in the music, I met Mike the DJ and I knew that evening I would marry him. Mike -- tall, dark and handsome, for sure. Mike -- a DJ. I learned he had a popular weekend oldies radio show on a local radio station. Oh, and I also learned that his *real* job was, as he put it, "traveling salesman." Sheesh, he couldn't even dress up the title, saying he was a manufacturer's representative or a sales consultant. He was, quite simply, a DJ on the weekends and a traveling salesman hawking a line of fashion jewelry during the week.

Mike was charming, in a quirky, funny and sincere way. He made me feel special. We exchanged business cards, and the next day when he called me, our life together began. We dated on and off for about a year, but it was a tumultuous relationship, and we had a bitter break-up. Mike wasn't ready to settle down.

Several years later, I still thought about Mike, though I certainly wasn't waiting for him. My career was everything to me, and I talked myself right into feature writing for *The Charlotte Observer*, then back to *Charlotte Magazine*.

I sold my stories as well as any Girl Scout cookie salesperson ever sold a box of Samoas, and soon I had clawed, back-stabbed and slept my way to editor of the magazine. Okay, it might not be quite accurate about the clawing, the back-stabbing and the sex. I think maybe I was the one most willing to put in the long hours necessary to put out a monthly magazine when we were perpetually "short-handed." But I loved the work, met some talented people, and had a grand time. My favorite task was writing the editor's column in every issue, and my photo ran with the piece.

One day, I was holding a meeting with some interns, and the receptionist interrupted to give me a note. It said, "Mike Kane is on the phone, do you want to take the call, or should I take a message?"

I took the call. I learned later that Mike had read the magazine while at his parent's house, and started thinking about me when he saw my picture. We got together that very evening and quickly became inseparable, moving in together after a few short months. Mike had grown up. Maybe I had, too, because we didn't have the turbulence we experienced in the past.

My Mike. My fiancé. He proposed by having me find an engagement ring hooked onto a (dirty) fork in the dishwasher as I was loading it after dinner one night. Okay, so it wasn't exactly a swoon-worthy proposal, and it didn't come with an accompanying Cartier box. But the exquisite diamond ring was an heirloom from his late Aunt Rose. It was a little on the snug side, but I was able to force it on my left ring finger. I later learned from Mike's mother that even though Aunt Rose was "just a little bit of a thing," she played piano and therefore had "*huge* hands." Apparently my hands were huger than hers. And though the ring was not, we were a perfect fit.

My wonderful Mike wouldn't wear a tuxedo or even a dark suit for our May wedding. He wore a natural-color linen sports jacket, navy pants, white shirt and yellow foulard-print tie. He looked great. I wore a tea-length lace dress that I designed and made myself. It was a beautiful Sunday afternoon wedding with about a hundred people, friends and relatives, and we encouraged them to bring their children. My plans for a pianist and string quartet at the reception gave way to Mike's fellow DJ playing mostly oldies. Our guests enjoyed it, and everyone was out on the dance floor. We had a lavish buffet table including a huge roast beef with a carving attendant. I'm sure we had plenty of other food, too, but I honestly don't remember specifics. We had a beautiful wedding cake with fresh flowers, but the highlight was a large fruit platter and a chocolate fondue pot for dipping. What I *do* remember is chocolate on the floor, chocolate on the flower girls' puffy dresses and general stickiness on most surfaces. (Suggestion: Never offer fondue when there are children in the building.)

Several people commented that it was the most fun wedding they had ever attended. I would never have believed that "fun" would best describe my wedding day, but it was true. We had a great time. My mother loved Mike, she said, because he made me laugh.

Life with Mike is never dull. In fact, it's fun.

———————

I have always been a good salesperson myself, selling either things or ideas, even though I seldom recognized it as "sales." My first real sales experience came when I was in the third grade. My older neighborhood friends were selling Girl Scout cookies, but I was still in Brownies and had another year before joining the cookie chaos. This just wouldn't do a'tall, I decided, and I commandeered my grandmother to take me to the grocery store where I bought fifty novelty boxes of cookies at a quarter each. There were three flavors of wafers – chocolate, vanilla and lemon. I remember the store manager asking me why I had all those cookies in my cart. I was probably very indignant and gave him a song and dance about my plans. I came home and made a sign and sales receipts and then hit the sidewalk. I sold my cookies door-to-door for the bargain sum of $1 per box or $2.50 for three boxes, one of each flavor. I beat the Girl Scouts. They merely took orders and customers had to wait weeks for the Thin Mints and the Do-Si-Dos, while my business was strictly cash and carry. I sold out in one afternoon. Well, I might have had a couple of boxes of vanilla leftover, but fortunately the inventory was edible. I wanted to re-stock (more chocolate and less vanilla and lemon this time), but my mother had gotten wind of this caper and put the kibosh on further plans. At the end of cookie-selling season, my Girl Scout friend had a patch on her sash for outstanding cookie sales, but I was smug knowing I had made more than $25 profit. Of course, what I *really* wanted was the patch.

The following year, I joined the big leagues, the real Girl Scouts, but I didn't last until cookie season rolled around in the spring. I did not like anything about the Scouts. I had a falling out with the troop leader, Miss Delice, over something or other, and for several weeks when my mother thought I was walking to the church where the meetings were held, I was playing hookey at a small park nearby. The jig was up one week when Mama came to surprise me by picking me up. Boy, was *she* surprised when I was nowhere to be found, and Miss Delice's big fat mouth told her I had not been to a meeting in a month or so. The whole southeast Mecklenburg County Hornet's Nest Council Girl Scouts was in an uproar trying to find me, but I was back at home watching TV, eating a Popsicle, and wondering where everybody was.

Selling is important, but it's also important to clearly know what you are buying. I've had some experience with fakes and counterfeits.

In sixth grade, I was writing, directing and starring in our class play, some type of historical epic. There was a girl named Angela in my play who had recently moved to our parts from California. She lived near me in a fixed-up and fabulous barn-turned-house (before fabulous barns-turned-houses were chic). It had been the talk of the neighborhood when work commenced in the summer, before Angela and company hit town. By the time school started, her family had moved into the barn with one wall demo'd and plastic sheeting was all that stood between their living quarters and the elements. Nosy neighbors just couldn't understand how they could live there during the renovation.

Angela and I shared the same bus stop, but she made it known she was far superior to us southern girls, and I didn't much like that. But I do recall she had the coolest wardrobe of the entire sixth grade: Tie-dyed babydoll tunics, extremely wide, distressed bell bottoms and a turquoise suede pocketbook with crochet accents and long fringe. Angela had the coolest knee-high boots that laced up the front -- real hippie boots from California that were impressive. I had trendy blue suede clogs with a cork platform, but the boots were far, far better. I was jealous.

I wrote and directed (and starred in) our sixth grade class play, some type of historical epic, and one day Angela brought a tray of rings to school and was selling them on my time. This was creating a distraction when we were supposed to be rehearsing. She claimed they were real diamonds, sapphires and rubies, set in real gold. They did look mighty appealing, well worth the five and ten dollars she was asking for each ring. A few girls got a ring for free, because Angela liked them. She told me if I gave her a big part in the play, she would give me a special ring that was so beautiful, she didn't have it with her that day. I didn't believe her for one minute and was irritated she was interrupting rehearsal, so I left the room, found the teacher and tattled. Not only was Angela's Jewel Emporium shut down immediately, but Mrs. Walker made all the kids give back the rings and then she confiscated them. I later heard that Angela's mother had been called and it turned out that the rings were samples and had been swiped from her father, a traveling salesman. (And no, of course, they were not *real*...) I don't know what floored me more: That she was passing off fake stones as real or that she did it during our rehearsal. That Angela had some nerve.

I was no naïve Nelly when I moved to New York City to go to college, but I was still in culture-shock mode when my dorm-mate showed me where to buy a counterfeit pocketbook. I was overwhelmed by the Canal Street Specials, as I perused the (fake) Gucci, Coach and Chanel bags. I bought a nice Bottega Veneta with an extra-long shoulder strap in a dark brown for $20 (bargained down from $28). The logos on some of the bags were too garish for my taste, even though I reckon that was rather the point of buying one.

By the time I moved back home to Charlotte, I had traded working in the arts for writing about the arts. I was a single girl reporter with a closetful of designer knock-off bags. You'd have thought I was making a pile of money.

After a while, the finish on one bag was wearing thin, the zipper on another failed, and the nickel was peeling off the hardware on my favorite bag. But I carried them anyway, as one simply couldn't go back to department store bags after being used to the big-name designers. I carried around my pens, pad and mini-tape recorder in the large bags. This was way before notebook computers and smart phones (though there was a brand new computer system in the newsroom confounding everyone).

A press release made its way to me: One of Charlotte's most prestigious women's auxiliaries was holding a bazaar to raise money for breast cancer awareness.

Bazaars! I was no stranger to the artsy-craftsy salesfest. Immediately after Labor Day, bazaar season starts in the South, and when I was a child, my mother and I would get in the car on a Saturday morning and go from one bazaar to another, checking out the merchandise. Usually held in a church hall, school gym or community center, the bazaar had tables manned by people selling anything from used toys to Tupperware and dolls made from Clorox bottles to crocheted potholders. My mother and I would snicker at some of the homemade craft items, but I was always on the look-out for a one-of-a-kind hand-made Barbie outfit. I also stocked up on used Beatles records and current pop songs on 45s I would buy for a nickel or dime. I remember buying a soundtrack from the musical "Hair." After playing it at home, my mother was so shocked at the lyrics, she took it away from me and gave it to my cousin, already in college. I still haven't gotten over that, but now I have CDs of both the Broadway show and the movie.

The most popular booth at these bazaars was inevitably the one selling homemade powdered Russian Tea mix in a Ball jar, complete with a fancy fabric lid cozy. (I never understood what was "Russian" about the tea, but that's what it was always called.) Just add a few teaspoons of the powder mix to a mug of boiling water and you had the sweet, delectable taste of fall. Sometimes the recipe for the mix was attached to the jar with a ribbon, and we always intended to make it ourselves but seldom did.

INSTANT RUSSIAN TEA MIX

Ingredients
- 1 jar of Tang *(it's what the astronauts drink)*
- 3/4 cup instant tea with lemon

- 2 cups sugar
- 1 tsp ground cloves
- 1 tsp cinnamon

Directions
- Mix all ingredients. Store in Ball jar (lid cozy optional). Use 2 to 2-1/2 teaspoons of mixture (to taste) with a cup of boiling water.
- Stir and enjoy!

The highlight of any bazaar day was always the lunch available for purchase. Volunteers of the sponsoring organization sold various sandwiches cut diagonally and wrapped in wax paper. Egg salad, pimento cheese and PB & J were standards, but the jewel in any southern sandwich menu was (and remains) the chicken salad sandwich. Chunks of white meat chicken flanked with minced celery and lots and lots of Duke's mayo was the benchmark against which all variations were judged. Occasionally, there might be a gourmet chicken salad with grapes and chopped pecans, but these fancy versions were just beginning to catch on. Yet to come were the days of whole wheat bread, wraps, light mayonnaise or yogurt, and fresh herbs. (Many locals blamed -- or credited -- the northern transplant invasion for these mutations.) For dessert, there was a brownie or blondie or maybe even a piece of chess or peach pie on a paper plate with plastic wrap over it. Typically, the desserts sold out before lunch-goers wolfed down the last scrap of chicken.

I pitched a story about bazaar season to my editor, and he gave me the assignment. We decided I should focus on the hoity-toity women's group, since it was their first bazaar and the money was going to such a worthy cause. It didn't hurt that many locally notable names could be incorporated into the story. My editor always reminded writers to "keep it folksy," and "readers love to see their names in the paper."

I called my mother and asked if she wanted to go with me. We had not been to a bazaar together in years, and I knew it would bring back many memories. Most of these affairs were Saturday-only events, but the women's auxiliary must have been expecting big crowds because their bazaar started on Thursday. We were at the elegant clubhouse shortly after they opened the doors that first day, and to our surprise there was an admission charge of five dollars and a line snaking out the door. Ahem… this had better be one fancy affair inside, Mama and I joked, as we had never been to a bazaar that charged for the privilege of walking through the door.

Oh, yes, it was very fancy, indeed. First of all, I noticed that most attendees were better-dressed than the average bazaar-goer. I didn't see gaggles of sweatsuits or mom jeans and T-shirts, nor were there sticky-fingered kids in tow, yammering and jumping around. No, these were beautiful young blondes, many pushing prams or jogger carriages, outfitted in preppy ensembles, most likely from Talbot's. The older guard, presumably their mothers, sported chic bobs or chignons and dressed with casual elegance: Perhaps a blouse and trousers and a lovely silk scarf knotted effortlessly around their neck. Everyone was meeting and greeting, with lots of pleasant small talk lingering in the air.

Tables were set up in various rooms, and let me tell you, not a single Clorox bottle doll to be found. Vendors peddled cosmetics and skin care, jewelry of all types and prices, and there was a table with adorable baby items. People bought candles, kitchen gadgets, knitting supplies, and monogrammed stationery. One woman was selling hand-painted and decorated tennis shoes, just too cute to be on this planet, and she had a large crowd patiently waiting in front of her table for their chance to buy. I saw a woman thrilled with her purchase of white tennies painted with pink and silver stars, pink glitter laces snaking through the eyelets and her name, Patsy, in script on the side of the shoe. She held them up above her head, as though in a victory stance, so everyone could see them as she left the room. There were lots of ooh's and aah's; Patsy had scored a winner.

Mama and I were browsing the fall scents of candles, trying to decide between Orange Cranberry and Cinnamon Stick, when we heard a ruckus at the other end of the room. Ladies were crowding a double table and hovering around to get closer; some weren't very nice about it, either. Scarves and belts were being tossed from one person to the next, tried on, and then either tossed back to the table or held tightly by the chest, the shopper waving frantically with the free hand trying to get someone to take her money. It reminded me of a trip to Boston where I had witnessed a legendary frenzy at Filene's Basement –back when there was a Filene's Department Store and Filene's really had a basement – where there was pushing and shoving and tossing and clutching of drastic mark-downs.

We couldn't get near the table, but we learned from the surrounding conflux that the storied vendor was selling scarves, belts and sunglasses by Hermés, Chanel and Dior, to name a few. The buzz was that a Hermés scarf could be had for only $25! What a bargain. I was stunned the legions of women seemed to think the merchandise was authentic, as these scarves generally retail for $400 and (way) up. Or maybe they knew the merchandise was fake and just didn't care. No wonder I had seen so many matrons wearing designer scarves when we walked in. Silly me – I thought it was because the women were well-heeled. I would like to have taken a look, but I am not a good pusher or shover, and my mother didn't know a Chanel from a Channel Two. We moved on to the tea room for lunch.

Actually a tented area behind the building, the tea room was decorated with hundreds of potted flowers -- also for sale, to benefit breast cancer research. Tables with linen cloths and napkins were beginning to fill. We each ordered mixed greens with a scoop of chicken salad on top and a glass of iced tea, the house wine of the South. While we were waiting for our meal, models wearing the latest fashions from a local chi-chi store came around to the tables to tell us about their outfits. "Available in sizes 2 – 10, $795" was all I needed to hear from the first model before I tuned out.

The plants were selling rapidly, and a truck pulled up to unload more colorful mums, miniature roses, and begonias. It was a good day for breast cancer research.

Lunch was served on a huge platter -- we easily could have split a meal. The chicken salad had cranberries and walnuts in it, which didn't make my mother very happy. She complained the whole time about the "things" in her salad, as she is a purist and prefers just the celery and mayo. But all was forgiven when her slice of caramel layer cake arrived. Mama said it wasn't quite as good as my grandmother's, with chopped pecans on the top, but it was still delicious.

I had work to do for my story, but I needed to sneak another peek at the designer scarves table. I craved a colorful Hermés, real or not. But the table was more crowded than before lunch, and the entire room was engulfed with people struggling to get to the front lines and possibly snatch up a Gucci leather belt for a song. The vendors at the other tables were sighing and irritated that no one was ogling their merchandise. In some cases, there was no access amidst the throngs anyway.

No way would I attempt to fight that good fight, so I wrangled some comments for my story from the organizer of the event, a pretty woman, perfectly coiffed, wearing an Hermés scarf atop her twin set. "Great, great! Fantastic turnout! We're thrilled!" she said enthusiastically, as though she had won the lottery.

On the way out, we found a table selling Russian Tea – thank goodness -- and waited in a long line to snag a few jars each. A bazaar just isn't a bazaar without Russian Tea.

For the next two days, my thoughts were plagued by the faux designer scarves I didn't have. I wanted one (or three). Badly. I had to go back. My plan was to be there early Saturday, wait in line for the 10 AM opening, and make a bee line for "the table." I wore comfortable shoes, paid another $5 entry fee, and had my scarf cash at the ready for a quick transaction. I felt smug seeing I was one of the first heading in the Hermés direction, but when I got inside the room, there were no stacks of scarves and no belts laid out on the table. In fact, there was no table at all, just a quiet dead end, a slightly scuffed section of buttercup-yellow wall. Had I imagined the whole thing?

"Excuse me, what happened to this table?" I asked a man selling stuffed animals.

"The FBI shut them down yesterday morning," he said in a weary voice as though he had answered the same question forty times. "All counterfeits."

I beat a hasty retreat and looked for my contact. My little feature story was turning into juicy news. On the prowl to get the whole story, I finally found my contact from Thursday and noticed she was not wearing a scarf. When I asked about the accessories vendor, my contact turned beet red, and told me that the salesman had run out of merchandise. "It was just a one-day thing anyway." I asked about the FBI story, and she acted like she didn't know what I was talking about. "Oh, that's silly," she said with a nervous giggle. "They just ran out of stuff to sell, so we took down the table Thursday night."

Uh-huh. What a fibberooni. I went home and called the local branch of the FBI and couldn't find out a thing. Everyone I spoke with claimed they knew nothing about it. Monday morning, I talked with my editor. He spoke with the reporter from the news division who covered such FBI-related things, and made a few calls, but there was no information to be found. It was as though the $25 designer scarves and belts at the First Annual Women's Auxiliary Bazaar never existed. The beat reporter, speaking to me privately, pointed out that many of the women of the esteemed women's club probably had husbands who were powerful politicians, lawyers or maybe a district court judge. I got it; the inference was clear, and therefore, the story was not a news story. "Let it remain a snappy feature," he advised, as originally intended. "These things happen." Seems folks like to see their names in the paper, but not in the same paragraph as "counterfeit" and "FBI."

For weeks, it smarted that I had not managed to wangle a few big-name scarves when I had the chance, but there were more faux designer items in my future.

Years later, after Mike and I moved to Baltimore, we took frequent weekend jaunts to New York City, and a new Canal Street bag was a requirement for each trip. I would find the best place to shop (but by our next visit, inevitably the entire block would be lined with all-new retail fronts). I learned to notice the look-outs patrolling the sidewalks and intersections and observed what I believed were secret hand signals. I learned not to buy the openly displayed unbranded copies; the *good* stuff with the name brands – the *real* counterfeits – were always in a secret place. I would whisper "Gucci! Coach!" to the tiny, hard-nosed woman minding the racks, and she would give us the evil eye trying to assess whether or not we were troublemakers. I did occasionally hear shoppers being told everything they had was displayed in full view, but we were always lucky enough to pass inspection.

On one such excursion, the proprietress barked, "Just one of you!" and I jumped ahead, to be escorted to a winding hallway, lit with bare bulbs dangling precariously from the low ceilings. Standing at 5'7", I ducked down like Quasimodo. I sensed we were somewhere under the street, but I wasn't sure. It occurred to me that I could be in a long tunnel to China, kidnapped and soon to be sold into the slave business, where I would likely be forced to clean toilets and wash linens by hand in a barrel.

I was starting to get a little uneasy, but then I saw a short door ahead with bright lights beaming through the cracks like a lighthouse beckoning us to the Holy Grail. My escort fiddled with the digital lock, and the door flung open. There they were, positively glowing. Coach! Fendi! Gucci! Tod's! Prada! Handbags were stacked to the ceiling in every style and color.

I felt privileged to be in this hallowed haven and instinctively knew not to ask too many questions or take the plastic wrap too far off the bag. I had planned to buy just one this trip, probably a Coach bag. But because of the long hike to get to Mecca, I decided I would splurge and buy two. I quickly negotiated a price and left with one Coach, one Prada and one Tod's, for good measure, tossed into a black plastic trash bag.

My next encounter with questionable merchandise wasn't quite as snappy or exciting; there were no long walkways involved, no bare bulbs and no handbags, either. Mike and I had started our jewelry and scarf store on V-Cart and we were working night and day sorting scarves, taking close-up shots of hand-crafted earrings, and listing items for sale. I bought the jewelry from various websites, mostly in China. I had bet the farm a customer would rather order a piece of jewelry shipped from Baltimore and get it in a few days, than wait a month or so to get it from, say, Mae Sot or Zhengzhou. I had established a following, with excellent feedback and many people asking for a wider selection.

Always on the prowl for new lines and styles, I was browsing V-Cart and saw some beautiful sterling silver earrings, necklaces and bracelets I could order wholesale. After a few messages back and forth to the factory, I purchased an initial order of $500. The website said it would take about a month to arrive.

Just a week later, Mike and I slept late following a nearly-all-nighter sorting and grading scarves while watching old episodes of *Law & Order*. We were sitting at the dining room table eating brunch, listening to CNN in the background. Mike suddenly developed a need for Kleenex and had to go out to our car, also known as our adjunct mobile storage unit (MSU), where we often stored extra supplies of Kleenex, toilet paper and paper towels.

"We got a package from China," said Mike as he walked in the door, precariously balancing a carton in one hand and a stack of five boxes of Kleenex in the other. I pushed aside my bowl of blueberries and yogurt topping. The silver jewelry had arrived.

HEALTHY YOGURT TOPPING

Ingredients
- 1 8 oz container plain, fat-free, unsweetened yogurt
- 1 tbsp (or to taste) SPLENDA Brown Sugar Blend

- 1/2 tsp vanilla extract (not "flavoring" please)

Directions
- Stir the sugar blend and vanilla into the yogurt.
- Spoon over a fruit cup or slice of pound cake, as you might with whipped cream. Or, pour into a shallow bowl and use as a dipping sauce for fruit, cookies or cake sticks.

"Mike, look!" I said breathlessly, as I tore open the package. It was sealed with enough tape to go from China to Baltimore and then some. As I cut into it and removed the packing material, I could see silver pieces gleaming in between the styrofoam peanuts. I took out all the bags of jewelry and laid them on the table, sorting according to style, counting it and matching the count to the packing list. It was all there. I picked up a pair of square hoop earrings. "These are beautiful!" I gushed. "We'll get a good mark-up. I'm so glad we discovered this source." I opened the little baggie and was going to put them on right away, claiming the first pair as mine. I took a good look and saw something etched on the earring. I assumed it probably said sterling silver or 925, the international code for sterling, but there was something else there, too. I held the earring closer and tried to catch the light. It was still fuzzy, so I went into the kitchen where I could see it under the bright fluorescent light. The earring said Tiffany & Co.

I tore open another bag holding a bold chain link bracelet with a heart in the middle and saw it was also etched Tiffany & Co. The silver high heel charm and the Scottie dog charm? T & Co. Every single piece I received was stamped with the famous moniker, either Tiffany spelled out, or T & Co.

I went online and took a gander at the current Tiffany sterling silver line. The designs were there, identical to my new jewelry, same etchings, though my pieces cost a fraction of the Tiffany retail price.

Suddenly I felt a lump in my throat. Were these pieces stolen from a factory making the Tiffany order? Was Tiffany jewelry made in China? Or were these flat-out counterfeits? Were they even real silver? My pieces looked beautiful and high quality – nothing tinny about my Tiffany. But I had a feeling the silver would peel off in short order and I'd have angry customers. Customers? *What was I thinking?* I couldn't even consider selling this jewelry. I could send it back to the factory in China, but I realized I would probably never see a refund. Calling the FBI to complain wouldn't get me anywhere because the jewelry would be confiscated from me altogether – that's the way it works with counterfeits.

I packed it all back up in the carton and put it in a corner of the room; I didn't want to even look at it. I told Mike we would think about it later and decide what to do. "Can we send it back? Are we out the money?" Mike asked. "What are we going to do?" Mike was relentless.

"I don't know. We'll worry about it later."

"Why wait?" Mike asked. "Let's discuss it *now*."

"Discuss *what*? I don't see a lot of options here."

Before you could say 'Tiffany & Co,' Mike was on the phone. "V-Cart won't take it away from us," he felt certain, "but we need to tell them about this immediately." I wondered if I should get dressed, because I had this (possibly) irrational fear that V-Cart would secretly notify the FBI, probably while we were still on the phone. Agents might arrive and bust down our door any minute, and I didn't want to be handcuffed and carted away barefoot, wearing my blue nightshirt with the bumble bees on it. What to wear… what to wear…. A black shirt, black pants and comfortable shoes seemed a much more jail-friendly ensemble. I shouldn't wear a scarf, I thought, because the cops might think I would use it to hang myself. No shoes with shoelaces, no belt. I knew the drill from years of watching cop shows. Should I wear lipstick and quickly fix my hair? Would it be humid in jail? Would they try to sweat the truth out of me in a little interrogation room? Maybe I shouldn't even bother with the hair. Besides, there probably wouldn't be anyone outside my door to witness the perp walk, unless the maintenance man was sweeping the sidewalk or Fed Ex was in the area making a delivery. I considered accessorizing with my new Tiffany heart necklace, which would look nice with the black top, but I decided it might aggravate the agents who could interpret the flaunting as an "attitude." It might not bode well for my future trial for trafficking in counterfeits.

If I went to the bedroom to get dressed, I would miss hearing what V-Cart had to say. Maybe if federal agents paid a visit, they would let me get dressed first. Or would they slam me against the wall, cuff me, and drag me out to the paddy wagon without any further ado? I would probably get bruises on my wrists from the handcuffs, just like Ana in

Fifty Shades of Grey. Okay, that was a slightly different situation, but the same steel cuffs (or so I imagine).

After I calmed down a tad, I thought I may have over-reacted expecting the SWAT team, but at the very least I fully expected V-Cart would immediately shut down the store that shipped the jewelry– and possibly my store as well, for punishment. This could bring VintageCartel.shop (and my company) to its knees, I thought. What have we done?

While we were on hold, it also occurred to me there could be a Chinese mob after us for whistle-blowing. I knew this contingent was alive and well in Baltimore, because not too long ago, we saw a white limo pull up to a Chinese restaurant in our part of town, and we saw several serious-looking men get out and go in the back door of the noodle house. That had to signal "mob" in my book, and if they got wind of my tattling about the counterfeiter in China who shipped the stuff to me – they had my address! I had replaced one fear with another. Was I more afraid of the FBI or the Chinese mob? Hmmm…. Might be easier to deal with the Feds.

I could spin my story, employ my flair for marketing, and get public sympathy on my side. Or maybe I would spill my guts and sing like a bird, in exchange for immunity. Would Mike be implicated, too? I had no desire for this story to be on cable news, with a panel of experts discussing my naiveté.

Though he would never admit it, I could see that Mike was nervous while we were on hold for the next available customer service rep (calls would be taken, we were assured, in the order in which they were received).

"This is Dave. Thank you for calling VintageCartel.com, how can I help you?" Dave was on our speaker phone.

Time to report the shocking news: "One of your V-Cart stores is selling counterfeit jewelry!" Mike blurted out, as though this was an emergency.

"I can fill out a report, if you like," Dave said, nonchalantly.

"You're not going to shut down their store?" Mike asked, all incredulous that maybe this wasn't the hottest news flash of the decade.

"Here's what happens," said Dave. "I get some information from you, and then I send in a report. The powers-that-be will investigate and decide what to do."

"That's *it*?"

"That's it."

Dave couldn't have driven home the point any clearer. This was, quite simply, not of major importance (or *any* importance). "We get calls like this all the time," he said, and I think I detected a yawn in there somewhere. We answered his few questions about the name of the store and item numbers for what specifically we received. Then Mike started interrogating Dave, who told us that they try to keep the counterfeits off V-Cart but if they close a store one day, the next day the same vendor will open a new store or two under different names. Dave suggested we also file a report with Paypal "for the record," since they handled the payment end of the transaction, but he didn't sound optimistic we would get our money back.

"So, you or someone else from V-Cart will get back with us and let us know what happens?" Mike asked.

"No. Someone may call you if they have any questions, but they aren't going to report back to you with their conclusions and any action they take. This is an internal matter."

Just like that, the conversation was over and my worries about the SWAT team coming for us – dead or alive – dissipated. There was no reason to get dressed after all.

The ladies in my family and select friends received T & Co jewelry as gifts for every occasion for at least a year. And no, I didn't try and pawn it off as the real deal. It was beautiful jewelry, not real Tiffany and probably not real silver, but the earrings sure sparkled when they caught the light, and the necklaces were bold statement pieces. Honestly, I'm just not sure what statement was made.

Whenever we talked about this in the future – and we did – somehow, the story grew bigger and bigger. My family knew there was always drama around Mike and Terri, and this story, when we were through with it, didn't disappoint.

6

FEEDBACK: WHEN IT WAS GOOD, IT WAS VERY, VERY GOOD

"The way to avoid criticism is to do nothing and be nothing."-- Anonymous

As one of V-Cart's highly-rated and stable sellers, we receive a thimble's worth of respect and attention, and our volume precludes a single negative Feedback entry from affecting our score. But in our early days with V-Cart, selling books and clothes, we were not immune from worrying about Feedback.

"Let's look at some Feedback," Mike would say, several times a week, whenever we needed a little boost. I'd go to V-Cart's Feedback page and read aloud the most recent comments.*

+ POSITIVE FEEDBACK FROM BUYER: tablecloth
You got it down TERRIART Perfect in all aspects Thats why I keep coming back!
Garlic and Sapphires by Ruth Reichl–Hardback, Read Once, Clean Hands

+ POSITIVE FEEDBACK FROM BUYER: rockingranny
Love This BLOUSE! Love This SELLER!
Black & White Abstract Print Silky Button-Down Blouse, EUC

+ POSITIVE FEEDBACK FROM BUYER: kyliesmom
Lovely sweater, nicely packed, quickly sent with nice personal touches. Terri is the best!
Black Chenille Cardigan, Collar, Pearl Buttons, Worn Once or Twice

---

* all V-Cart messages are reproduced here exactly as I received them, including spelling and grammar errors and typos, but the names of the buyers and their VintageCartel.shop account names have been changed.

+ POSITIVE FEEDBACK FROM BUYER: monabologna
This seller is awesome. Great Stuff, Fast shipping, Awesome Prices. WOW!
A Year in Provence by Peter Mayle — EUC, Loved it! Want to Move There!

A person could get used to this. But one time when we took a gander at our Feedback page, I saw our very first negative comment, with a big gray minus sign in a circle preceding the message: "Book wasn't wrapped, was shoved into small envelope." I was crushed to see our rating had slipped from 100% to 99.9%. I looked up the listing and saw that it was a hardback, an excellent book I had flipped within a week. How does one "shove" a hardback book into a small envelope? Fold it in half? Roll it up? I always wrapped a book in several layers of tissue paper before Mike packed it in a large envelope for mailing. But because I was fearful of the V-Cart "machine" and the possible ramifications of an unhappy customer, I immediately gave a refund for the book and dashed off an apology to the buyer.

Dear sweet-tart1020:

I am very sorry your book arrived inadequately packed. I gave you a full refund in Paypal, and I hope the damage wasn't so bad that the book isn't salvageable. I am a new seller, and I will make an effort to pack the orders better so that this doesn't happen again. I appreciate your bringing this to my attention.

Terri

Within five minutes, I heard back from sweet-tart, who seemed to me much more tart than sweet.

Dear Terri,

I wasn't asking for a refund, and I sent the money back to your account. I only meant to warn you. The book was not damaged in shipment, but you need to know it could have been, and you should always pack a book in bubble for best protection.

sweet-tart1020

A *warning?* Who was this tart person -- the packing police? I pictured a middle-aged man, balding, very small. He fancies himself an inventor, but his split-level house is littered with abandoned projects and his frustration level is high as he feels no one will listen to his ideas. He thinks he could be the next George Foreman, if only he had a chance. He vents his sourness online, posting negative comments on message boards, chat rooms and of course, in Feedback to sellers of his online purchases.

Sure, the book could have been damaged. It *could have* fallen out of the mail carrier's bag and landed in a sewer. It *could have* been left just outside the front door, and the nosy neighbor could have carefully opened it to see what the sour tart was ordering. It *could have* been stolen by a boy riding his bicycle through the neighborhood when he spied a package on the patio steps. (Boy, would he be disappointed when he saw it was a book!) It *could have* been chewed up (and spit out) by Buster, the pit bull from down the road a bit that always manages to escape the fenced-in backyard. But no, sweet-tart, you say the book was not damaged; yet, you felt compelled to teach me a lesson, taking it upon yourself to warn me of what *could have* happened. Yeah, I'll take it under advisement.

Dear sweet-tart1020,

Thanks for your suggestion and for sending the money back to my account. It was very considerate of you. Please know that I will be more careful in the future.

Terri

Since this negative comment was made before V-Cart allowed a buyer to revise his Feedback, the matter was closed and the damage was done. (Damage to me, the seller; clearly there was no damage to the book.)

The serious V-Cart seller lives in fear of negative Feedback. Every customer is asked to leave Feedback about their experience buying or selling an item. This information is posted and available for all to review and therefore greatly affects the reputation of both buyer and seller. The Feedback form asks a buyer if the experience was positive, neutral or negative, giving up to five stars each for several questions about product description, communication with seller, and delivery time. The form then asks for a one-line comment about the transaction. V-Cart says: "Honest comments gives members a preview of what to expect when dealing with other buyers and sellers." The HELP pages include an explanation about how Feedback scores are calculated, but it all sounds complicated and frankly, over my head. I just like to see the pretty gold stars and "100% positive" posted on my listings.

I learned to live with a less-than-perfect rating. After six months, I was well underway in the scarf business and had not received any other negative Feedback. My score went back to 100%.

+ POSITIVE FEEDBACK FROM BUYER: primadonna2
Terriart is the best! as always, sent clean, sweetly packed, and FAST. A++++
Golden Khaki, Blue, Lavender Flowers SILK 54" x 9" Long - LIZ

+ POSITIVE FEEDBACK FROM BUYER: karmachameleon
Absolutely stunning! Photo did not do this scarf justice. Thank you so much!!!
Turquoise, Purple, White Anchors, Stripes 32" Square

+ POSITIVE FEEDBACK FROM BUYER: comeonhomenow
Gorgeous-classy-loving it!! thanks again to a fave seller—u r the best!!!
Pink, Purple, Multi Abstract Flowers SILK 55" x 11" Long - ECHO

+ POSITIVE FEEDBACK FROM BUYER: bowwowser16
Cannot beat a great dog theme-this one is wonderful and so is the seller!!!!
Caramel, Blue, Beige Doggies COTTON 30" Square - OSCAR

Ah… so it is. When one reads and believes the good reviews, one must take note of the bad reviews as well. Many people ignore reviews altogether and simply do the best work they possibly can, but I imagine it takes years to elevate to that level, and V-Cart does not offer any stars for that attitude.

It had been some time since our temporary fall from grace, but I still got a slightly sick feeling in my gut when we did our frequent

Feedback checks, only to feel relief when we read the glowing reviews. But one such check-up showed the grandeur wasn't so grand and the luster was lacking.

- NEGATIVE FEEDBACK FROM BUYER: misssublime
Description of this "scarf" was deceptive. I was sold a useless small square of cloth.
Black Organdy, Gold Butterfly Applique 16" Square

When I saw this, the bile was rising in my throat as I rushed to find the original transaction so I could review the order and contact the customer. Mike stood over my shoulder, repeatedly asking: "Do you think this will hurt our score?" as though the end (of our business… of the world …) was near.

The V-Cart site was moving slow that morning as I scrolled through the sales archives. Meanwhile, the phone was ringing constantly in the background, but we ignored it. It could be said that Mike and I have a tendency to over-react, but at the time, it seemed everything was in a state of flux over one case of negative Feedback.

Ring…ring…ring…
"Are we going to be kicked off V-Cart?" Mike whined.

Ring…ring…ring…
"What's the worst that can happen?"

Ring…ring…ring…
"Terri? Terri!! Are you worried?"

This was not helping my newly-minted headache or my tense shoulders. I was still seething and perhaps possibly foaming at the mouth by the time I found the original order. Her handle was 'Miss Sublime' (I'll be the judge of that) and she had purchased a small, very pretty vintage scarf for $5.95. It was black sheer organdy-like fabric with a gold butterfly embroidered on one corner. The description in my listing clearly said it was 16" square. Sure, you can't toss this over your shoulders or tie it into a fluffy decorative knot, but occasionally someone wants a small square scarf to tie on a handbag, drape over a small bedside table lamp or re-purpose as a decorative pillow top.

This situation was maddening, and I could not shrug it off. Not only did Miss Sublime overlook the scarf size when she ordered, she violated V-Cart's buyer guidelines: Only if a solution cannot be found, V-Cart advises, is the buyer free to leave negative Feedback. I always remind the customer of this with a sticker on the packing list: *POSITIVE FEEDBACK is greatly appreciated. If you are unhappy for any reason, please give me the chance to resolve the issue before you leave negative or neutral Feedback. Thank you. — Terri, Your Scarf Maven.* Next to the blurb is a cartoon of a cute, young girl with dark hair and a ponytail (presumably me) working at her computer. Had Miss Sublime simply contacted me and said she was unhappy with the scarf, I would have refunded her money with a smile in my message, and told her to keep the scarf anyway. "No unhappy customers" is our policy, and we have willingly refunded money any time a buyer was unhappy for any reason. Usually it is a friendly situation, the buyer insists on mailing the scarf back to me, and we part friends.

I would be willing to serve my time in punishment bay had the complaint been at least semi-valid. Suppose Scarf Maven overlooked a hole or a stain the exact likeness of the Virgin Mary? *That* would be grounds for a complaint. Suppose Scarf Maven mailed out a Vera with a noxious perfume stench malingering on the silk? *That* would constitute a just grievance. Suppose the package traveled during a rainstorm and arrived soggy with tissue paper stuck to the acetate, perhaps causing a stain or two? A most legitimate hoo-ha that Scarf Maven would surely take up with the Post Office. But to serve a six months sentence of a 99% Feedback score because a customer didn't read the dimensions of the scarf in the listing? (And then did not post her complaint directly to me?)

The Feedback from Miss Sublime was burning a hole in my retina as I re-read it. This is war, I thought, as I crafted a biting return message to the offending V-Cart-nik. I wrote several versions of a response, each nastier than the next and barely fitting into the allotted message space. My favorite draft was just sarcastic enough:

Dear Miss Sub,

The dimensions were clearly specified in the listing, so if this scarf was "a useless small square" perhaps you shouldn't have ordered it. V-Cart policy is that you contact the seller and work something out if possible before leaving neutral or negative feedback. I don't know how in the world you can say you were taken advantage of. Had you followed policy, you would have a swift refund for anything you were unhappy with. Under the circumstances now, however, I will not refund your money, and if anyone was 'taken advantage of,' clearly it was me.

-- Terri

Before clicking on the SEND button, I stared at this dispatch for a few long minutes. What would be more gratifying, I thought, as I weighed the satisfaction quotient of sending this vitriolic message to the buyer vs. graciously writing a mildly apologetic note asking her to please consider changing the Feedback to positive (V-Cart had changed the rules to allow this). It was a tough decision between immediate gratification (typically my choice) or the greater good of my business. The clock was ticking. If I waited much longer, the immediacy of the response would dilute. Should I make a dumb or smart decision? Even after making a good-size dent in a large bag of Peanut M & Ms, I just couldn't decide.

Mike and I discussed it, and we agreed I should delete and re-write. While the nasty note would indeed make me feel better, I would take the high road (I am quite unfamiliar with this avenue) so that Miss Sublime may be inclined to change the Feedback and we could all live happily ever after.

Hello,

I am very sorry to read you are unhappy with the scarf. I am putting through a full refund immediately. Would you consider revising your Feedback due to my swift handling of this situation? I would very much appreciate it, as I don't want any unhappy customers.

Thank you.
Terri

In less than an hour, I had a reply:

Dear So-Called 'Scarf Maven':

The item you sold me, the black square with gold butterfly, is not in any way a "scarf," even a small one. I own a collection of true scarves and wraps from all over the world (at last count 2,356) and the item you portrayed as a small scarf is actually a cocktail napkin. There was no reason for me to expect to receive a cocktail napkin described as a small scarf. If you did not know what you had, you should have consulted someone before listing them. There is no place on this planet where what you represented as a scarf qualifies as such. Although I hope that this was not deliberate, it is still inexcusable and I was plainly taken advantage of. For this reason, I will not change my Feedback, and was actually kinder than I should have been under the circumstances.

misssublime

"Cocktail napkin?" Okay, just call me Cocktail Napkin Maven. And, by the way, why do you have a collection of 2,356 "true" scarves? (Ha-ha, I have more scarves than you do.) And what is a "true" scarf anyway? Anything over 16" square? Are my small scarves "false" scarves? Judgmental, aren't we? Apparently, Miss Sub wasn't meeting me on the high road. I knew I should have wallowed in the mud and started a full-on fight with this woman. Why doesn't everybody play fair? Oh, how satisfying it would be to shove the computer out the window and get out of the business altogether. Once again, my meter was tuned to angry and upset.

"Cocktail napkin?" *"Cocktail napkin?"* That's ludicrous. And, let me tell you, I do happen to be familiar with cocktail napkins – we have a history. Mike and I received a dozen monogrammed white linen cocktail napkins as a wedding gift, and I even used them several times in my pre-scarf, pre-warehouse-dwelling days. I pulled them out for desserts and coffee, as well as for wine or cocktails. I starched and ironed the napkins to use when serving Prosecco and basil pesto bruschetta for eight in the living room, before dinner in the dining room (with my matching white, monogrammed dinner napkins). Someone wiped dark lipstick on a napkin (I am thinking it might have been me); it didn't come out in the wash, even with bleach, so now I have eleven cocktail napkins and incidentally haven't used them since. And though I acknowledge I never actually served a real "cocktail" – say a Chocolatini or Midori Sunrise - alongside the napkins, the point is, Missy Sublimey, I am familiar with cocktail napkins. And the black organdy scarf with the gold butterfly applique *isn't* one.

I worked up quite a frenzy thinking about this as I waited on hold for a V-Cart customer service rep. I had a mental picture of Miss Sublime: Late 40's, single, living in the same home where she grew up - now, sadly, in disrepair. A bit of a loner, she is a court reporter, making good money and though her extended family often asks her for loans, she declines and banks most of every dime she's ever made. Her claim to greatness is making a small roasted chicken last for a week's worth of meals. Two things you can count on when assessing Miss Sublime's fashion fitness: Her long brown hair (with some gray showing) is twisted into a smooth and tight bun (no sexy, messy updo for her!) and her shoes with flat, rubber soles are comfortable. Oh, she would prefer to wear high-heeled pumps, but they hurt her feet and she is a firm believer that happy feet make a sane person. She wears severe outfits on her statuesque frame - perhaps a navy slim skirt with a blue polyester blouse (easy to wash and wear) and she always, always wears a scarf around her neck, snugly tied. It's her security blanket. Often there is a stain or a hole showing below the knot, but Miss Sublime assumes people do not notice the imperfections, as she feels they do not often notice her at all.

I am still on hold, and because I have the line on speaker phone, my entire apartment has the pleasure of the fuzzy musical concert. V-Cart interrupts every now and then to remind me my call is important and a representative will be with me shortly. I am too deep in thought to be miffed about the wait.

I return to my daydream. Miss Sublime enjoys her job, because she doesn't have to mingle much with other workers, preferring to communicate with the eleven cats that rule her home. She spends time with each one every night, telling them about her day and asking each kitty if they enjoyed their supper. Sharing the sofa with the family felines as they smooth their fur coats against the faded velvet upholstery, Miss Sublime watches *Jeopardy* and knows most of the answers. Or... questions, rather. She has learned much trivial information from reading her books, too many to fit into the built-in bookcases lining the living room. She longs to be a contestant (though she has never applied), and believes she could probably...

"Hello, my name is Polly." *Of course it is. Short for Pollyanna, perhaps?* "How may I help you today?" an all-too-cheerful customer service woman with a high-pitched voice asked, jarring me from my musing. I poured out the story. Polly confirmed that by not contacting me, my buyer did not follow Feedback guidelines. But, she explained, "this is a suggestion, not V-Cart policy," and it would bear no reflection or consequence on the buyer's rating. Polly further explained that my volume as a seller was very high at this point and just one negative rating would not affect my overall score (as it had in the past). At least this was good news, but I realized there would be no resolution with the noxious customer.

My head certainly knew it was nearly impossible to maintain a 100% score and most other sellers operated quite well with a 99% or even lower score. But when negative Feedback was *not* justified, my heart beat out a message telling me it isn't fair. The words of my Daddy were ringing in my ears: "Life isn't always fair, Terri." I guess I never quite grasped that.

I got over it (somewhat) and, like Polly promised, my 100% rating stayed intact.

+ POSITIVE FEEDBACK FROM BUYER: luvmyscrapping24

AGAIN!!! I am a HAPPY CUSTOMER!!! Terri, i know you see that i have ordered a lot
Blue, Pink, Multi Flowers, Butterflies SILK 28" Square

+ POSITIVE FEEDBACK FROM BUYER: queenoftherodeo

Looks great with my daughter's dress! Super-great seller!
Black, White Mod Swirls SILK 30" Square - Jones NY

+ POSITIVE FEEDBACK FROM BUYER: parisrocks1982

Beautiful scarf,pretty packaging,fast shipment,happy 3X returning customer!
Caramel, Blue, Beige Graphics COTTON 32" Square - OSCAR

+ POSITIVE FEEDBACK FROM BUYER: deservinglady29

A+++ seller - your scarves are always top notch-everyone asks where I got them:)
Olive, Black, Brown, Gold Tiger in Jungle 21" SILK Square - VERA

A few weeks passed, and I was uploading photos for the listing of a *"Red, Green & Purple Tropical Flowers Print SILK 54" x 11" Long Scarf by Liz Claiborne -- no stains, but there are a few pinholes. Feels good!"* I was feeling good, too; we had a healthy bump in sales for the week, and Suzanne, my new assistant, was really working out, entering V-Cart store listings from her home. I finished the last sip of my iced tea, closed the blinds and turned off the TV, ready to call it a day.

"Come on, Mike, let's get going!" We were going out for a pit beef sandwich at a food truck across town and wanted to get there before dark. He was online checking into coupons, probably plotting a stop at the grocery store on our way home.

"Wait a minute," Mike said, "we haven't checked Feedback in a while." I think he needed to be reminded how great and wonderful we were. I sat back down at my desk, with a huff, and went to the comments, reading them aloud.

+ POSITIVE FEEDBACK FROM BUYER: needsasnack
Such a lovely scarf! Thank you Terri. Also enjoyed your newsletter.
Navy, White Box Stripes SILK 26" Square – OLEG CASSINI

+ POSITIVE FEEDBACK FROM BUYER: hubbyissuper
Wonderful scarf - another TERRIART deal for me! much nicer than pix, BUY HERE!
Blues, Browns Marled Blocks SILK 30" Square – ALBERT NIPON

+ POSITIVE FEEDBACK FROM BUYER: chubby4331
will wear this with my new suit ...thanks
Pink, Vanilla Stripes, Flowers SILK 22" Square- ELSA SCHIAPARELLI

* NEUTRAL FEEDBACK FROM BUYER: teensie500
Never even got the stupid scarf
Orange, Periwinkle, Gold Paisleys SILK 26" Square

Oops! I was getting a little smug there for a minute. Teensie? Really? First of all, teensie500, if it was a "stupid scarf," then why did you order it to begin with? Oh, that Teensie. She's just a little bit of a thing, I thought, but what hell on wheels when she gets angry and the wrath starts spewing! Teensie has lots of friends; after all, she was active in the Gamma Phi Beta sorority in college and frequently looks back on her glory days.

Next question, Teensie Weensie: Why didn't you just write to me and tell me the scarf never made it to you? The transaction was six weeks ago, and you're just now getting around to telling me about it? Do you think it takes six weeks for a small package to get from Baltimore to Dunwoody, Georgia? Why would you notify me via Feedback? Do you think I never put it in the mail at all? Do you really think I intentionally swindled you out of $6.49?

I called V-Cart to complain about the unfairness of this Feedback affecting my score. I was assured that this Feedback would not affect a score one way or another. But I didn't like the comment on my "permanent record." I laid out my case like a defense attorney pleading for the life of a wrongly accused killer. I was reading from a list of bullet points I wrote, supporting my stance.

The customer service rep allowed me to finish my tirade, and I felt rather proud of my performance. I was clear, concise and sure the comment would be removed at once.

"What, exactly, are you disputing?" the rep asked. "Are you saying the buyer *did* get the scarf? And do you have any proof, like tracking results?" I did not. We were self-insured, as it was too costly to track and insure a scarf costing $6.49 including postage. (Note: V-Cart has since changed the rules, making tracking mandatory if we want to keep our "elevated status.")

"Therefore, what the Feedback says is accurate," the rep asserted, presumably using legal verbiage to match my opening statement.

"Well," I said, "I don't think it's accurate to call it a 'stupid scarf' - it's very cute, though there is a small run near one end..."

"But you cannot document the buyer received the scarf."

"She should have contacted me on a timely basis," I said, "and I would gladly have given the refund." But my plea fell on deaf ears, as this V-Cart rep was both judge and jury and the decision had been rendered.

"I'm sorry, but I can't delete the comment." The verdict was final.

Or was it? Mike wanted to appeal the case to a higher court - a supervisor for the customer service line. Mr. Quick Draw was already on hold waiting for that higher power before I had a chance to respond. With the phone on speaker mode and the hold music blaring, Mike and I debated. I said we should forget it and just live with the rating. Stupid scarf - stupid Feedback. Mike felt it was a miscarriage of justice to let the verdict stand. But after twenty minutes on hold, he quietly hung up, and we never spoke another word about it.

Dear Miss teensie500,

All you had to do was notify me via message. I have refunded your money through Paypal. The package went out on a timely basis, but apparently it was lost in the mail. I am very sorry for the problem, but would you consider changing your feedback?

Terri
Your Scarf Maven

I never heard back. Just when I thought I had moved on from both the Teensie and the Sublime problems, I received a V-Cart message from the cocktail napkin woman:

Scarf Maven,

I owe you an apology. In my newness to the V-Cart world, I believe that I had some incorrect ideas about using it. I was extremely harsh in my expectations of thinking every individual seller should operate like a retail store. I never understood fully what you go thru until a new friend from China gave me wise advice. I do not want to harm you in any way, so if you would be kind enough to send me a revision form for the first feedback, I would be honored to revise it to all five stars.

At your service,
Laurie
misssublime

While I was not sure I understood what she meant by "operating like a retail store," or what advice her "new friend from China" could possibly have given, I was pleased to get her Feedback revision before she changed her mind.

A few days later, I got another message from her, like we were now BFFs:

Dear Terri,

Glad we worked things out... Have any other scarves for sale?

Laurie
misssublime

Now she has a name: Laurie. Although I wasn't thrilled with the prospect of selling this woman again, I wrote back, directing her to my store.

Yet another message arrived from Her Sublime Chattiness:
Hey guys! I'm an idiot! I had no idea all I needed to do was go to your store! I don't have time to look at everything right now, but I'll be good for several purchases a month! Also, I'm filling out the feedback revision form right now! Have a great one!
Laurie
misssublime

We both agree she's an idiot! That's progress. And later, another message:

Just ordered 4 scarves, gave positive feedback already!!
L

Now, we were so close that she simply signed it "L." But fortunately, "L" became a good customer, adding to her massive scarf collection.

I noticed there were two words that frequently popped up in our Feedback and messages: "awesome" and "perfect."

+ POSITIVE FEEDBACK FROM BUYER: funblonde1
Gorgeous silk scarf, LOVE IT!! Ship'd Fast & Free!! PERFECT SWEET SELLER!

Green, Gold, White Stripes & Crests SILK Long - Vintage Ellen Tracy

+ POSITIVE FEEDBACK FROM BUYER: 77craftersewer
Terriart rocks! Awesome seller! Great price!! Shipped fasssst! Buy here!
Moss, Lavender, Pink Nautical COTTON Square – Vintage Ginnie Johansen

+ POSITIVE FEEDBACK FROM BUYER: swimmingluv
Can't say enough about this seller and the products…Perfect!
Small Novelty "Happy Birthday" SILK 10" Square - Vintage

Things appeared to be so easy, buying and selling used scarves, many people said they wish they had a "fun" business like ours. I loved the business and wouldn't have traded it, but we worked hard to make things look easy (and "perfect"). Diligence trumped other skills, and we both spent a lot of time and care buying and flipping our vintage scarves. Having your own business wasn't all *Judge Judy*, Cheetos and afternoon naps. (Well, actually, some days it was, though I was more of a sweet than a salty.)

I'd like to be like you, in such a fun business! You're awesome!
I love your store! I want to live in your awesome world of scarves!
Do you need help? I'd love to work for you in your perfect niche!

Previously, with our candy clients and customers, we would get comments, though there was no formal Feedback:

What a fun business!
Wow, must be great to be in the middle of that candy all day long!
Bet it's a happy place to work!
I could never work with my husband all day long like you do.

We learned early on that the scarf business, like the candy business was not a laid-back, easy-going field. Ever hear of a candy crisis? We have.

I grant you, hawking candy isn't as important as, say, driving an ambulance or fixing a leaking sewage system. But when someone's livelihood is a retail business, they count on the candy sales for a large part of their income, particularly over the holidays. If an order comes in late, or is short, it affects their profit.

We spent years working in-house with candy companies to elevate the sales and marketing teams and at the same time, implement changes in procedures and customer service to best handle the growing business. But we've faced screaming matches and tears from unhappy retailers, distributors and candy employees -- scenes so dramatic we'd be left embittered and exhausted.

There are small "emergencies" in the scarf business, too, though fortunately, these are addressed via V-Cart messages, and not in person or by phone with the attendant theatrics.

Dear Mrs. So-Called Scarf Maven,

I was very disappointed in this item. The scarf was really a kerchief. I don't want to write a bad review, so until I hear from you, I won't put one in.

infashion854

We rushed to refund her money and sent her a nice note. (I did not ask for clarification on the difference between a scarf and a kerchief.) She was happy - negative Feedback averted.

Occasionally I cannot identify the scarf fabric, so in the listing, I speculate: *Fabric unknown, feels like silk*. I do the best I can, but sometimes it isn't enough:

I am most unhappy with this scarf. There was no label, and I do not believe it is silk, as you say. I am going to turn your business in to the US Trade Government Commision if I don't get a refund for your deceptive practises.

Waiting for response,
kitfromcal88

I should have laughed this off, but I have a difficult time doing that. It was hard not to send her a nasty return note saying "I never said the scarf was silk" or "Hey, dumbass, these are USED scarves!" or "Every

fashion stylist will tell you to cut off the tag before you wear a scarf."
Really, what I wanted to say was "Great! Turn me in!" But I refrained
and immediately sent a refund and a non-sarcastic note explaining why
there wasn't a tag on most of the scarves.

It can be a big fashion emergency when a scarf doesn't arrive on
time.

Good morning:

Your listing says I should had this scarf by Friday, and I do not
have it yet. I planned to wear it to a wedding tonight. It's not fair
that you sell something under false pretence and it doesn't come
on time. I want my money back, and I do not want the scarf
now – you can let the post office know. You really shouldn't say
it is going to be here when it isn't.

oneproudcanuck

This customer was in Red Deer, Alberta, Canada. We say in our
listings that we put the item in the mail within 24 hours of receiving the
order (excluding Sundays and holidays). Look peeps, we do not control
the mail! And complicating shipping time in international shipments
is the "unknown" of customs, which we also do not control. A package
can slip through very quickly, or it can be delayed indefinitely. Often we
can mail a package to our frequent customer Anja in Lucerne, and it will
be received in a week, yet sometimes it doesn't get to its destination for
a month. Dolly in Perth, Western Australia always lets us know when
she gets her scarves, usually about ten days after we put the package in
the mail. Lucy, a good customer in Tallinn, Harjumaa, Estonia who
collects Vera scarves, doesn't expect her orders for a month or more.

Mike and I wallowed in the positive comments, and fortunately,
we rarely received a disparaging one. But I came to accept that the
occasional negative phrase would not throw us into bankruptcy.
Everyone faces criticism, reviews… Feedback.

———✦———

I am a loyal watcher of the Academy Awards, but the part that
most captures my attention is the red carpet walk. Feedback of every

carefully-styled outfit is posted online within seconds of the star exiting the limo. Millions of people comment on the dress color, hairstyle, sweat stains, lumps and bulges (that is, those few stars that have lumps and bulges). I love the clothes, and also reading about the best and worst-dressed of the evening and the occasional ridiculous ensemble by some little starlet. I have also spent time over the years with my head in the clouds, wondering what I would wear if I were an Oscar nominee for, say, costume design or writing a screenplay (or both).

In my younger days, when I actually thought the Red Carpet might be a possibility, I recall visions of a bronze lace gown with a boat-neckline, a full skirt and sleek long sleeves. Then at some point the idea seemed only marginally likely, but I was thinking I would ditch the ballgown and go with a knee-length dress, something spectacular in black; Extreme Little Black Dress (in a large size). By the time I was "of a certain age," and an Oscar nomination was a mere fantasy, I thought I might go for the retro Streisand-in-concert opera diva look: Perhaps a midnight navy silk taffeta coat-dress with a wide portrait neckline, suitable for showcasing exquisite jewelry. And by the way, I wouldn't *borrow* jewelry from a famous designer and arrive with an armed bodyguard to protect the jewelry. I could put together a stunning faux pearl and jewels concoction that wouldn't have to be back in a vault by curfew. (All the while, knowing my own curfew would be earlier than the jewelry's.)

Lately, however, I'm thinking that given the opportunity, I'd prefer to slip in the back door. I would feel pitiful in my "mature woman look," maybe a beaded black sheer lace duster and camisole over a long skirt or wide pants, avoiding the cameras (that would be avoiding me). I could also add that perhaps it doesn't much seem like dressing for the Oscars is in my future anyway. With no more costumes in sight and no screenplay in the offing, it seems unlikely they will decide to give out an Oscar for Best Vintage Scarf Worn in a Movie (or even a movie *theatre*) anytime soon.

But listen, sister, the Oscars are not the only game in town: The V-Cart world has its own awards and honors we dubbed the Carties. About a year after we started our business, we received a V-Cart message that Terri*art* was recognized with the award of POWER SELLER. Given to those sellers "who consistently meet minimum sales revenues with above average Feedback ratings," a POWER SELLER is given special customer service hotlines, good citizen fee discounts and a dust-free glittering VintageCartel.shop banner proclaiming its elevated status.

My goodness, I didn't even know I was nominated. I accepted the award on our behalf. I thanked V-Cart, I thanked my parents for having me, and I remembered to thank my husband and partner, Mike. I would not be one of those ingénues the tabloids criticize for "forgetting" to thank their significant other. Truthfully, I would not be considered an ingénue, period, but that's another issue. My *thank yous* were done via my newsletter to fans…uh… excuse me, customers, and I didn't have to stress over whether or not to wear mascara or high heels. I accepted the award at home in my long cotton T-shirt with the lavender hearts print, safe and secure (and hidden). It was perfect. Well, I did miss a grand Carties party, hobnobbing with the other winners and dining on fancy chow (though, for the record, I do not eat ceviche, foie gras or caviar).

We came to learn that, possibly because of the money saved by not renting a hall or catering a large dinner affair, V-Cart can give their awards much more frequently, on an as-earned basis. A year or so later, the Carties recognized us once more, this time in the TOP RATED SELLER category. I thought of it as Box Office Favorite and Miss Congeniality awards rolled into one. The day we won, I happened to be wearing the long T with the blue stiletto heels print – a fancier selection befitting the occasion of being a two-time award winner. As I accepted, I thought: *They like me. They really like me.*

* 7 *

THE BIG "GET"

"The 'show me' slogan is used to indicate the stalwart, conservative, noncredulous character of Missourians." -- Website of the Missouri Secretary of State.

We had not been able to reach Travis, our contact in Missouri. Mike was calling every day, finding no answer or voice mail. We sent several emails asking him to call us. It had been over a month with no reply, and we were worried.

After a lengthy session with Google Search, we found a newspaper story and a police report that told us what had happened. Travis and his wife, Tori Ann, were in jail. Seems their auction operation was in a warehouse and office park, and they "B & E'd" the sports memorabilia business next door. We gleaned the term B & E – police lingo for Breaking and Entering - from the online account of the crime. The logistics sounded so simple; they removed a ceiling vent, shimmied through the heat and air duct where they removed another vent and jumped down into the neighboring unit. (I was thinking they must be small people.) Travis and Tori Ann were loading the computers and rare sports loot into their pick-up truck when the cops arrived.

Simple operation, indeed, but apparently Travis forgot the probability of a burglar alarm. What kind of idiot was he? And just like that, our source for vintage scarves was no more.

A follow-up news story revealed when the stolen merchandise was appraised for the insurance claim, another surprise was discovered: The autographs on every item seized the night of the crime were fakes, though they were being sold as "genuine," and "certified." Huh! Counterfeits! Seedy bedfellows in the "show me" state.

———

People ask where we get the scarves. It's not the most frequently asked question, but it's certainly in the Top Ten. They often posit I peruse flea markets and canvass yard sales and thrift shops, buying every scarf I see. Whether it be friend, family or customer, I always answer the same way: "Oh, I get them here and there." Like a jeweler puts the diamonds and rubies in the safe, I guard my sources. I do not design the scarves or make them, so all I have are my connections and relationships with vendors on one end, and my connections and relationships with customers on the other end. Sure, anyone can do what I do, in theory. If a person wanted to start a vintage scarf business on VintageCartel.shop, through due diligence (and luck) they might find the sources we use or others. But I'm not afraid of competition because I know that no one can do it quite like Scarf Maven.

So, again, where do I get the scarves?

VintageCartel.shop Messages: INBOX
Dear scarf maven,
I am thinking about starting a V-Cart business simular to yours selling scarves. Where do your scarves come from?
Kay

Dear Kay,
How dumb do you think I am?
Sincerely,
Your Scarf Maven

No, I didn't really answer that, though I wanted to! I wrote:

Dear Kay,

A good Scarf Maven doesn't give away her secrets!

Good Luck,
Terri

During our first year in the online sales business, we bought our vintage scarves in lots of 20, 50 or even 100 on occasion. Surprise! I bought them on V-Cart, right there where anyone else could buy, too. We opened a second account because one of V-Cart's big flaws is that anyone can search and find every vendor from whom you have purchased, effectively revealing your secrets. This way, the Terriart store was not officially connected to the second account. We purchased scarves, some at very low prices, some not so low.

Most every day, Mike and I spent hours at our computers, answering emails, updating paperwork, reading news or just browsing around. Sometimes one of us read the other an article about one of our pet issues and then we might debate an issue. Or if an episode of *Perry Mason* was on and we hadn't seen it (lately), we might pause to watch Della hopelessly swooning over Perry.

"Terri! Come over here, you have *got* to see this!" Mike startled me, as it had been quiet for a while.

"What is it?" I really didn't want to get up.

"I think this might interest you!" Mike was so enthusiastic, I thought I'd best go to his desk and take a gander.

Mike had found a V-Cart listing for an auction of fifty vintage handbags. He showed me the seller's other listings: Large lots of belts, children's clothes, T-shirts and prom dresses. We were not interested in adding any of that to our store, but we both wondered the same thing; what about scarves?

"Call this place, now!" I said, and I hobbled on my sore leg back to my desk to study the listings up close. We could always send a V-Cart message, and hope we got an answer, but we were too impatient to wait. Mike researched the web, found a phone number for the vendor, and was talking scarves with Travis in less than ten minutes.

"Scarves? You mean *kerchiefs*?" Travis asked. "Oh, yeah, sure. I just don't ever get around to listing them. I have hundreds of kerchiefs right now." (I hadn't heard the word *kerchief* since the days when my grandmother donned one, tied under her neck, on a windy day before driving to the grocery store.) Mike put the call on speaker phone, and I was introduced to an exciting new source.

Travis and his wife, Tori Ann, specialized in surplus clothing and accessories bought from estate auctions throughout the country. They separated the pieces into lots and sold them online or locally, at their own Friday-afternoon auctions.

A few phone calls later, we made an agreement right then to be exclusive buyers for the scarves Travis accumulated from estate auctions. Mike negotiated a great price, with the understanding that the quality was very mixed, and not all scarves would be salable. The shipping cost more than the merchandise, but we factored that into the price and took a chance.

It was a good bet. We bought every scarf Travis had for nearly two years. Tori Ann would call every three to four weeks, and whether it was a small batch of a hundred scarves, or a one time "get" of three thousand, we were in. Funny, she always asked for me, but then the men got on the phone to tackle the negotiations.

"Hello, Miss Terri," Tori Ann would say, every time. "How are you today?"

"Just fine, thank you," I was a bit small-talk-challenged, but I managed. "How's your weather out there?"

"It's freezing," she might say, adding "you're so lucky you live at the beach!" I had explained to her the first time she said it that we were about a three hours' drive from the shore by car. I guess when one is living in the fly-over zone, all of Maryland seems like a beach.

"Yeah, the beach. Uh-huh…. So what do you have in stock for us?"

"We have six hundred scarves for you today."

After the necessary niceties, my thanking Tori Ann and she thanking me, Tori transferred the phone to her husband and he and Mike would negotiate the prices. They varied, based on Travis' mood (and perhaps what he had paid for the scarves, too). It was a little like *Let's Make a Deal,* and we bought the leftovers from Door #3.

We were always very pleased with our shipments and the business was growing and making a profit. We hired an assistant to handle our listings and a social media specialist to maintain our online accounts. But we made a big mistake, one that could be fatal to any business; we became complacent about our source and didn't spend time looking for another one. We knew better.

"Have you checked other auction houses for leads on scarves?" I occasionally asked Mike.

"Have *you?*"

"No, not really," I might fess up. "I'll work on it later in the week."

"I'll make some calls tomorrow afternoon," Mike said.

"We really need to find another source."

"Yeah, we really need to."

"Yeah…"

"Yeah."

A month or so later, virtually the same conversation would be repeated. Despite our new help, we were busy working long hours and finding a new source apparently was low on the priority list.

Now we had a colossal problem: Our only current source was sent to the county jail (and who knew where after that). We were left without a back-up and were getting low on inventory with darn little reserve in the warehouse.

"Why didn't you ever find a back-up source?" I asked.

"Why didn't *you* find one?" Mike replied, and then we both laughed. The situation wasn't funny, but it was helpful to share a laugh before one of us became paralyzed with panic (which, believe me, would have been very easy to do). We immediately went on a manhunt. Or a womanhunt, we weren't picky. We had to find another source. We were stalwart people (even though we were not from Missouri) and wouldn't let a little thing like losing our only source derail our success. I went to the web to see what I could find, just to sustain the business. I started buying the smaller lots like I had done when we started. They were more expensive than we were accustomed to, but we could make it work.

Mike used his favorite tool -- the phone – to scout out possibilities. He found various auction houses and they, in turn, referred us to other auction houses. Eventually, Mike discovered a few places where Travis bought the scarves, and we were back in business with several sources. We even saved a few cents per pound with the hooligans cut out of the deal. In short order, we had more than a thousand scarves in transit to us.

We survived that bump in the road and learned a valuable lesson. Back in the days when Mike and I first went into business together, we would sit around with his parents and business talk was inevitable. My father-in-law periodically helped us (or thought he did) with "business lessons," where there were frequent heated discussions in their den. Both of Mike's parents got on their high horses and repeatedly told us how dumb we were because we did this or that, or because we *didn't* do this or that.

"Michael! How can you *not* know that?" was one of Dad's favorite lines. This was never said to me, because I guess it was a "given" that I was ignorant about business.

"I just don't." Mike typically didn't argue, because he knew he couldn't win.

"Michael! Listen to your father!" Mom always had to chime in.

"For god's sakes, Michael!" Dad always said, "You grew up hearing about business every night at the dinner table, so you should have learned something!"

I was proud of Mike when he stayed calm, and I was usually too petrified to say a word unless directly spoken to.

"Terri, did Michael tell you how he wasted time in college?" Mom asked, as though we hadn't had this conversation before. "He took a course on the history of Zaire! Can you imagine? How far did he think that would get him in business?"

We weren't as dumb as Mom and Dad always thought we were, though we made our share of mistakes, as we're sure Dad must have, at least a couple of times. (He never acknowledged anything.)

Years later, in our consulting business, if Mike and I had worked with a company heavily dependent upon only one source, we would have helped the client adopt a back-up plan immediately. And we might have shared a private snicker over the ineptitude of *some people*. I was glad my father-in-law was not around to tell us how stupid we were to get too comfortable. I think we would have deserved his wrath.

———ww◦⟨◦⟩◦⟨◦⟩◦ww———

It was always exciting when the UPS truck brought the large cartons to our apartment. We had tracking information so we were prepared for the delivery and tried to be home so we wouldn't irritate our UPS man by his having to keep the large boxes in the truck until the next day. We greeted him with a bottle of water or soda and sometimes a little snack to keep us on his good side. It was hard work for him to drag the cartons up the steps to our building, and then down the steps to our apartment. Each box was about 26" square and rather heavy; sometimes we got one, and sometimes we got six or seven.

Our first shipment from Travis was three large boxes with a total of a thousand scarves (*uh... kerchiefs*). Mike helped the UPS man drag the cartons into our hallway, and I felt excited as well as a bit intimidated. How long would it take to sell this many pieces? Could we even do it? I was thinking we might not need to buy any more scarves for at least a year.

"Can you bring one of the boxes in here, please?" I asked Mike, as I sat in my comfortable chair, ready for an afternoon of sorting, akin to dumpster diving, not really knowing what to expect. I was watching my home improvement shows, learning how to turn a basement into a rental unit, and how to stage your home when you put it on the market.

"I need to rest a minute, first," Mike said, huffing and limping a little bit for good measure. He made his way into the living room, took his seat on the sofa and turned the channel to an old rerun of *Kojak*. "Just let me watch this for a few minutes."

After working primarily with candy companies for many years, and receiving sales samples, it was a relief to get merchandise that did not melt, perish or break in transit. But one time, after the UPS man left, we noticed a box had split on a corner, and some scarves were hanging out. When we set out to the post office shortly after the delivery, there was a trail of scarves from the parking lot to our front door. The more scarves we picked up, the more we saw that had blown to the far corners of the property and even into the busy street.

"There goes an Anne Klein!" I yelled, as Mike tried to catch each scarf.

"I can't help it! I'm trying!" He had a few scarves under his jacket, but the wind kicked up and just when Mike would reach for another scarf on the pavement, it would blow away.

"Hurry, I think that one might be a Laura Ashley." I could guess, anyway, because of the beautiful pastel flowers on silk. Mike was out of breath as the scarves drifted farther and farther away, into the parking lot of the medical park across the street and beyond.

"Forget it, Mike! It's okay – they'll just keep blowing. Come on, let's go." After he grabbed two scarves stuck in the fence surrounding the dog park, he came back to the car and we went to the post office. We never again served refreshments to the UPS driver.

When Mike eventually brought a carton from a new shipment into the receiving room (living room), we would sit the box in the middle of the floor and place organizing bins in a circle all around it. The bins were labeled Chiffon, Small Squares, Solids, Hold for Later, Ready to List and the largest container was for Garbage -- those scarves badly stained, torn or just mangled to death. Lest you think they came clean, ironed, folded and neatly placed into the carton, I will tell you they did *not*. The scarves were tightly stuffed, often wadded and matted together. Many times, there were surprises sequestered in the box, like an errant vintage girdle, a tablecloth, pillowcase or even a stem of plastic flowers. Garbage.

I learned how to work a big box of scarves. It was an art, really, to work quickly and efficiently so the process wouldn't take all day. First, my deal with Mike was that we would never open a box unless we agreed to put everything away after it was sorted and vacuum the area, getting rid of the dust and grit. I couldn't stand to have piles of scarves everywhere. (Stacks of bins apparently didn't have the same effect on me.)

I often slathered on a thick coat of rich, vanilla-scented hand lotion before donning a couple pairs of white cotton gloves, one pair over the other. This saved my hands from getting so dirty, and it gave my hands a desperately-needed spa treatment while I worked.

We would rout through the scarves, one at a time, holding it up to the light of the patio door checking for holes. Once it passed the hole test, we looked it over for stains. Small spots or even a few very small holes would pass muster, particularly if the scarf had a designer name on it. I would later describe any minor flaws in the listing and often post a summary like: *I would wear it!, Luxurious!, Exquisite!* or *Not as bad as it sounds.*

I loved the feel, or "hand" of fine fabric. Silk has the best hand: Chiffon or twill, either will do, but there is silk and then there is *silk*. There are lesser silks, thin and flimsy, and a swift movement can often produce a hole. Yet, just the word silk evokes a cachet that leads many to shun anything else. There are other fabrics with a good hand: A soft dotted Swiss polyester scarf, with its textural dots and maybe a pastel floral design is delicious for spring and summer. Silk, being the strongest natural fiber, was reserved during World War II to make parachutes, so acetate was introduced to the fashion world. It's still popular today because it has the look of silk with a less expensive price point. Nothing has a crisper print than an acetate scarf. Some acetate fabrics are very fluid, almost impossible to distinguish from the silks, while others can be thick and cumbersome to tie. Acetate fabric also doesn't breathe, so it can be hot to wear around the neck. Rayon has good drapeability, often mimicking silk, but I find it does not hold its shape as well as other fabrics. Cotton rules when using a scarf as a headband. Cotton breathes and helps keep the wearer comfortable. It is not ideal for draping around the neck, unless one likes the look of a wrinkled mess akin to a linen dress by the end of the day.

—⁓⦁⦁⦁⦁⦁⦁⁓—

I learned to sew when I was in fourth grade and soon started making my own clothes. I won a blue ribbon for dressmaking at our county fair (as well as a blue ribbon for my pound cake). I would linger for hours in the fabric department of Belk Department Store, back when every major department store of any repute had a fabric, or dry goods, department. My mother would let me stay there looking at pattern books and fabric while she traipsed around the mall looking for that elusive something she *had* to have.

My fondness for fabrics strengthened when I formed a strong interest in costume design in the seventh grade. I studied every book I could find on costumes and fashion history, but I soon exhausted the supply in the school library. When my mother was at the grocery store, I went to the public library at the other end of the shopping center. My book search was always rushed because in about 45 minutes, my mother would storm in and get me, angry I hadn't watched the clock and been outside waiting for her. When I discovered that a bus could take me to the big downtown library, it changed my world. All I needed was a ride to and from our suburban mall which was the end of the bus line, and I could be browsing fashion history books in a half hour. I would stay there all afternoon feeling sophisticated and scholarly, like I fit in with the many high school and college students studying at the tables. It was heaven.

Once I completed driver's education and got my license, there was no stopping my newfound freedom. My father bought me a brand-spanking-new Ford Pinto hatchback in an olive green that I picked out. It was a great world. (Little did we know the Pinto would eventually become a big laughing-stock in the auto world due to its notorious problems, but I never had any trouble with my little car.)

The high school drama department produced "Our Town," Thornton Wilder's classic set in 1901 Grover's Corners, New Hampshire, and I designed and sewed costumes for the key characters. According to the neighborhood weekly newspaper, my costumes were the real stars of the show. With that experience under my belt, I volunteered as costume mistress for a community theatre production of "The Mikado." It was exciting fabric-shopping for the bright and colorful kimonos. The main characters and chorus alike wore the clichéd traditional Japanese garb, popular in the mythical town of Titipu. Each costume required four to five yards of a cotton or blend, as inexpensive as possible. Woolworth's was always a good source, and while I was there, I always got a small bag of orange slices for sustenance while I cut and sewed.

I snagged my first paying job as a costumer with the (then) venerable Pineville Dinner Theatre, in the countryside just out of Charlotte. I was in eleventh grade and already taking a few classes at a local university, but I always had time for costumes.

Even though my sewing and quilting days are on hold (possibly forever), I still enjoy seeing the new fashions each season, more interested in the fabrics than the styles.

—⁓⁓⁓⁓⁓—

New is nice, but vintage is prime. Fishing through the new shipments was the best part of the job. It was like Christmas, Hanukkah and my birthday, all rolled into one. The larger square silk scarves were the crème de la crème. I instinctively fished for those. When I pulled a square scarf out of the box I recognized to be an Oscar de la Renta, Liz Claiborne or Anne Klein, I held my breath while I shook it out and held it up to the light, hoping there were no stains or holes. These would sell quickly for the best prices, and they went into the Ready to List bin.

The long, rectangular silks were also good numbers. Several times, I went to Facebook for some fun, and asked, "Are you a Rectangle or a Square?" and after years in the rag biz, I learned a few characteristics of people with either preference. Historically "people of the scarf," the French and Italians love the classic foulards, silk and square. Women in Brazil seem to order larger scarves – squares or longs, just lots of fabric in bright colors and designs. I would estimate American women are split evenly in their preferences for squares or longs. The street style today calls for ultra-long scarves that wrap around the neck several times, but vintage-wearers tend to eschew the current trends in favor of a mod 60's pop art print or maybe a soft floral Ralph Lauren design. Women who gravitate to squares are fashion-forward and know a half dozen ways to tie it, while the Practical Janes and the less fussy among us usually stick with a long scarf that is much easier to tie. Of course, women "of a certain age" who rode the scarf wave in the 80's (remember Oprah's scarves?) know all about scarf-tying and may still have Kathie

Lee's VHS tape to prove it. However, they may no longer have the tape player for a refresher course.

Mike's job was to pull the chiffons out of the box. This was one type of scarf he could easily identify. Chiffons came in very sheer polyester and silk, squares and sometimes longs. Most were nylon in vibrant sherbet colors, neutrals, and an occasional print. Typically, this scarf was worn tied close to the neck, perhaps with a sweater twin-set and maybe the scarf even matched the lipstick (think poodle skirts and later, tight straight skirts). The bobby-soxers dressed accordingly when swooning Sinatra; on *Happy Days*, the TV series set back in the 1950's, Joanie often wore a chiffon scarf when wooing Chachi. And trendy TV babes *Laverne and Shirley* were seldom caught without one while Americans reminisced about the transition from the 1950's to the 60's. Even younger people who never had the pleasure of knowing Laverne or Joanie may have noticed that Sandy and the dancing girls from the ever-popular stage show and movie musical "Grease" wore a chiffon scarf while daydreaming about the boys.

The price we could get for one chiffon scarf was way too low to sell individually, so we bundled them in lots of fifty or a hundred. We probably threw away more than we kept, since the nylon was very fragile. I burnt more than a few while ironing; the nylon melted and shrunk like cotton candy. I threw the remnants away, but it took some time and elbow grease to get the burned nylon off the soleplate of the iron, and the smell malingered for a day or two. (Eventually, I stopped ironing all scarves we sold in lots.)

The small, square scarves were also too inexpensive to sell one at a time, unless it was silk and in good condition, so we bundled them in lots, too. Our description said most were around 19"-20" square, but we took a few liberties with the word "small." We threw in a few fine cotton or silk 16" mini-scarves with adorable prints like poodles or shoes. These could be used on a dresser, draped over a lampshade, or maybe tied to the handle of a pocketbook. All of our lots included several free scarves to cover for any badly flawed pieces we might have missed. Customers loved that.

+ POSITIVE FEEDBACK FROM BUYER: luv2sew4u789
Fantastic assortment! Love my gifts. u r the best!!!
Lot of 50 Assorted Chiffon Scarves - Vintage

+ POSITIVE FEEDBACK FROM BUYER: selmainthehood
So much fun going thru the bag - like Christmas. ☺
Lot of 50 Assorted Chiffon Scarves - Vintage

The bins holding solids were a mish-mash of long and square silks, polys, rayons. I came across the occasional silk velvet scarf, a few long silk charmeuse pieces, and several iridescent organza wraps. Once in a while, I found a gorgeous shawl embellished with beads or sequins, and it would sell for a good price. An exquisite white beaded silk bridal stole came across my threshold in like-new condition, and it fetched $150. When a solid color scarf was a silk or poly in a popular color in very good condition, I might sell it individually. Stains and other flaws showed up more on solids, so there were fewer "very good" scarves, and solids with minimal damage sold in lots of thirty or fifty.

We listed the lots under both ladies accessories and crafts. As a former quilter, I thought the scarves would be great for crafters and others who make art from textiles. "Yes, you *can* cut the scarves!" I said in the listings, having received notes from many buyers telling me they used scarves for making tote bags, collages and other artwork. One fashion designer from New York posted photos on the Terri*art* Facebook page of exquisite dresses she had made from vintage silk scarves. A frequent buyer from Kyoto, Japan told me about the tapestries she made and sold in an art gallery, and a good customer from Cottlesloe Beach near Perth, Australia purchased only silk chiffons for her *felting* arts and crafts. She explained to me what she does, but I didn't quite understand (the language difference, you know). Fortunately, Martha Stewart cleared it up for me on her website; if it's crafting, Martha *knows*.

My V-Cart shop included the Vintage Vera Boutique. Make no mistake, I was not referring to Vera Wang or Vera Bradley, as some customers thought. One such buyer wrote to me saying she loved my Vera Wang scarves and wanted to start collecting them. Serious scarf customers know "Vera" is Miss Vera Neumann – American diva, doyenne and designer of scarves from the 1940's through the 1970's. Famous for her brightly-colored pop art designs, Vera was a fine artist who wanted to roll out her designs to the masses and chose scarves as her vehicle. Most prized were designs with her trademark ladybug drawing in the corner by her signature. Lots of folks frame a Vera scarf for dramatic and affordable artwork. Vera's are plentiful, due to her wide distribution and licensed lines, so they typically don't command high prices. An unusual print will garner more attention, as Vera collectors are always looking for that special gem. Vera was the only designer with her own boutique in my store.

Fa-la-la-la-la.... There were scarves for every holiday: Halloween, Thanksgiving (yes, really, I've found two or three), Christmas, Hanukkah, Valentine's, St. Patty's Day and Easter. My V-Cart holiday shop opened around October 1, and the whole spectrum of holiday scarves was listed for sale. I didn't want to keep seasonal scarves listed year-round, as they were received; I felt they would sell faster being fresh and novel. From small square polyesters sporting mittens and snowflakes to a large, elegant silk with a Dickens' scene, Christmas scarves were in demand. V-Cart has an annual humorous tradition of people offering (and actually selling!) "Ugly Christmas Sweaters," but not once did I see a holiday scarf called "ugly" – even ones with Jingle Bells attached or one that "sings," courtesy of a micro-chip enclosed in a plastic button. I felt it necessary to include a warning in the listing of the singing scarf: "Be careful not to fiddle with the tail of the scarf while you are in church, or in a meeting, because the song could play (and there's no turning it off until it finishes!)."

Not only did scarves come with designs for every holiday, there were special occasion and special interest scarves, too. I've seen scarves celebrating birthdays, book clubs, back-to-school, homecoming, sports teams, conventions and religions. I sold a beautiful sunrise print silk scarf from the United Methodist Church and several Roma Catholic Consortium commemoratives from various years. Special interest scarves typically sold quickly, like a brightly colored poly for the Florida State Gators or a refined silk for Yale University – the older, the better. I even found a silk scarf commemorating St. Andrews University in Scotland, where both Prince William and Dutchess Kate went to school. (I wondered if Kate had one like it.) It sold in one day for $19.99.

Many corporate scarves for Asian airlines were beautiful and artistic – all silk, of course -- while US carriers like Carnival Cruise Lines and Delta Airlines are usually patriotic colors in polyester. Over the years, I've seen several dozen polyester scarves for Red Hat Society, the empowerment group for boomer women. I thought they were cute, but not one ever sold. A hospital in the Midwest had its name on a high quality silk scarf with cartoons of stethoscopes, syringes and clipboards. It flew out the door.

Souvenir scarves were a special category. Highly desirable for serious collectors and kitsch collectors alike, the more common scarves were souvenirs of Mexico, Paris, London, Puerto Rico, Hawaii and Florida (most often made in China). More interesting were the scarves from the 1962 World's Fair in Seattle and a New York City souvenir scarf I believe was from the 1940's. I've also sold souvenir scarves from countries that no longer exist: Czechoslovakia and Yugoslavia.

Scarves denoting historical dates or events were good numbers, and I listed them under both accessories and history. I sold many American Bicentennial scarves, plentiful mementos from 1976. Less common scarves included a Richard M. Nixon campaign souvenir, a long scarf with pineapples sporting the Daughters of the American Revolution logo, and varieties of D-Day remembrances. I found one navy and white scarf commemorating the 1972 Olympics in Munich, which was so very tragic. After it was listed, I debated whether or not I should take it down and throw it away, as it didn't seem like a "souvenir" I should be selling. On the other hand, there are many who collect Olympics scarves. My confliction didn't have time to fester, because it sold the first day. The sweetest scarf I can remember was from the Korean War era and brought a tear to my eye. It was a small aqua silk scarf with an embroidered country scene and message, "To my sweetheart, from Korea with love."

We've all heard stories about a young ingénue who was an awkward, geeky teen and, seemingly overnight, blossoms into a glamorous movie star. The same can happen with a scarf. A plain red and white striped square was bought by a costume mistress and worn in an off-Broadway show, she told me. The buyer asked for – and received -- a small discount based on this brush with fame, and it was my first *celebriscarf.*

Dear Scarf Maven,

I just got the scarf I ordered. Just wanted to tell you it will be worn by a character in a video game. I am the wardrobe coordinator and it's exactly what I was looking for. Thanks so much!!

Scott

I wrote back asking him what video game this would be, but I didn't get a response. Scott later ordered a few more pieces, and I hoped they became *celebriscarves* as well.

Several buyers told me they were stylists, and the scarves would be featured in a fashion show. One said the big floral scarf they purchased was for a print ad shoot. For every buyer who gave me a story, I imagine there were many more who didn't alert me about the special status of the purchase.

"Hey, Mike, get this!" I said, boldly interrupting *Hawaii Five-O*. "We sold a scarf to a Supreme Court Justice!"

"You're kidding!" he said.

"Would I kid about a thing like that?"

The scarf in question was a classic and conservative navy and wine paisley silk square – a serious scarf, very fitting for the position. As much as I'd like to see an item about this online in "The Huffington Post" or maybe gracing the pages of "Women's Wear Daily," I must protect the privacy of my customers, so I cannot divulge the name.

A note came from a man in Paris named Alain, who told me he was a fashion designer with his own atelier. He said he loved my polka dot scarves and was, in fact, doing a study of "the dot." He ordered several times, and I did a Google Search on him. Lo, and behold! He was on a list of the most important living fashion designers of France. He had cut his teeth designing scarves for some big, big names. Later, under his own label, he received several distinguished awards for his line of *foulards*. I wondered what in the world he did with the scarves he bought from us.

It may be a stretch to consider the exchange with Joel, from California, a brush with fame, but I loved his story:

Hello Dear,

I am looking for a particular scarf and I hope you can help me out. I am going to have a photographer take some portraits of my 83-year-old grandmother riding with me in my red convertible. Sometimes we go for a drive down the Pacific Coast Highway going very fast and furious, and Granny loves it. But she won't ride with me unless she wears her Chanel sunglasses and a scarf over the head to protect her hairdo (she gets her hair done twice a week). So for the photos, I need a glamorous scarf with red in it. Any ideas?

Joel

Dear Joel,

Love the visual here! I have a few suggestions in the attachment -- a classic paisley, a contemporary graphic design, a floral and a dotted scarf, all squares. Any one of them would be appropriate. All are in a matte-finish fabric so they will not slide around easily. Hope this helps, and good luck.

Terri
Your Scarf Maven

I was tempted to ask Joel to send a picture to me, but I decided not to. Buyers should be allowed to order without being questioned. Joel chose to share a little bit with me, but I didn't want to push it. I remember how irritated I was once when I bought groceries and the cashier had a comment or question about almost every item. I felt slightly violated, and I didn't want to impose that upon any of my customers.

Talk about an imposition, this incident (almost) left me speechless:

Hi there,

As you know, I have bought at least 20 scarves from you over the past year. I am a good and loyal customer. I have a large scarf collection, but now I am running out of space to display my special scarves, and I have to cut back. Here is a proposition for you: Can I return some of the scarves I bought from you? You will have new inventory and I will be able to clean up a little bit. They are still in great condition – hardly worn. If you agree, I will send them to you and I don't expect to get the full price I paid, just send to me whatever you think they are worth. I think it would be a good deal for both of us. Let me know.

Thanks,

Karen
Boulder, CO
mamaof12345

What a bargain! This woman had some nerve, as this was no "good deal" for me. I wanted to say no, thanks, and *should* have said that. But instead, I wrote:

Dear Karen,

Sounds great. Send them!

Thanks,
Terri
Your Scarf Maven

A few days later, I got the package in the mail. A box about 12" by 18" stuffed with 43 scarves, I did not recognize most as coming from my stock. I never agreed to accept a return of "other" scarves! Furthermore, about a third of them were large, tropical-looking swimsuit wraps with fringe hanging down. Not a good look, and one I knew from experience wouldn't sell. I often trashed similar scarves when they came to me from an auction. My first impulse was to send a biting note to Karen, but then I made a decision: Karen was a good customer and a frequent contributor to my Facebook page. I didn't want to lose her or make her angry, even though she had clearly taken advantage of me. I reluctantly sent her a dollar per scarf, and she seemed very happy about that.

Mike's dad had always known we placed a high value on customer service, and he was constantly warning us that "the customer is always right – *until it costs you money.*" I thought about that when writing the check to Karen for her unscrupulous returns, but I felt I had done the right thing.

Dear Terri,

Thank you for the swift payment for my scarves. I have a great idea. I could work for you as a scarf picker. I can scrounge the thrift shops and flea markets in the Denver area and buy all the scarves I think you can use. I will sell them to you for a low price – under $5 each, most likely, plus shipping. We have the same good taste, so I think this arrangement will be ideal. Please let me know if this sounds good to you so I can get started immediately.

Looking forward to working with you,
Karen

Dear Karen,

I appreciate your offer, but I don't think it will work for me. I have sufficient sources at the moment, plus I have never paid anywhere close to $5 per scarf (plus the shipping would raise it even more). So it's not an option at this time, but I will definitely keep it in mind in the future. I know I could count on you to be a good picker!

Thanks for thinking of me.
Best,
Terri
Your Scarf Maven

I never received another order (or return) from Karen. However, several other customers over the years made similar offers to sell a few scarves back to me. No, no, no, no, no.

After sorting a big box of scarves, I was usually left with about half the scarves deemed unsalable. Some, with large holes, stains or those that had been ripped in half were obviously garbage, but others were so pretty, maybe silk, and three-fourths of the scarf was in good condition. I thought a crafter could make good use of these, cutting out the pretty designs for collages, decoupage or quilts. I bundled several together and called them "Oops Scarves," listed them with good descriptions, low prices, and thought they would sell. Only a few lots sold, and one lady asked for a refund because she hadn't realized the damage was *that* bad. Oops! That little experiment came to a swift end.

Part of the excitement over a new carton of old scarves is that you never know what you might find. I've seen my fair share of knock-offs, some of which are street-quality polyester with big logos and an even bigger designer signature (fakes), while others are made with silk and copy designs of the real deal (counterfeits). I toss them immediately, unless it's in that latter group, in which case it may or may not go into my personal collection.

One day, I was sorting and reached deep into the box and pulled out a beautiful baby blue silk scarf with horses and carriages and a filigree border, entitled "La Promenade de Longchamps." This brand is the mother of all scarf brands, and it had the Hermés logo on it, but I assumed it was counterfeit and tossed it. (I do not wear pastels.) But then I gave it a second look and wondered if my sister-in-law might like it. The scarf was in excellent condition, not a single flaw on it. And I noticed the plump hem was not rolled *out* toward the back, but *in* toward the front, just like the high-end European brands. Illegal bounty usually has a small tag saying "Made in China," but this one had a larger tag with a logo and said "Made in France."

I went straight to my computer to do some homework, researching details determining if a scarf is real or not. Authentic Hermés Scarves… Hem rolled in, check! Made in France, check! I also learned the artist's name is embedded in the design somewhere on the real ones… check! (This one was by an artist named Ledoux.) In addition to the main Hermés logo, there is usually a small logo with a copyright embedded as well. Bingo! It was an honest-to-goodness authentic Hermés 90 cm (about 35") square silk twill scarf in perfect condition.

"Mike! Hurry in…."

"What happened?"

"I found a real Hermés scarf!" I squealed.

"Huh?" Is it possible a fashion stylist like my husband didn't know about the Hermés scarf?

I explained the brand: If we walked up to the door of the Hermés boutique on Madison Avenue in New York City, we would probably not be nicely-dressed enough or glamorous enough to be buzzed into the store. (I read that Oprah was denied the buzz on a Paris shopping trip.)

"Oh, one of *those*," Mike said. I had told him about these exclusive shops before, and even read an article to him saying some stores note your handbag, your manicure and the quality of your haircolor before letting you in the shop. And after all, I read it on the Internet, so it had to be true. Mike was shocked to learn there were stores like that. I told him he was naïve.

"Sit! Let's see how much this is selling for on V-Cart," I said as I typed into the search block.

The famous, titled designs of these scarves generally come on a variety of background colors. I found a few other scarves this same design with backgrounds in pink and slate, but there wasn't a beautiful blue one (yet). Prices ranged from $595 for a New-In-Box with Tags pink piece down to $100 for the slate selection, which had several noted imperfections. I decided to go for a $300 price tag, Buy-It-Now.

Mike and I quickly took photos of the whole scarf, the logo, the title, the design, the hem, the label, and the artist's name. I listed the scarf myself rather than put it on the log for Suzanne's work. It sold within the hour to a buyer in Lausanne, Switzerland.

Other gems have been unearthed, including a few more authentic Hermés scarves. Several Burberry's have come my way. One, a stunning pale yellow with purple irises, was in great condition and it sold in less than a day for $60. I may have been able to get more for it, but I wanted to ensure it sold quickly. A colorful, beaded Judith Leiber scarf sold for $45 in about a week. I've always wanted a Leiber crystal-encrusted minaudiere evening bag and bargains could be found on V-Cart for as little as $1,200. (I could carry it to the diner on meatloaf night.) This scarf didn't quite do it for me.

I found an exquisite long scarf in an abstract bronze, gold and brown print with the designer name FENDI. The hem on one end had come unrolled, but I noted it was an "easy fix." I also passed along a tip -- because the scarf was so large, a blouse could be made from it. I was later sorry I didn't keep this one for myself, though I don't typically wear browns. It was just so exquisite and felt like a million euros.

A Coach scarf always sold, and I found many of them, but over half were bad fakes. Other prized finds included scarves from Gucci, Valentino, Ferragamo and 1960's icon, Emilio Pucci. Although I was confident these designer pieces were authentic, V-Cart made me a little nervous; when listing a big name, high end scarf, a special screen popped up warning the seller about fraudulent claims. However, one glance through V-Cart's stable of scarves showed an abundance of easily recognizable fakes.

The "big get" was just one aspect of the business that made my job so entertaining.

* 8 *

FREQUENTLY ASKED QUESTIONS
(AND COMMENTS)

"No question is so difficult to answer as that which the answer is obvious."
-- George Bernard Shaw

Where do you get your scarves?
Ha! Ha! Ha! Ha! Ha!

Are your scarves available in any stores near me?
No, they are vintage scarves, sold exclusively on V-Cart.

What does 'vintage' mean?
Previously Worn, Pre-Owned, Formerly Loved, Recycled, Time Honored…. In a word, "Used."

Does this come in navy?
Once upon a time, it may have been available in navy, but I do not have another color on hand.

Do you have another one like this, without the silkspots?
No.

What is a silkspot?
Silkspots: There probably is a proper name – I sort of made this word up! It's not necessarily a hole, though it could be, but it's a worn spot that is sort of puckered maybe, and maybe some threads showing. Almost any silk (or other fabric, too) of any age will have these. Sometimes they are from wear, sometimes from overhandling, ironing too hot. You can't usually see these silkholes or silkspots unless you hold the scarf up to the light. Sometimes a scarf will have only one or two silkspots, and sometimes a great many. Wish I had a better description!

What are the dimensions of this scarf?
Dimensions of all my scarves are in or the body of the listing and often in the title.

I get asked this a couple of times a month, and somehow, it always surprises me. I started putting the dimensions in the title after I realized it was difficult for a cell phone user to scroll down the whole listing. But the question persists!

Can you tell me what the dimensions are in centimeters?
I'm not good at the math, but 1 inch = 2.54 centimeters.

Do you have a store in Baltimore?
No, but I live in a warehouse. I would open up to retail customers, but security is impossible around here.

Do you make your scarves?
Yes, in a little corner of my warehouse, I have a sewing area where I make all the scarves myself. Sometimes, I finish with a nice rolled hem, and sometimes I am feeling lazy and finish with an overlock edging. I am careful to add stains, silkspots and holes so my scarves appear to be vintage.

Can you send a gift box with this?
Hey, missy, this aint Macy's! I am wrapping it up and putting a bow on top, what more do you want from me?

Do you give a discount for combined shipping?
There is never a shipping charge for domestic orders (though I get this question from US accounts!). For foreign orders, the buyer pays the shipping charges on all scarves ordered, and then I refund the difference in the amount paid and the actual shipping cost, if any, upon shipment.

How much does it cost to ship to Hawaii? (Alaska, Puerto Rico)
I believe that Hawaii is now part of the United States, so it's free shipping.

Why do you spend money on a newsletter, tissue paper and ribbon? I don't know how to recycle all this.

This isn't truly a *frequently* asked question, though I have had two complaints about it. Natasha, in Minnesota, said the wrapping was cute and all, but the extra thickness made it hard for the mailman to fit the envelope in her door slot. She requested I leave out any "extras," including a packing list. She ordered frequently, and I tried to remember to send her scarf "naked" in an envelope.

Another buyer, George, was a fashion show stylist from New York City, and he ordered a dozen or more scarves at a time. After he received his first order, he wrote me that he loved the scarves, but didn't love all the fru-fru that came with the order citing the recycling issue. George asked that I send the scarves only, with no tissue paper or ribbon. I taped a note on the side of my computer to remind me about the request. I wanted to keep his business!

I could save time and money by eliminating this "fru-fru." But I've had scores of customers share what they did with the ribbons, like make a hair bow for a child or use the ribbon for crafting cards, bookmarks and other items. I've received many Facebook and V-Cart messages, emails and Feedback telling me the beautiful packaging is appreciated and that they triple love my newsletter. All this made the customer feel special and confident they were unwrapping a treasure from a valued seller.

In addition to the general information questions, we received very specific questions and special requests. I wondered if anyone ever bothered to think (or spell-check) before asking:

Do you remember the Christian Diore silk scarf you sent to me a few months ago – the large square scarf with the black and fusia paisley design? Can you get me a dozen of them? Same condition, just a few pinholes and silkspots.

Surely you jest.

I received a message from a buyer in Portugal. I wondered if she actually wrote the note in broken English or if she used V-Cart's automatic translation program:

Dear Scarf Maven,

TRogering you for helping poor old fool.
I am thinking maybe perhaps there is a scarf for me?
I am wanting small and tiny little flower heads, no stems.
Any color for me is fine but must not be sad color like yellow
sometimes can be.
Please tell me what of your loveliness there is for me? Send me
number or picture, is okay?

Many fine wishes for your happy day!
Mogli

Because I didn't want to risk starting an international incident, I replied
with a few links to scarves Mogli might like, but she never placed an
order. Maybe my colors were too sad.

Do you have a 35" scarf with peach and green pastel flowers and nature?
I would have to do a search and browse through my scarf inventory
online, same as you can do. Or, I could plow through thousands of
back-stock scarves and take a look-see, just for you! Oh, wait a minute…
I think I have one, but it's only 32" square.

I need the scarf by the weekend. If I order it in a few minutes, will I get it in time?
I cannot tell by your message where you are located, which, of course,
has bearing on when the scarf may arrive. If we get your order shortly, I
can promise we will put your scarf in the mail today, and you can follow
its progress by using the tracking number for the package under your
list of purchases. But beyond that, you understand we cannot control
how long the mail takes.

V-Cart frequently makes changes in format without notice or input
from sellers, even top-rated power sellers (like us). One such tweak was
to put a new field on the listing page that shows when the buyer can
expect delivery of the package, should they order then, based on their
zip code:

Delivery: Estimated on or before Thu.
Oct. 09 to [buyer's zip code]

This is problematic because if customer does not get the package by that date, it is open for some comments like "I didn't get the scarf on time," "you were late sending the package," or "it's past the receive-by date and I still do not have my scarf." We have refunded money a few times, just to avoid a dispute and have endured several comments in Feedback alluding to our lateness when the truth is, we did our part shipping it on time, but the mail took longer than expected. Overall, we found the mail to be very reliable, but there is no guarantee on delivery dates for regular mail. (We occasionally had people ask about overnight mailing, but when they heard it was upwards of $20 for one scarf, they always retreated.) Fortunately, V-Cart would take down the negative feedback comments if we called customer service and they confirmed we indeed sent it out within our next-business-day shipping policy.

I saw a woman on the street wearing a scarf that was square (I think), and it was a medium blue with little lavendar flouwers along the edges, and it had larger yellow and white flowers all over the middle portion. Do you have anything like this in stock, or do you know where I could find it?

Does not ring a bell. I would suggest monitoring listings of scarves and maybe checking out your local thrift shops. Good luck!

I came across a gray, black and red 41" x 29" polyester scarf with a photo and logo of Led Zeppelin. I thought it might be a decorative flag or a piece of wall art. I had sold similar pieces in the past, featuring Kiss, Jimi Hendrix and the movies "Twilight Breaking Dawn" and "Stand By Me." I called these novelties wall scarves and they sold quickly. The Led Zeppelin scarf sold in one day, and I got this message from the buyer:

I just ordered the Led Zeppelin wall scarf. Can this be worn around the neck, like a regular scarf?
Certainly. It is the same-type polyester as many of my other scarves. Try it and see what you think!

What I really wanted to say was, "Look, Lady, you bought it, you own it. [Unfotunately] there are no accessories police. You can wear it around your big toe if you want to!" But I guess she really wanted to know if the fabric was suitable for draping.

Can you send me a list of all your 30" square silk scarves?
Go to my store, write 30" in the search block, and see what happens.

Some people don't have the sense to come in out of the rain, as my mother used to say. On a Monday morning, I staggered into the office to find this threat via V-Cart message:

Dear Miss Scarf Maven,

I have been watching your store for a long time and just placed my first order last week. I received the scarfs and they are very pretty, but there are no labels. I am of the understanding that every textile sold in this country must come with a label stating the fabric contents, contry of origin and other pertinent info. It is important for consumers who care about anything to know these things. I am sorry to tell you that I am going to notify the government agency for manufacturing and let them know about you are selling scarves without labels.

Respectfully,
gingin2002

I asked Mike if we should call customer service about this message, but he said to ignore it. (I couldn't resist just a little reply!)

Hello,

My grandmother had a dog named GinGin.

Terri
Your Scarf Maven

Despite all our efforts, Mike and I occasionally made a little, itty-bitty mistake. In this case, we sent the wrong scarf to a customer. Two scarves in the same storage bag had a burgundy background, one with paisleys and one with flowers – and we packed up the wrong one. When the customer received his scarf, he wrote to tell me about the mix-up, and I refunded his money along with an apology. Soon afterward, I got a note back:

Hello Terri,

This is Tom. I didn't want a refund, I just wanted to buy the scarf in the photo. I want to keep this one you sent me as it don't look to bad. I like these type of scarfs to wear on my head as a bandanna when I ride my motorcycle. I will either send you back the refund or I will buy another scarf from you and you can add the $8.99 to shipping? How ever you want to do it? Im sorry for the confusion, I just liked the pattern in the photo better. I will wait to hear back from you-

Tom in Ariz.

Keep the refund, and keep the scarf, I told Tim. Maybe you can think of my store whenever you need another scarf. Later that same day, Tim ordered seven motorcycle-riding bandana scarves from me. This time, we shipped correctly and now Tim is a regular customer. (Lots of riding going on in Arizona.)

Hello,

I really need this scarf, but I don't have enough money. would you think about sending it to me with no charge? I really wnt it.

Thank you in advance.
Heather

When I read this message, my first reaction was to ignore it altogether. *The nerve!* But I kept thinking she must have some sort of problem(s), and I decided to honor her brazen request. It's not like she was asking for a ham sandwich or a blanket for staying warm -- no one "needs" a scarf -- but if she had the *chutzpah* to ask, let me be the sucker to give it to her. I never received a thank you (other than the one she sent "in advance"), and I never received Feedback, either.

In spite of my sarcasm and complaining, the V-Cart community – or at least the scarf enclave -- is a pleasant, honest and loyal group. I have "met" some very nice people who do not hesitate to share their stories. I sent an order to a woman in Charlotte and on her packing list, I wrote that I was a native-born Charlottean and had moved to Baltimore several years ago. Her name was Audrey, and after seeing my note, she wrote:

Hi Scarf Maven,

I was born in SanAntonio Texas, then 15 years in Minnesota, then family moved to Peru S.A. then back to college in Minnesota where I met my North Carolina husband. He was in the army so we moved around for 8 years - mostly southern - but while in N.C. I experienced a neighbor who showed me what a 'Damn yankee' meant. Never would have believed it. My husband Roger and I are retired. In 2004 Roger fell 14' straight down through 3 sets of scafolding squeezed between the house and the fence. We had a house (money pit, but wonderful) and he and our contractor had been up assessing and planning when a board broke and down he went, breaking bones in his feet, femuer, and two vertebrea. His days of self employment were over. A few months later, the facility where I worked was closed. All our eggs had gone into one basket. A friend from Mauritania, West Africa, suggested we go to his country where we could live on what little early SS we could get...

Audrey went on to tell me they stayed abroad several years, but her husband needed medical care here in the States, so they moved back to Charlotte and have stayed put. We had several back and forth "conversations" through V-Cart messages, as though we were chatting at Starbucks over a ten dollar coffee drink. We agreed we had at least one thing in common, other than a liking of vintage scarves: Both of us were strong women.

Sadly, I have received more than a couple of messages such as this one:

Hello,

I'm hoping you can help me. I am a chemo patient and am looking for several head scarves. I need them large enough to cover my entire head and I do not want slicky ones that will slip off too easily. Can you recommend some?

Thank you in advance for your time.
Angie

I get a knot in my stomach just thinking about this. I always wrote back right away with suggestions and a 25% discount offer, too. My mother had breast cancer at age 42 and survived without a recurrence. Her sister had it a couple of years ago at 78, and is also a survivor. I owe a debt of gratitude for their good fortune, and I hold my breath, hoping I will not get it. Angie and the others in her shoes are the *real* strong women of the online shopping community.

A woman from California named Miri ordered a dozen scarves individually, and the following week, she wrote that she needed 30 more scarves. "All solids, and small imperfections" were okay, she said, so I put together a lot at a special price. After receiving her order, she wrote:

Dear Scarf Maven,

You are probably wondering why I've been ordering so many scarves, and I thought I'd write and let you know. I teach dance and yoga to young children, and they wave the scarves around while they are moving. It helps hold the interest of the kids and makes the class so much more fun. The scarves you sent are great, but I only have one purple scarf and several little girls argued over who got the purple. Do you have a few more purples I can buy?

Thanks,
Miri

Mike and I got a good laugh over this, just picturing the girls at the dance class. I sent Miri three purple scarves right away. She was very pleased and is still a good customer. She said she has started using scarves for her movement classes at a nursing home: "The seniors love it!"

Terri,

Thought you might like these back to re-use.

G.K.

This customer requested that every order be packed in a baggie inside the envelope. One day, I received a package in the mail with the above note and five empty baggies. It was a very thoughtful gesture, and I felt good someone was looking after my interests. Any time I saw a V-Cart message from a name I recognized as someone who had been shipped recently, concern about a possible problem immediately set in. But it's always a pleasure to read a friendly note while I breathe a sigh of relief.

The most outrageous (but not uncommon) messages were along these lines:

Can I order a dozen like this one? or **Can you get more of these?** or **Can you let me know if you get another one like this?**

"Hello, this is Terri, with Terri*art* Sales," I said into the speaker phone while continuing to work my online jigsaw puzzle. "I'd like to place an order please."

This is a call to China, and I am phoning in my weekly scarf order. My contact, Su Lyn, is always cheerful and glad to hear from me.

"Please repeat each item back to me. I'd like…"

6 pieces of the Small Bronze, Turquoise & Fuchsia Signature SILK Square by Vera

- 3 with fraying hems and minor silkspots
- 1 with fraying hems, minor silkspots and two short runs
- 1 with a 1" diameter beige stain in the lower left quadrant
- 1 in mint condition

4 pieces of the Light Olive & Peach Paisley Border Print SILK Long Scarf by Echo

"Excuse me? Oh, that style comes by the half dozen only? Okay…"

6 pieces of the Light Olive & Peach Paisley Border Print SILK Long Scarf by Echo

- 1 piece with the hem unrolled in a 4" section of one end
- 2 pieces with minor silkspots and no stains
- 2 pieces with pale gray smudgespots here and there that may or may not come out
- 1 piece with a v-shaped cut towards the middle and a few silkspots – too pretty to trash

"What? I can't hear you. Su Lyn? Well, just send them. If I have to toss more than two, that will be okay."

8 pieces of souvenir scarves

- 2 Navy Blue, Red, Multi-Color Souvenir of Tijuana Rayon Square Scarves with several tiny holes near the middle and a few minor runs
- 1 Green, Gold, White & Black Greetings from South Dakota Souvenir Silk Square Scarf with subtle green bleeding on the white – not too noticeable – and threadbare areas along the borders
- 1 piece of an adorable Pink & Gold Paris Souvenir Square Scarf that I can throw away, too damaged to sell
- 3 pieces Green, White, Multi-Color Souvenir of the New Jersey Turnpike Silk Square Scarves – this has been popular because everyone deserves a memento of their ride on this iconic strip of highway
- 1 piece of Blue, White, Multi-Color Skiing in Switzerland Souvenir Square Scarf. The hem should be ripped in one place, with a few blue paint splatters here and there, and the scarf should be 'out-of-square' stretched diagonally from tying.

6 pieces Purple, Green & Black Floral Print Sheer Square Poly Chiffon Scarf by Woolworth's

- 2 pieces in good condition with the old price tag still affixed (99 cents)
- 3 pieces with various silkspots, small runs and a few puckers
- 1 piece with a 3" section of the rolled hem torn off and a small beige-ish spot about 7" from a corner – salvageable

5 pieces Green, Black & White Geometric Print SILK Square Scarf with self-fringe by Oscar de la Renta

- 1 piece with a green spot on the white center and a whitish spot on a black corner, minor silkspots and a run here and there
- 2 pieces with silkspots and a minor run or two
- 1 piece with some thread-bare areas with a few almost-holes
- 1 piece with a lump of what looks like hardened chewing gum stuck to a corner and with dust and grit stuck to the gum, that will make my hands sticky and gross me out a little bit, will need to toss this piece

"And Su Lyn, those solid color scarves you sent to me last month have really been selling. I need to add some to my order:"

- 5 pieces red sheer polyester long scarves with minor silkspots and a few short runs
- 2 pieces caramel-color silk chiffon square scarves with a small stain near a corner and several pinholes
- 6 pieces of royal blue sheer poly long scarves with…

"Out of stock? So, you think the royal blues will be ready to ship a week from Tuesday? Okay, then, hold the entire order until you can ship it complete." It is at this time, Su Lyn gives me the penalty "buy" that is mandatory with each order.

I have to order and pay for

- 14 pieces of various colors of poly/cotton bandanas, most unsalable with large holes, filthy and/or faded

- 9 long poly chiffon scarves that are printed with gold metallic stamping and say "Praise the Lord," "I Love Jesus," or "What Would Jesus Do?" These come in black, white, purple, royal and red. They will be in various conditions, and I won't even be able to give them away. I'm sure I have many customers who are good Christians but apparently they don't want to broadcast it around their necks.
- 7 pieces representing the Red Hat Club, in designs of red and purple hats printed on polyester sheer stripes long scarves. I've read about the club, and it's cute and all, but these scarves are a bust and I've never been able to sell one.

But to offset the penalty scarves, Su Lyn says she can send to me:

- 6 pieces of assorted floral print scarves, assorted colors and designs. But the thing is, some or all of them may or may not be in too poor a condition to sell.

"Su, a couple more requests before we hang up. Do you have any scarves with books printed on them? Well, if you see any, let me know. And do you remember the Christian Dior silk scarf you sent to me a few months ago – the large square with the black and fuchsia abstract paisley print? Can you get a dozen of them for me? Same condition, just a few pinholes and silkspots."

"Okay, just keep me in mind if you do."

And I have completed the order until the following week, when I do it again.

I wish it were that easy.

* 9 *

IT'S NOT EASY BEING AWESOME – LESSONS LEARNED ALONG THE WAY

"Success isn't about the end result; it's about what you learn along the way."
– Vera Wang, Fashion Designer

My father owned a construction company, and from a very young age, I learned three things from him about business: When you have your own business, you have to work long days and often on the weekends; you have to treat your employees like valued human beings; you are always waiting for that "big check" to come in the mail.

I have memories of going to work with my father some Saturday mornings when I was five or six. I particularly remember one time wearing a red corduroy jumper and a white blouse, with the dreaded short white socks and navy blue Mary Jane's. My dark blonde ringlets were probably a tangled mess, but my mother was still asleep and I was on my own getting ready. We would leave the house before anyone else was awake, and I cherished our time together, not having to share Daddy with my two younger brothers. We always went to the Coffee Cup Diner in uptown Charlotte for breakfast. We sat at the counter on the worn turquoise spinning stools, and I ordered a Cherry Smash (cherry syrup in Pepsi-Cola) and a cinnamon bun, pointing to the specific one I wanted from the glass domed-pedestal. The hostess was Miss Jane, and she winked and called me "Sweetie."

My Daddy seemed to know everybody – the workers and other customers. There were typically men from his Masonic Lodge and his Rotary Club drinking coffee and maybe eating a bacon biscuit and a bowl of grits, while chatting about business and politics. One time, he even introduced me to the mayor, who pulled up a chair and joined us for a while.

I was ready to go, probably about the time my attention from others wore thin, and we went to the big downtown post office where Daddy had a box. He gave me the key and let me open the ornate brass door to the box and pull out the mail so he could flip through it. "Mornin' Mr. Bob," a postal worker would call out from behind the bank of boxes. "All the mail's up, sir." Sometimes the big check was there and sometimes it wasn't, but it was of little consequence to me.

We would drive around town, visiting some construction sites. Daddy said you always have to watch everything when you have a business. He checked to make sure the workers were on the job, and asked about any problems. Sometimes he would have to call a client or a foreman at home. This was long before cellphones, yet Daddy had a phone in his car. It was a black tabletop model with push buttons and a very long cord so he could keep it near him at a site if he was expecting a call. There was a long antenna snaked over the top of the car, and the phone actually worked! I always found this thrilling, as I didn't know anyone else so lucky they had a phone in the car. This was a Daddy-special that he had jerry-rigged himself. After a few hours, we would head home, often stopping at the Krispy Kreme to get a box of warm glazed crullers (we called them tractor wheels) for the rest of the family.

Around suppertime one evening, Mama and I were cooking, and the doorbell rang. I ran to the door. It was Ol' Tom, one of Daddy's long-time employees. We knew him well, as he spent time at our house fixing things and working in the yard. Tom always had a butterscotch Life Saver in his pocket for me and a story to tell. But today, Ol' Tom brought a watermelon from his garden, and when I opened the screen door, he handed it to me. I turned around to take it to the kitchen and promptly dropped it. Splat! The watermelon cracked and the red juice splattered all over me and all over the new wallpaper in the hallway. I was screaming and my mother was hysterical. My father disappeared out the front door with Tom.

Turns out Ol' Tom didn't come just to bring the watermelon. He needed to talk with my Daddy about "barreyin" some money. I later heard Daddy telling my mother, "Tom's a good man, and I had to help him out."

One night, we were all sleeping and the phone rang. A few minutes later I looked out my window and saw Daddy in the car, pulling out of the driveway. I asked Mama where he was going, but she was half-asleep already and kept repeating "go back to bed… go back to bed."

Daddy was home in time for breakfast, and I learned it was one of the construction workers who had called from jail and needed to be picked up. *Jail?* This was exciting news, and I asked a lot of questions. Daddy said it was one of his men who was drunk and rowdy, that's all, and you have to take care of your good employees. Then he said he didn't want to talk about it anymore. Being the house busybody, *I* wanted to talk about it, but to my chagrin, didn't get any more information.

My parents were divorced a few years after that, and I never went to work with Daddy again. But these are vivid lessons I remember from him about being a business owner, and they still ring true today.

In the early days, starting our business with my father-in-law's help was an exciting project. Mike and I would sit with him at the kitchen table and review our sales and expenses and discuss whatever business principle was on Dad's mind. We were doing a good job, Dad often said. "You're making money, Michael, I never would've believed it." Dad couldn't quite let a compliment rest; he had to tack on a qualifier.

Goodness knows, Mike and I were hungry for any scrap of praise we could get. Mike felt he never had approval from his parents, and I heard his mother say many times they were hurt he wasn't a lawyer, doctor or a CPA so they could be proud of him. Her attitude on this baffled me, because Dad had neither of those distinctions, but Mom revered him as a very shrewd businessman. Their other son was a stocks and bonds wiz without an advanced degree, and they referred to him as "brilliant." When I was in her good graces, Mom sometimes conceded that with my help, it might be possible for Michael to run a successful business.

Mom said there was, however, another major qualification my husband was lacking. He needed to learn to play golf. Almost every time we saw her, she was fixated on Mike's disinterest in the fairway game. "Most sales are made on the golf course," she said. Mom's knowledge about golf and sales apparently came from her teacher's degree and thirty years as a homemaker. "Michael will never be successful if he can't schmooze with the other men on the golf course."

"Ma, I'm not interested in golf! And most of my buyers are *women*," Mike responded, the same way he did every time the subject was raised, and he could never resist adding. "Dad never played golf."

"Michael, your father was a CEO and an owner, not a *salesman,*" she said with disdain, also pointing out that Dad was from Boston where golfing wasn't popular in his day.

When I was alone with Mom, she tried to work through me: "You've got to get Michael to take some lessons." I debated this with her many times, and finally I learned to change the subject rather than repeat previous conversations verbatim.

Our sessions with my father-in-law quickly faded from "interesting" to stressful. Dad decided he should meet with me alone and keep Michael out of the business end. "Just let him sell," he would say. I didn't like this, as the intimidation factor rose considerably when I was the only prey. He would lose patience quickly and didn't take kindly to questions, most of which he thought were disrespectful. I asked when I didn't understand something he said, but he just assumed I was questioning his knowledge. I remember one conversation when I asked about ways to know if we were making money when we were growing (thus the simple money in, money out equation didn't cut it). Dad seemed exasperated and said, "*I'll* let you know when you are making money." Once again, he was trying to make sure we remained dependent on him.

One thing my in-laws never understood was that Mike and I were a team. Dad called for a clear and distinct division of duties, while we often had need to overlap or share duties. One day, Mike called his father, aglow with some good news. The buyer for a small chain of junior stores was interested in our accessories and asked us to make a presentation to their committee. They asked *us*! We were movin' on up.

That evening we visited Mom and Dad thinking maybe they would have champagne and kudos for us. (Of course, we knew that was a fantasy and would never, ever happen.) As soon as we were in the den, Dad summoned Mike to the kitchen, and Mom started in on me.

"Dad's very upset," she said. "He doesn't want to hurt your feelings, but Michael should go alone to the appointment."

"Why?"

"He's the one in sales. It's a project for *him*. Let him do it."

"But we work together," I said.

"Look, you don't want the buyers to think he had to bring his *wife* with him on an appointment. Let Michael be a man and do this by himself."

"It's not like bringing his wife," I asserted. "We're business partners."

"Yeah, well, it looks bad," she said, "taking your wife on a sales call, like he can't handle it himself."

"No…" I started my rebuttal, but she interrupted.

"Your father-in-law never took *me* with him on an appointment."

"That's different!" I said. "You weren't a part of the business!" Uh-oh. I had really stepped in it now.

"Oh, yes I was!" Mom said, and this was news to me. "Dad ran everything past me before he made a decision." I flatly knew this to be untrue, but I decided it was time to pipe down.

Quietly and calmly, I said, "We will make a more powerful presentation as a team."

"Well, *we* don't think so."

It occurred to me that this was very ironic since obviously Mom and Dad used their tag team act when they wanted to manipulate us.

We made a rare decision to buck the dictators, and we both went on our appointment. It was a very successful meeting; we gained a new customer and left the buying office with a purchase order. But we still had to contend with the in-laws. Typically, they would want every detail of every appointment (repeated several times – another effective interrogation technique), but we gave them the gist of the meeting and they didn't ask us any questions at all. We did something our way, it worked, and they didn't want to hear about it.

In spite of the adversarial relationship with my father-in-law, I managed to learn from him about the business world.

Check for reasonability.

When working with figures, Dad told me, always check for *reasonability*. That is, if a long column of figures adds up to $23, there might be a problem and it should be double-checked. This will help prevent careless errors on invoices and purchase orders. When scanning a purchase order, for instance, rather than tediously checking each line item, a check for *reasonability* could spot an obvious error, like 5 dozen instead of 50 dozen or 100 pieces instead of 10 pieces.

Depreciate and move out inventory that doesn't sell.

Our inventory of scarves and jewelry didn't melt or break, get stale or moldy, but you could say there was an expiration date on some of the trendier pieces. I remember the large plastic button earrings, the architectural dangles with the green patina and large hoop earrings in fluorescent colors. With a few exceptions, though, accessories were timeless, so thinking it could still sell for full price to new customers, we didn't feel pressured to move out the old inventory at the end of a season. Dad had another philosophy, we learned.

"You have to move out the old inventory," he would say repeatedly. "Take whatever you can get for it." When we countered about the advantage of durable goods, he bristled at being challenged. "Move it out! And I don't want to hear another word about it."

Dad didn't like explaining things, but after a while, we realized he was right. Keeping previous-season items in the line meant more sample boards to carry around and longer to show the line. The look of a new season should be clean and fresh, but when the "old" pieces were in the mix, our line looked a little bit stale.

Years later, we would face the same situation with our online store. Our listings were set so that anything not sold in 30 days was automatically renewed. Everything was new to the people browsing our store for the first time, but we determined about half our sales came from repeat customers who may have seen many of the same listings for months, some as old as a year or longer. We wanted everything to look fresh and exciting, so occasionally we would mark down the older listings to move them out of inventory. If that did not work, we would take them out of the store for a while. Sometimes we donated the scarves to a charity thrift shop and sometimes we would liven up the store by taking new photos and re-listing the "old" scarves.

Your customers often buy from you because they *like* you.

Dad said the *opposite* all the time. "Michael, you can be buddies all you want with your customers, but if they find something for a nickel less, they will drop you like a hot potato." We both frequently got into debates over this point. We did not agree. Price was certainly important, we acknowledged, but we were also building relationships, selling the Terri*art* experience, the ambiance and the feeling.

"That's a bunch of bull," Dad said. "Don't kid yourself. They're buying on price and price alone." My father-in-law had no experience with a small business; he was used to competitive contracts with big companies where pennies really added up. In contrast, I believe our marketing prowess has been the key ingredient to our success in all our endeavors.

Be flexible on receivables.

In our accessories business, we extended open credit to stores after a simple credit check; we sent an invoice and expected payment in 30 days. Most of our independent store owners were very conscientious and proudly paid right on time, but about 10% of our customers were always late. Often a reminder phone call was all it took to have a check put in the mail.

When a good customer seemed sincere and told us they simply didn't have the money to bring their account up to date, we always tried to be understanding and work with them. A payment plan often was the ticket. Or, we suggested they could put us first in line for payment right after the holidays. Maybe we would suggest a sale and mail point-of-purchase signs to place in the store. A good weekend sale could raise enough money to cover the invoice.

We tried to exercise good judgment about continuing to extend credit, and often it was a crap-shoot -- an *educated* crap-shoot -- considering our history with the customer and the amount of money in question. We learned to trust our gut.

Early in our jewelry-selling days, I had an experience in a store that helped shape my understanding of customer service and human nature. We were showing our jewelry line to the owner of a small dress shop in "uptown" Beaufort, South Carolina. When a bell rang to announce a customer coming through the door, our appointment was interrupted so the customer could be helped.

Even though we were in a rush to get to the lunch buffet at a hometown restaurant on the edge of town before it closed, we smiled and chatted with the customer, an older woman with a kind face, and showed her a few samples of the upcoming fall line. We could see the extra bit of attention made her feel good, and then she turned to the store owner and said, "I want to pay on my lay-away," and then ambled her way to the register. We saw her take a dollar bill out of her pocketbook and proudly hold it out to the store owner. While waiting for her receipt, she turned back to me and joyfully told me about the beautiful raincoat on lay-away that she would be able to get by the time the weather turned cool. She described the coat as knee-length, gray with a touch of black, a nice collar and a belt that made her look "skinny." She was proud of her find. After she left the store, the owner said the coat was $19.99 and the woman had been paying on it every Friday. It occurred to me to pay the coat off for her, but something told me her pride would be crushed. The store owner was a good steward working with her customer.

We made it to lunch with time to spare and enjoyed sweet potato casserole, okra, succotash, chicken fried steak and iced tea. This was good southern fare before the term 'soul food' was popular. (We bypassed the chitlins, nearly gagging after asking what that was on the steamer table.)

Sooner or later, you're going to be sued.

Despite our best efforts on collections, when we exhausted offers and suggestions, and when a stern letter didn't garner payment, we had two choices: We could forget the whole thing and write it off, or we could file papers in small claims court. If the store had closed its doors, we generally didn't pursue a case. But if the store was still open and we were in a game with the owner, being repeatedly told they never got the invoice or playing telephone tag, it was time to get tough and proceed through the legal system. Fortunately, we only had a few such accounts over several years' time. We were young and naïve and thought if we won a court case, we would be paid. It wasn't that easy. We didn't use an attorney for any of these cases, so we had to travel to the courthouse, trying to schedule some selling appointments along the way. Many times, once we got there, we would find that the case had been postponed, costing us more money and time. When we won – and we usually did -- it was costly and complicated to execute the judgment. Cynicism set in when we realized the customer doesn't really have to pay unless they're so inclined.

We surely could have used Perry Mason's help when we filed papers in small claims court against a store in Fayetteville, NC (pronounced FED-vuhl) called The Toggery, a busy store in a hoppin' military town where we had several accounts. We were owed $1,500 that was six months past due. Just a few weeks after the store owner was served, we ourselves were served papers by two sheriffs who came to our Charlotte showroom. It was an embarrassing show during a bustling day with people roaming the hallways of the apparel center. The papers said we were being sued in district court for a "frivolous lawsuit." We learned that the store owner's husband was a well-known attorney in Fayetteville, and he claimed we sued the wrong entity. The store was a part of another corporation, and we had caused "humiliation and suffering" for the owner. The suit was asking for $5,000 from Terri*art*.

Mike and I both were quite agitated after we read all the paperwork. We called our attorney immediately. Actually, James was *Dad's* attorney as well as a family friend who had helped us when we set up our business. First, he admonished us to calm down, saying we could probably win the case, and he asked that we fax the papers to him. James said he would get back with us when he had time to look into the case. Mike and I were frankly irritated that James didn't seem alarmed about our emergency. We were being *sued!*

That evening, we visited Mom and Dad to discuss the lawsuit. Dad had already heard about it from James, and asked why we were so upset.

"For God's sakes, Michael, being sued is a part of life," he insisted, "and any business that's been around for a while will eventually be sued for something or other." Dad snickered a little bit and added, "Michael! Geez, you're acting like a criminal!"

The injustice of it all hurt, but what really hurt most unfolded in just a few days. We received a letter and copies of papers from James showing the case had been settled. Mike called, and James took the call immediately (he always did, thanks to Dad's account).

"Didn't your father review this with you?" James asked, incredulously.

"The first we learned about settling anything was in this letter we just received."

James explained that Dad had told him to settle the suit immediately, saying it was ridiculous for us to make repeated trips to Fayetteville, a three hour drive to the eastern part of the state. Since James was on Dad's retainer, he took his orders directly. Of course, James *thought* we concurred with the plan. So, the decision to settle was made, and we had to pay $1,500 to the store owner, drop our case against the store, and then pay a $1,000 fee to James.

That evening, we made a B-line to the in-law's. Angry and frustrated, Mike asked Dad why we weren't consulted about the decision. He waved off the question. "You don't need anything hanging over you," he said. "Besides, you had to be taught a lesson." We never filed another small claims suit.

I believe my father-in-law had a grand time dabbling in this case and playing with us. Checkmate! Something's got to change, we vowed.

———

Most of what I know about business, I learned on my own from experience, voracious reading and a motivating drive to get things done. Although I am not a believer in firm "rules," it helps to have some guidelines for an inventory-based business.

Fast shipping wins.

When we launched our first accessory line, we capitalized on fast shipping. Many other distributors would gather all seasonal orders from retailers and only then place an order with the manufacturer, at home or abroad. Inevitably, the order would come in late or, sometimes, very incomplete, leaving the retail store with shortages. This was the most aggravating complaint from buyers that we heard, so we decided to work differently. We ordered inventory earlier, based on our estimates. We didn't oversell, and therefore the orders were ready to go out complete and on time. This gave us a healthy edge over the competition; we were dependable and the stores loved it.

"They don't really need this now," we frequently heard when working with candy company owners who would say this repeatedly when they were late shipping or delivering an order. For example, most retailers wanted their Christmas candy to come in immediately after Halloween so they could take down the leftover candy corn and peanut butter goblins and put in its place the chocolate Santas and eggnog-flavored chews. When the Christmas order didn't arrive on time, according to the date on the purchase order, the store had bare shelves. Further, the candy office staff would go nuts with all the customer complaint calls.

"This stuff doesn't even sell until much closer to Christmas," was the justification we got when we emphasized the importance of shipping *on time*. If the customer wanted the candy order on September 1, we said, either do not accept the order if it couldn't be done or *ship it on time*. We eventually sold the concept of shipping on time to most of our clients, and it lead to significant sales increases. But one well-known seasonal candy company we worked with never quite believed the value of giving the customers what they asked for – so they never quite grew their sales, either.

Our fast shipping philosophy carried through to our V-Cart sales, too. "Lightning fast shipping" is a phrase we often read in comments from customers. "Fast and free!" "I had my scarf the next day!" When we were very busy, Mike made more than one trip to the post office in a day, and he joked about needing to build a condo for us above the main post office in downtown Baltimore.

Our listings touted we shipped within one business day. *Do what you say you are going to do* seems so simple, but we've constantly been surprised how often others ignore this basic business principle.

Tools Really Do Help.

An artist needs a canvas, an easel, a palette and a treasure trove of oil paint tubes, chalk, pencils and brushes. A construction worker wears that ubiquitous belt holding a tape measure, screwdriver, hammer and chalk line. A person selling time-shares may need a laptop or CD player to show a video of the property. She may also need a golf cart for personal tours, and then there's that big key ring. In all our business consulting, Mike and I made it a priority to be certain the correct sales tools were available. A lack of proper tools is very common with small businesses and is one of the first things we "fixed."

A small candy company owner instinctively would say they couldn't afford a catalog or website. We would immediately prove them wrong and show that sales tools do not have to be expensive productions. We designed and produced many sales kits over the years, with sell-sheets, easy-to-read price lists, and general info sheets. This was accomplished by using minimal graphic design skills, digital photos or drawings, and a color laser printer. Though not comparable to a glossy color catalog, these efforts got the job done just fine – and on a shoestring budget.

Another tool I often used was a newsletter for customers. I started this early in our career, back when desk-top publishing was becoming widely available. Customers loved the newsletter, and it generated sales with every monthly issue. Some of the stores asked for their own personalized version of the newsletter to give out to *their* customers. This goodwill led to many exclusive relationships selling accessories, and we carried this over to the candy business. "Every time an invoice is mailed to a store," I insisted, "we must include a newsletter or other promotional flyer." It didn't require any extra postage, and it was a valuable sales tool. Later, we also used email for getting out the message (but nothing beats info in the customer's hand). When we opened our store, we started a Scarf Maven newsletter and sent it with each order. We have two versions customized to the buyer – one for new customers telling them about us, and another for repeat customers with seasonal fashion information, such as trends, colors and maybe even a recipe or some trivia.

We finally woke up and hired a woman to handle our social media. Feeling our age, neither Mike nor I knew much about Facebook, Twitter and whatever else is new and exciting. For a year or more, we vowed we would learn. "Yes, we really should," we said. "Uh-huh, soon we will learn." We both took a four-session class called "How social media can increase your business." It was very worthwhile, but the instructor assumed everyone had a general knowledge of social media, so some of the material was lost on us. We never had the time to devote to what we feared would be a massive project, but we found Elle, a great computer person and fashionista, who set it all up. She is having a grand time maintaining the "fun" and reaching out to potential customers.

"Raise your prices, dear!"

Our scarf business was only a few months old when we received a message from a customer who had bought a couple of times. She loved our selection, she said, but insisted the prices should be higher. "You'll never make any money at these prices," even though she didn't have a clue about my costs and expenses, and I didn't have a clue about her background. Was she a businesswoman herself? Retailer? CPA? I immediately discounted her comments, but later, when I was wide awake at 3 AM, I started thinking about it. My father-in-law used to warn us about selling too low. "You need to have fair pricing," he said, "but be careful not to underestimate the value of your product." Another of his frequent sermons started out, "Your time is worth something; don't forget to charge for it." Indeed, I had learned over the years that many businesses do not even know the true cost of their items, including their own time, and then they wonder why they aren't making money. While I felt we had a handle on our expenses and overhead, I began to wonder if we were fully aware of the *value* of the scarves.

Vintage scarves are often stained, ripped or scratched. The colors sometimes bleed and the hems can easily ravel away. But there are undeniable attributes, too. For the most part, they are one of a kind. Of the approximately 45,000 scarves we've sold, I estimate we have come across duplicates only a couple hundred times. I am constantly amazed at the variety of prints and designers that have made their way onto scarves. From post-war florals to 60's pop-art, to the large, boldly-colored geometrics and florals of the 80's, scarves have long been an avenue of artistic expression.

A new scarf to rival a golden oldie is difficult – if not impossible -- to find today. And if you do find one, it is typically in a (locked) glass display case and you have to trip up a salesperson to see it. You try to act non-chalant when you are told it is $225. That is, unless you are in a very chi-chi store and learn the gorgeous Hermés scarf is $795. Even if you don't get sticker-shock, you can't find a Tracy, Vittadini, Schiaparelli or Balmain at the mall. On the other hand, you can shop at a big discount store and probably find a selection limited to today's trendy, very long wrap-arounds. Nothing wrong with the *mise en scène*, but sometimes you just need a classic silk. A vintage scarf is also a way for a woman of average means to wear, say, an Oscar de la Renta design. In addition to the big price tag for a designer dress or suit, big name designs often come in sizes 0-10, effectively ignoring a majority of American women. A scarf *always* fits.

All of this contributes to the value of vintage. After I put more thought into value and worth, I raised the prices gradually during my first year. Our scarves shipped without an additional shipping charge, but common sense says it is included with the price. So, when postage prices went up, I raised prices accordingly. These honest increases didn't hurt my sales one bit.

You Do Not Have To Do Everything Yourself.

Delegating has been a difficult thing for me to master over the years. I admit I am a bit of a control freak, but I'm much better about it now than I used to be. Even before "micro-managing" became a popular catchphrase, I felt I could do a task better, faster and more efficiently than anyone else. And though that may (or may not) be true, I realized it was a matter of priorities.

When working with one of our candy companies, boxed chocolates going to an upscale store were shipped gift-wrapped for holidays, with a bow around the box. I showed the chocolate-packing ladies how to tie a pretty bow. I showed them over and over again, but it didn't "take." I tried and I tried, but their bows never looked quite like mine. After much angst and effort, I finally realized it didn't matter one way or another. Not really. Their bows were pretty "enough." I learned to choose my battles.

And this holds true now, with our scarf business. After we hired our assistant, I nagged her a bit over the minutia. Did it really matter if the color of a listing title was violet or darker purple? Could jacquard be shortened to either jacq or jacq'd? Suzanne was very dependable and did a great job, so I asked myself, did it really matter? It did not. I make suggestions and work with Elle on social media promotions and sales, but for the most part, she has an open slate, and I'm very happy with the results of her creativity. I've learned to hire the best people possible and then *let them do the job.*

The Personal Touch.

Mike and I called on clients and customers in our consulting business, and we always met face-to-face before commencing on a project. Even though all the work could be done via Internet in the more recent years, we felt it was important to bond so we would know who we were talking with when communicating via phone or email.

When Mike or another salesperson working with us called on a buyer, particularly one with multiple stores, we tailored the sales kit and literature to that customer. For example, the front of the kit folder had a label with the company name on it and inside was a special flyer listing the promos or specials we could provide for them. The price list had the store's name at the top, saying "special pricing." (Chain stores generally received discounted pricing.) This usually garnered favorable reactions from the buyers.

There were no personal meetings with our online customers. (Though I've had invitations to visit Australia, Britain and Salt Lake City, I'm waiting for the invite from my customers in Florence or the Côte d'Azur before making any plans). We still tried to form a connection with the customer by using a personal touch. We were mindful of the fact that our customers didn't really *need* to buy a scarf, and they sure as heck didn't have to buy it from us. We appreciated the order and wanted them to know that. I hand-wrote a personal note on each packing list thanking the customer for the business, signed "Terri, Your Scarf Maven." For international orders, I wrote 'thank you' in their language:

"Grazie!" *Italian.*
"Arigatou!" *Japanese.*
"Takk tusen!" *Norwegian.*
"Spasiba!" *Russian.*
"Efharisto!" *Greek*
"Obrigada!" *Portugese.*
"D'akuju!" *Ukranian.*
"Toda!" *Hebrew.*

Many comments have been sent to us regarding our extra efforts. "Mi piace!" ("I like" in Italian.)

Accommodate Special Requests (whenever possible).

When talking about customer service, the most common comment I've heard from business owners over the years is "They [our customers] have to understand that's not the way we do business." My snappy reply is always strong: "They don't have to understand *anything* other than the fact that there are plenty of other candy companies that would love to have their business."

A small company needs to be flexible. This can be essential to a buyer who has a special request, since a large company probably cannot or will not go the extra mile to make the buyer happy. For example, when a store wanted boxed chocolates with half milk and half dark orange crèmes, we said *do it!* It wasn't on the price list, and there weren't stock labels for it, but a little bit of knowledge of computer graphics programs and a good printer can produce special labels for anything needed. And, by the way, we added an extra charge for any requests that actually have costs involved, such as the labels – but it's important not to be petty, and explain the charge well in advance of accepting the order.

I've argued with candy company owners over smaller requests, such as mailing the invoice and not just packing it in the box with the order. This was a common need when the store had a clerk who opened up cartons and checked in the candy; often the paperwork never made it to the person paying the bills. "That's not the way we do invoices," I'd be told. "They'll just have to find it in the box."

But it was a reasonable request, and I'd say the way it should be done with all customers. Why couldn't the invoice be mailed separately to accommodate the request? All it took to make the customer happy was the cost of a postage stamp! Furthermore, if the right person didn't get the invoice, how did you expect to be paid (without having to send a copy of the invoice via mail, email or fax)?

A woman named Etta owned a small shop on the Maryland shore, and she ordered candy every week during the season. The candy company offered regular beach deliveries, but the truck had recently been re-routed and pulled into her area around 10 AM. Problem was, she didn't open until noon, but Etta had a ready solution: She worked mornings as a volunteer firefighter, and the driver could drop off her order at the firehouse about a mile down the street from her store.

"We don't go that far down the beach road," the candy truck driver said. "The traffic is always backed up, and there's nowhere to park." Etta would have to meet the driver at the store, he insisted.

There was no logic in that rebuttal. *What difference did it make if the driver stopped at the shop or at the firehouse?* Etta was a very good, loyal customer who ordered heavy during the summer, a time when candy companies desperately needed business. Finessing this change wasn't easy, but we made sure Etta's deliveries were made to the firehouse. (Darned if the same argument didn't pop up after Memorial Day the following year.)

Some business owners we worked with "got it" and some never did.

We frequently fielded special requests from V-Cart customers, too:

"Can you please put my scarf in a plastic baggie? If it rains, the package could get soaked and ruin the scarf."

"Please send this to my friend in California and write a note saying HAPPY BIRTHDAY."

"Can you please hold this scarf until payday on the 15th? I'm good for the money."

"Please write the long V-Cart number on the outside of the envelope."

But there's one request we received repeatedly from some international customers:

"On the customs forms, can you please claim this is a gift?"

No can do. That's illegal. (Not as illegal as the rampant counterfeits on V-Cart, but illegal all the same, and Scarf Maven did not want to be featured in a *Prison Lockup* episode on cable TV.) We didn't have to fill out customs forms when the order fit into an envelope, but we did if it shipped in a carton or an oversize plastic pouch. Either way, the dollar, euro, pound, ruble or yen value of our scarves was relatively small, so typically it was not an issue.

Is it worth losing a customer over $8? (or $10, or $28...)

When dealing with a difficult customer with a real or imagined problem, there was rarely a reason to stand firm on principle. Make the customer happy, if you possibly can. For a complaint about a hole or stain we must have overlooked, we typically refunded the money right away and suggested the customer just toss out the scarf. We believed most customers were fair and honest.

Sometimes, though, it just wasn't possible to make a customer happy. We sold a lot of 50 assorted small scarves for $28 to a woman in Oregon. About six weeks later, we got a V-Cart message where she said, "I brought my package home with me to Russia, and I just opened it to find bad scarves. I can't use these for making socks. Most are too thin. I only have about ten I can use."

Making socks? How did she use silk and poly scarves to make socks? Did she knit them from scarf strips? This was perplexing; I have made dresses, suits, quilts and a slew of craft items, but I have never attempted to make socks, and I don't know if Martha has either. Had this been a friendly exchange, I would have asked about her sock-making, but this was not a chatty message. She demanded a full refund. V-Cart requires a 14-day return policy for Top Sellers, but even though this far exceeded the time frame, Mike wrote to her saying we would give her a refund as soon as we received the return.

The Russian sock-maker wrote back right away, sounding very agitated, and said she was in Russia and it would be too expensive to send the scarves back. She felt we should give her the refund anyway. Mike and I mulled this over for about three seconds and decided her request was unreasonable. We had sent the scarves to Oregon, as ordered, not to Russia, where we would have added on an appropriate shipping charge. There was nothing about the scarves that wasn't fully described in the listing, and all other customers who had ordered the lot had been very satisfied with their purchase. We did not issue a refund.

A customer from Boston asked to return a scarf, saying it was much smaller than she thought it would be. I wrote back, very carefully reminding her that the dimensions of the scarf are clearly in the listing, but I agreed to refund the money after I received the return. She was grateful, she said, and would put the scarf in the mail that same day. Her Feedback, left after she received her $7.99 refund, raved about our superior customer service.

While a happy customer can refer your store to others, a customer who feels "wronged" can spread a negative note to friends, online message boards and social media. When there's a kerfuffle, we ask ourselves, "Is it worth losing a customer over $8?"

* 10 *

FROM PAISLEY PALACE TO
CHIFFON SHANTY (AND BACK)

"My sun sets to rise again." – Robert Browning

I was eighteen years old and living in Samuel Rubin Residence Hall, a dorm of New York University, on the corner of Fifth Avenue and East Tenth Street. It was a pretty tony address for a theatre geek from North Carolina, well on the path to a life of glitter and glamour winning Tony Awards as a costume designer to Broadway.

Dorm residency required a food plan, and while it was *de rigueur* to complain about the cafeteria food, it was actually quite good and where I discovered new and exotic items like yogurt, blueberries, and pumpernickel bagels with cream cheese, onions and tomato.

But it was always better to eat out whenever possible, even on a student's meager allowance from home. A falafel or "a slice" were always within reach. So were the big chocolate chip cookies from the deli around the corner, until I realized they had schmaltz (chicken fat) in them. *What's that chicken smell?*

There was always something exciting to do, which was one of the reasons I went to New York to begin with. Oh, other than school, of course. I went to the San Gennaro Festival in Little Italy and had zeppole (fried dough with powdered sugar) and espresso from street vendors on Mulberry Street; I saw Patti Smith play at the famous CBGB's nightspot; and occasionally our instructors gave away free tickets for a show on or off-Broadway – often a show for which *they* had designed costumes, lighting or sets.

Just as exciting, though, was the night my friend Judy, a film student, invited me to go with her to dinner at a classmate's apartment. An apartment? An actual New York City apartment? I was intrigued that someone our age had her own apartment. After walking up three flights of steps, the studio was no larger than my dorm room, but the caché that went along with an apartment of one's own was palpable.

There was no kitchen table; matter of fact, there was no real kitchen, just a doll-baby-size set of appliances in the corner of the room. Furnishings consisted of two folding lawn chairs, a bookcase, and a twin mattress on the floor.

Apartment Girl Amy cooked risotto in her tiny kitchen and set out dinner on an ironing board. An ironing board! How clever… how chic! I thought it was the epitome of cool and creative. Judy and I took the chairs, and AG (Apartment Girl) Amy sat on a large pillow while we ate. The whole evening was very cosmopolitan, and I added risotto to my repertoire of new foods. I developed a minor girl crush on AG, the new and novel city girl, a junior Marlo Thomas from *That Girl* the TV show I grew up with that taught me all I knew about Manhattan.

A couple of decades later, my husband and I got together with my still-close friend Judy and her husband for dinner at a casual French bistro in New York City. Amy joined us, with her teenage daughter. Judy had stayed close with Amy and passed along frequent updates about her family, but I hadn't seen her in years. No longer cute and cool AG Amy, she had morphed into elegant Mom and Society Amy, the volunteer, the doer of good deeds, currently of a sprawling faux farmhouse in Connecticut (continually under renovation) and a pied-a-terre in the City, handy for long days and nights of supping, shopping and shows.

While nibbling the *amuse bouche*, I couldn't resist telling Amy's daughter the ironing board story and how cool her Mom was back in college. She rolled her eyes and mumbled, "That's such an embarrassing story."

"Are you sure that was *me*?" said MS (Mom & Society) Amy, who seemed befuddled over this tale. Good Lord! I thought for a minute I might really be starting something here. Judy quickly confirmed my account of the evening, with the ironing board and the risotto. Seems Amy *did* remember her first apartment (you never forget your first). My, how times had changed.

Well, *some* things changed. I was recently reminded of this urban ironing board tale while eating dinner in our suburban Baltimore apartment while Mike and I enjoyed our nightly dose of cable news. My Chinet plate with a rosemary balsamic boneless chicken breast and couscous microwaved dinner sat on the ironing board at a low height, right in front of my chair. I cut the chicken into bites with a black plastic knife from the deli and ate with a plastic spoon, since we were temporarily out of plastic forks. Oh, sure, we had a genuine dining room table with custom-made table pads and six matching chairs. I had a closet of table linens, from exquisite vintage pieces to some I designed and made myself. But the table had become Mike's laptop desk on one end, with the rest holding tall stacks of scarves: Ready to iron, ready to photograph, scraps, and the largest stack, "Worry About Later."

We had a genuine kitchen, too, with twelve place settings of stainless (not one piece missing!) and sterling silver service for twelve. My "everyday" wedding dishes sat on an upper shelf in the cabinet because on the lower shelves, we had packing tape, labels and mailers. A glass serving bowl held customs forms. Mike relocated my antique majolica pottery salad plates to the bottom cabinet with the pots and pans. Several pens and Sharpies sat in a Baccarat highball (my mother-in-law gave me her tumblers and said I would get the stems when she was gone, but it never happened). My china cabinet was in storage, otherwise we would've no doubt showcased our collection of various types of packing tape and envelopes.

The kitchen cabinet doors could be closed hiding our V-Cart materials, but there were additional supplies on the countertop. My Kitchen Aid mixer sat in the corner and the bowl held the paddle attachment plus 6" x 4" manila envelopes for single-scarf shipments. The hand-made tiered fruit basket I bought in Curacao held scissors, a stapler and a coffee cup of paper clips in the top level, while the lower level held a stack of triple-fold pink newsletters for inclusion in every package. Mike used a large cutting board as his wrapping base and a wood-handled steak knife as a cardboard cutter. And he rarely used the same one; when he couldn't find it right away, he would open the utensil drawer and pull out another knife. By the end of the day, there were typically a half dozen steak knives on the counter under a mess of label backs, despite the garbage can being only a couple feet away. We had to clean all this up before we could prepare and cook – or even microwave – our dinner. Often we would order Chinese or a sub to avoid tidying up, since we already had a new stack of orders.

One afternoon, I was looking for something in the kitchen, and I spotted a box of crackers in the cabinet. Mmmmm, crackers! (Contraband in our home.) Suddenly hungry, I thought I might as well have a few. I opened the box and found a stack of address labels. Even the refuse frequently served a purpose. Talk about going green!

I looked around the living room. We had 17 rectangular plastic bins filled with baggies holding scarves folded, numbered, catalogued and listed on V-Cart – over 1,600 scarves at any given time. The bins, which we called file cabinets, lined the edges of the room, in front of the bookcases and entertainment center, and snaked along the pathway from the sofa and chair to the hallway. These narrow pathways made it look like an apartment full of crop circles (though if anyone wanted to know, it was no mystery just how our crop circles were made).

I repeatedly asked Mike to help me keep the pathways unencumbered, but more often than not, there would be an obstacle, like his big brown corduroy slippers sitting in the way like a construction blockage on I-95. One day when Mike was out, I was taking a path, navigating around some zip-lock bags filled with ironed and folded scarves ready for listing that had been stacked up on the side. The slippery stockpile had spilled into the main road… no, I mean path… and I slid a few feet on a puffed-up baggie. I barely caught myself with a hand on the glass-top sofa table, then tripped over the table leg onto the coffee table, then to the bins of scarf files on the floor. The whole fall (or series of falls) felt like it took five minutes in slow motion, though it was only a few seconds. I quickly took inventory to make sure I was still alive and that my limbs and digits were intact. I looked around to find my headband, which had flown off in the fall so that my hair was flopping into my face. It was only at that point I noticed blood dripping into the bins. My immediate concern was checking to make sure the scarves were safely zip-locked in the bags and wouldn't be stained. Then I noticed my leg had a bad scrape all the way from my knee to my ankle and though it wasn't a deep or serious wound, it sure hurt. I also discovered a carpet burn on my arm and a small scrape on my forehead.

I was so stunned, I just sat there a few minutes, taking it all in and wondering how best to get up, since I was in a pile of slippery plastic and didn't want to fall again. I was too busy to wallow further, so I managed to stand up and get back to work. Mike was on his way home, and I had orders to complete so he could take them to the post office. All in all, it was a fairly typical day at the Paisley Palace.

When scarves needed to be washed, the polys would go in the washer on delicate and then in the dryer on low. I would glove-up and wash the silks in a plastic tub in the kitchen sink. I would pull up a chair and sit there contentedly, maybe singing a washer woman song like "His eye is on the sparrow, and I know He watches me," or maybe "Two little babies layin' in the bed, one play sick and the other play dead." It did occur to me on occasion that with my background and years of experience in marketing, this work could be considered below my pay grade, but I didn't mind. I enjoyed the whole business. I loved the scarves. I loved being Scarf Maven. I loved working whenever I wanted from my computer (though actually, I was working most of the time). After years of talking to customers on the phones all day, it was a relief to communicate with buyers exclusively via email or V-Cart messaging. I got to a point where I wouldn't even answer our phone, I so resented the intrusion. Talking was Mike's department.

My husband and I had our own continuous debate (or argument) over the thermostat setting, as we have all of our years together, but ironing was hot work, and I insisted on keeping it cool. Sometimes I accused Mike of trying to sweat me out when I felt he fiddled with the thermostat the minute I wasn't looking. I started giving him instructions on taking over ironing duty, explaining how to steam certain polys, not to steam the silks, and not to burn the chiffons. This was the charm: Mike got up and made the room cooler every time.

Our business spilled over all areas of our apartment. About ten feet of hallway was narrowed by the plastic bin files line-up, though we (usually) had enough clearance to open the front door. If UPS or the mailman brought us packages, say a carton of 500 scarves, this would be stacked in the hallway so that one had to squeeze out the door. The coat closet would have to wait until the first frost to be pried open. The master bedroom was our one escape that thankfully did not have evidence of a business, at least until you opened the door to the large walk-in closet, where you would find a few cartons of overflow scarves blocking my well-ordered (and pared down) shoe cubbies. This left me to wear only my freed black loafer-types on days when I actually left the apartment and felt I needed to wear shoes.

Our second bedroom, officially our office with the computer desk, two printers, several bookcases and two file cabinets, had every square inch filled beyond reasonable and customary capacity. A large carton by my desk held ironed and folded scarves that were ready to list. I would work on this often during the early morning hours of 3 – 6 when I was awake, tired of reading and had nothing better to do.

We had a small storage room off the patio we called our garage. It was filled tight with luggage, a few storage boxes and a carton of estate sale silk scarves with an unbearably heavy perfume smell I was trying to air out. And we had plenty of back-up scarves in a mini warehouse we leased, a few miles from our apartment.

With all that, we were still short on storage. One day I reminded Mike we had an impending crisis: We were almost out of toilet paper.

"We have plenty," he said. "It's in the car." He went on to say he was also storing several 12-packs of canned sodas and a dozen cans of chicken stock in the car. We began referring to our SUV as a DMSU (detached mobile storage unit).

During the spring, our apartment manager announced major renovations for all the units in our building. We cleared way for the bathroom and kitchen renovations, but we could not see moving all the furniture for new paint and carpet in the living room, dining room and bedrooms. Our business would need to be shut down for a week or two if the layout was disrupted. The kitchen and bathroom updates were stressful, but we managed, and these rooms looked great. When we got wind the workers were running way behind with paint and carpet for the rest of the apartment, we talked the contractor into "forgetting" about our apartment. We could live with the walls getting a little dingy and the old carpet buckling in places; the alternative was just too overwhelming. (A few months later when our lease came up for renewal, our rent increased because of the "substantial upgrades.")

With the excitement of our V-Cart success, all this folderol had not bothered me until that evening when I found myself having dinner off the ironing board. I gazed around the apartment and wondered why I was living in a warehouse. All of my adult life, one of my dreams, should I win the lottery, was to buy a large industrial space, maybe an old warehouse, and turn it into a fabulous loft home that would surely be considered for a photo spread in *Architectural Digest*. I don't know how I would, in fact, win the lottery when I have never bought a ticket, but that's not the point. My Terri Dream Home would be one tremendous room with clever space dividers, glorious sixteen feet tall windows and a real cook's kitchen. Guests would marvel that this luxury apartment was previously a warehouse.

Meanwhile, it dawned on me that we were currently living in a warehouse that was previously a luxury apartment. I know the word *luxury* applies, because the sign at the entrance to our complex says so; otherwise I'm not sure I would describe it that way.

We found our apartment on a quick trip to Baltimore before our actual move, and when one of our new friends asked us where we lived, most of the time they were impressed when we told them the name of our apartments.

"Oh! You live *there?*" often citing the well-tended flower beds, the sprawling clubhouse and the brick guardhouse at the grand entrance. I have to admit it was very nice. (It *was*, indeed.)

Though we weren't in the city, the 'burb of Pikesville was much more urban than we were used to. As we settled in, Mike loved to tell people, "We can walk to the grocery store, the post office, and Staples!" NOTE: We never once walked to the grocery store or to Staples, but Mike did walk to the post office once.

We put much of our furniture and belongings in storage, since we moved from a three bedroom house with a garage to a two bedroom apartment, thinking the apartment was temporary.

Years later, I was thinking about all these things as I was finishing my balsamic chicken and one tine broke off the plastic fork. What had happened to my exquisitely set dining room table? I hadn't eaten off a real plate at home in ages. We should do something about this, I thought, as TV talking heads sparred over the consumer confidence index. My personal confidence index was shot to hell as I remembered how much I enjoyed entertaining, pre-apartment and pre-V-Cart. When did our Paisley Palace become a Chiffon Shanty?

All discouraging thoughts flew out of my head when I heard the beeps from my computer in the next room, indicating we had emails, most likely with new orders. The sound of money snapped me right out of my nostalgic mood.

A few days later, one of those beeps (not to be confused with a ding) brought shuddersome news. It wasn't from V-Cart; it came to my personal email account and was from my cousin Rita in New Jersey. She said she and her 10-year-old daughter, Leah, would like to visit us the following week. Rita needed a break, she said, from caring for her mother-in-law in a rehab hospital, her two young children and her fulltime stressful job as a college recruiter. "I'm taking a week off work and I *have* to get away," she wrote, reminding me that over the years I had encouraged everyone in the family to come up and visit any time.

Oh, sure, I said that. I specifically remember writing it to Rita on a "We've Moved!" postcard after we settled into Baltimore. And I meant it – I *really* meant it. I may or may not have said it a few more times over the years when we saw her at family occasions and get-togethers. "We'll take you all around Baltimore and Washington," I may have said, while Mike always added we might be able to arrange lunch with the president.

I pictured a guest room with peach peonies in my crystal rose bowl sitting on the bedside table. I would have a basket of lotions, bath oils and chocolates sitting on the bed waiting for my guests, and I would offer a large breakfast spread at nine each morning before we headed off for the museums and other cultural attractions of the greater Washington-Baltimore area.

I heard old friends say they envied the semi-urban lifestyle we had here… we were so brave to pick up and move somewhere exciting and different. My mother, my brothers and their families had all visited at times, and had stayed at the Hilton around the corner. Over the years, several other people stopped in Baltimore to visit us, usually en route to New York, perhaps coming by the apartment briefly before we all went out to dinner at the Inner Harbor or Little Italy.

No, we didn't have a guest room, but never once did I envision living in a distribution center. It was Monday, and Rita and her daughter were driving to Baltimore Saturday and staying through Tuesday -- if it was okay with us. The countdown was on. Five days until their arrival.

I wrote her back saying come on up, it would be great to see them. Okay, okay… I can handle this, I thought. A plan began to form: We would simply put them up at a nearby hotel. Maybe they could come over to the apartment one night for dinner. Surely we could rake the scarves off the dining room table and tidy up enough to serve a proper dinner. We could do that. Yes, we could do it, Mike concurred, all the while wondering how much it would cost us to get a hotel room for three nights. Middle of the summer in the suburbs couldn't be too bad. That's what we'd do. But I didn't want to tell Rita she would be staying in a hotel until later, because I was afraid she wouldn't let us pay for it, and her own financial situation was strapped, she had told me. A hotel, yes, that's the answer. A hotel. Perfect.

Four days. We began executing our plan the very next morning. I sorted through scarves, transferring the table stacks to small cartons while Mike checked into hotel rates. Between phone calls, Mike wedged a carton or two in the "garage" (aka patio storage closet). By lunchtime, he had checked rates online and called the 800 numbers of all the acceptable hotels and motels within a 10-mile radius of our apartment. He even called the local numbers, speaking to the manager to see if they could cut a deal (we have found this often works), but there were no bargains to be found.

"It's going to be $160 a night for two people, including taxes and fees," Mike said. "And that doesn't even include breakfast."

We were going to San Antonio for Mike's cousin's wedding the following week, and we had reserved a junior suite at a major chain with daily breakfast for less than half that price. But that was Texas; we were in expensive Baltimore now.

A reservation was made as a back-up, but Mike felt determined to find a bargain before our guests arrived in town. "I think the rates go down on Thursdays if things look slow for the weekend."

Meanwhile, Rita said they were looking forward to seeing us and said Leah was spending all her time online scoping out Washington and making a list of places she wanted to visit: The Space Museum, the Holocaust Museum, the Treasury, the Smithsonian….

Three days until they would pull into town. Wednesday, I got an email from Rita asking if her 13-year-old daughter, Elise, who was coming home from camp early, could come, too. "Are you *sure* you have room for her?"

"Of course," I answered, thinking why not? Three could sleep in a hotel room as easily as two. She wrote back, grateful both daughters could come. I told Rita that being out of town the following week, we had work we had to do (and then, there were the increasing problems with my leg infections, making it painful for me to walk), and we might not be able to go sightseeing with them. Fine, she wrote. They would take off after breakfast and be gone all day. She asked if we could get information about the train from Baltimore to DC.

"A *third* person?" Mike said he would have to call the hotel back and let them know. "You have to tell them," Mike said. "Do you want Rita to have a hassle when she checks in with two children?" No, I definitely did not. It would be $10 additional per day for the third person, but Mike talked the manager into including breakfast for all, so it was actually better. We would only have to be responsible for daily dinner.

"Can we stay until Wednesday?" Rita wrote later to ask. They wanted to go to Chinatown and shopping in Georgetown, so they really needed another day, if it was okay with us. "No problem," I wrote back as a lump began to form in my throat. *Cha-ching.* Another $170.

"Well, did you tell her yet that she's staying in a hotel?" I ignored the question, so Mike knew I hadn't told her. Frankly, my "plan" all along was to tell Rita when she got here.

Two days. Rita wrote to say both children - the history buff and the shopaholic - had long lists of places to go, both in Washington and Baltimore. "There's just so much we want to do. How would you feel about us staying until Thursday?"

"She's got a lot of chutzpah!" Mike said, but I reminded him she thinks she is staying here with us. Another round of checking for hotel rates ensued. Mike thought a weekly rate at a suite hotel might be less than the daily rate for five nights, so he got on the phone calling hotels again.

When I got back from my book club Thursday, Mike proposed a new plan. Saturday night, we would book Rita and the kids at a hotel in Virginia a few miles south of Washington– we would arrange it and pre-pay. It would make more sense, since we could get a good rate, and they could get up Sunday and go right into Washington without back-tracking. Mike found a good rate in the Virginia suburbs for the next two nights, and after more time in Washington, they would come to Baltimore Tuesday afternoon. This way, they would stay in Baltimore at top dollar only two nights. It would also be easier on them (and, let's be honest – us) staying closer to their destination for those few days.

We wrote down all the details of the itinerary and emailed it to Rita. Within minutes, she called, choking back tears. "I can't let you put us up in a hotel," she said, insisting it would be humiliating to have us pay when they couldn't afford to. I told her we *can* do this and we *want* to do this for them, explaining that we didn't even have a guest room or a sofabed.

"We'll bring blow-up beds," Rita said. "It's no problem sleeping on the floor." I didn't want to tell her we barely have any floor. It would be hard to fit a blow-up bed in an arc of a crop circle, but I could see this visit was indeed going to happen.

"Remember, we go camping a lot," she said. "But if it's inconvenient, we can come another time."

"No, of course not!" I said, and I really meant it. "If you don't mind the floor... We're looking forward to it."

So, blow-up beds it would be: Three people sleeping on the floor of our living room for five nights. Mike and I both were up many times during the night for bathroom visits, drinks (then bathroom visits again), and I, being moderately insomniac, often went into the office (through the living room) for several hour stretches before dawn. Mike would frequently join me for a little while, checking in with the TV news. When we got up in the mornings, Mike immediately tuned in while I checked the voice mail and email to make certain we weren't waking up to news of a problem with one of our marketing customers or vendors. We would usually get right to work and rather than breakfast, we would have brunch mid-morning, or just wait until lunchtime. Pitifully, Mike and I had grown into such creatures of comfortable routine that a disruption could take recovery time. With three guests for five nights, our routine would need to be altered, to say the least. Even so, we were excited about having guests.

The dining room was company-ready, but we had to move everything out of the tool shed -- rather, the back bathtub where we stored the vacuum cleaner, the steam cleaner, a large tool box, and various other necessities. These people may want to take a shower while they are here, I thought, and we didn't want all five of us sharing our master bath.

We continued to de-warehouse the living room and dining room. Our apartment wasn't dirty – Mike is meticulous and kept up with the vacuuming and dusting. Nor was our place remotely like those of the hoarders you see on TV. We just had all our merchandise and doodads all over the place, nice and neat and perfectly organized. But it was there, alright, in the way, rendering the apartment decidedly un-guest-worthy.

I was in a panic over getting the apartment in showroom condition. I didn't want a bad report going back to the family over my fallen big city glamorous life. I was hand-washing all the serving pieces from the étagère while considering dinner menus: Grilled Greek lemon chicken breasts, spaghetti and meatballs or maybe just a meatloaf.

Kids eat a lot, I was thinking, so every day I would serve a sumptuous farmhouse breakfast, perhaps a buffet on the counter like you might find at a quaint Bed & Breakfast (despite the fact we were offering only a floor in our un-quaint combo warehouse/distribution center/apartment). I would need eggs, turkey sausage, hash browns, a couple kinds of juices and Mike could pick up some fresh bagels every morning. I wondered if they would rather have biscuits. I would make them (not too many biscuits flying around Baltimore bread bakeries). How would they like their eggs? Should I make a platter of scrambled or just cook to order? What fresh herbs go best with eggs? Could I learn to fry a sunny-side-up egg by the time they arrived, in case that's what they like? My omelets are iffy – maybe I need a new small frying pan. Is non-stick better? I would make a large fruit bowl. Should I put cantaloupe or honeydew in the mix? Some people like their melons separate from other fruits. Some people don't like melon at all. What if I spent hours cutting fruit and Mike ate it all the night before, which believe me, could easily happen. Sometimes he nibbled during the night, and then in the morning, he would act like he had no idea what happened to the fruits of my labor. (*Who, me?*)

I couldn't ease up; my mind was running on overtime. Maybe grits would be better than hash browns. Grits are trendy in the northeast, so maybe I should cook a pot of grits. Maybe grits and hash browns both, since Mike won't eat grits. Would I serve grits on the main plate or in bowls? My majolica bowls or regular cereal bowls?

I was still planning the menu and Mike asked, "What if someone has allergies?"

"Then it's their responsibility to tell me," I snapped.

"But what if one of the kids can't have wheat? What if the kids are vegans?"

"Well, if they can't let me know in advance, then they can eat a can of diced tomatoes from the pantry. Or they can go out to eat. I am not going to worry about *possible* allergies."

My husband has a dairy allergy and I firmly believe we need to let people who host us know about it. I'll never forget the time we had another couple over for a Passover dinner shortly after we moved to Baltimore. They also were new in town and we thought it would be nice to celebrate together. I made a big meal starring a BBQ brisket, and as we were filling our plates, my new friend announced she did not eat red meat. I felt deflated and irritated she hadn't told me, because I could just as easily have made chicken.

I continued with the campers' menu, compulsively making lists. I think it was when I was stumped over garnishes and the grocery list spilled over to the third page of a legal pad, I took a minute to breathe and reconsider everything.

Did I really need to keep up this charade of perfect hostess? The situation was quite clearly *not* perfect anyway, and we would prove that the minute they walked in the door. Did I want to further wear myself out cooking all day every day when there was business to be done and I had to prepare for our Texas trip the following week?

Deep breathe. Simplify. Deep breathe. Simplify. Did I even know how to simplify? Rita had shown her cards (or simply been honest, I should say) by telling us that they were hurting financially. They were off the pedestal I had them on for years. Maybe I could relax and be more myself while they were visiting: Scarf Maven rather than Martha Stewart. There is no way (at least at that point) I could conjure up a couple of robin's egg blue guest rooms with a vase of white hydrangeas and roses on the nightstand. I couldn't get new carpet in the next day or two either. I might get dressed in the mornings rather than show up for breakfast in my nightshirt with the cupcakes on it, but need I seemingly roll out of bed in a total "outfit," fully made up, to fry an egg or two?

We decided to do what was marginally necessary, pretenses and protocol be damned. It was time to show our authentic selves. We were growing a new business out of our apartment and, for the time being, that involved living amongst inventory. They would be able to accept it just fine, I thought in earnest, but I admit it was a hurdle for me, stepping out of my former world. I consoled myself by realizing we were healthy and happy and our new business was prospering. Nothing else really mattered, and I shouldn't worry about making a good impression. We would make them welcome and comfortable, and they would have a good time. After all, I reasoned, this was *family* coming a'callin'.

We moved the scarf bins into the office, stacking them one on top of the other and eliminating the crop circles. Mike suggested when the troops were out on their daily excursions, we could spread out the bins and pack scarf orders, stacking them back up before suppertime. We moved the laptop station onto a folding table and carried it into the bedroom, planning to carry it back out during the daytime when our workday commenced. We made the office bathroom into a full bathroom again, temporarily stuffing the bathtub-stored items into the bedroom walk-in closet. We hung nice guest towels and put scented soaps on the vanity, making it a very adequate guest bathroom.

I ran the original grocery list through the shredder and planned another menu. On Sunday, Mike and I would make large batches of chicken salad, pasta salad, romaine mix and assorted cut fruit. Sliced tomatoes would line a tray with pickles, olives and deli turkey slices. Every night, the spread would go on the dining room table and everyone could serve themselves whenever and whatever they wanted. Maybe the last night, we would order Chinese food.

Mike suggested we use plastic forks and spoons and Chinet plates (he gets them nearly free after sales and doubled coupons). For breakfast? Fruit and cereal, served in my majolica bowls (which had to be hand-washed – but worth the time). Rather than pulling out one of my Peterboro baskets, perhaps lined with a nicely starched 40's vintage cutwork napkin, a loaf of bread and some button rolls for sandwiches would come right out of the plastic bags.

The romaine was served directly from the Tupperware salad keeper, and the other salads were in disposable aluminum pans, wrapped in foil and stacked in the refrigerator. In lieu of using pitchers for milk and juice, we'd just put the cartons and bottles right on the table. (*Horrors!*) We would stack the plates at the end of the table, put the cutlery in plastic cups and be ready. No one ever told me entertaining could be so simple.

We were prepared for the onslaught by mid-afternoon Sunday. I felt a sense of pride that we had restored the Paisley Palace into a home again -- at least to some extent. (OMG, don't try to open the door to the bedroom closet!) Shanty no more! It was time to raise the victory flag and announce the shanty conquered. Flag? Let's try a scarf. A paisley scarf.

I harbored delusions that we might be able to take a short nappie before the crowd converged. Maybe a snooze in the chair would be just the refueling we needed. Surprise! An *L & O* marathon was on cable, and we settled in. Mike was snoring in minutes, and about the time I closed my eyes, the phone rang. "We're at your gate."

"Welcome to our warehouse," I said when they arrived. They were so happy to see us, I don't know if they even heard me. They each carried pillows, backpacks, blankets and tote bags; you'd think they were camping in the wilderness for a week. Well, maybe they were. (A new frontier.) After the song and dance I gave Rita about our small apartment, she'd made sure they came prepared. We lined the hallway with their bundles, effectively making crop circles again. The kids plopped down, and Rita opened her bottle of wine and poured it into a Hefty cup before I had a chance to offer her a real wine glass. I know casual, but this was pushing the envelope. *It's okay, Terri. It's okay.*

Effortlessly, we pulled out dinner and put it on the dining room table where I was using an olive tapestry cloth I had brought out of the linen closet and ironed. Everyone was hungry and ate plenty, commenting all along about the great spread. Leah, the little one, told us she was a budding chef – "and astro-physicist" – who watched the Food Network in her spare time. She was perplexed by an interesting taste in my chicken salad she didn't recognize. I told her I added a few dashes of curry powder. "Curry? I don't think I've ever had that before," she said, which led to a conversation about other dishes that had curry. She asked for my recipe. My first impulse was to mimic my grandmother and say, "Oh, just a little bit of this and a little bit of that," but I remembered how irritating that was, so I told Leah exactly how to make the salad, while she copiously took notes.

CURRIED CHICKEN SALAD

Ingredients
- Boneless chicken breasts
- Coarse-ground black pepper
- Garlic powder
- Celery, including some of the leaves
- Plain, unsweetened yogurt
- Low-fat mayo
- Curry powder to taste
- Fresh flat-leaf parsley

Directions
- Sprinkle chicken with garlic powder and black pepper and bake at 350 degrees for about 40 minutes, depending on size. Let

the chicken cool off and then cut in squares – small or chunky pieces, your choice.

- Chop the celery, matching size to chicken chunks
- Stir together yogurt and mayo, using equal parts each. Add the curry powder. Taste and adjust.
- Carefully fold everything together until mixed and sprinkle finely chopped parsley over the salad.

Elise immediately looked through my DVD collection, saying she liked to watch a movie while she was in bed ("on floor" here, but I didn't correct her). I showed her my collection of exactly three DVDs: *Phantom of the Opera,* a bootlegged copy of Hitchcock's *To Catch a Thief* that I bought from a Hong Kong V-Cart seller, and *It's Complicated* with Meryl Streep and Alec Baldwin. She said she loved the latter film, and wanted to watch it again. So while that played in the background, we all played word games the girls had brought with them.

I couldn't take my eyes off the kids, they were so amazing. I had only seen them a few times over the years and never really had a conversation with either of them, so this was a real joy. It was also important to me being reacquainted with my cousin. Rita and I had been close when we were children, growing up in Charlotte, and had many shared memories. A few years older, she had been my childhood idol. I wanted to do everything she did. Rita took ballet lessons, I took ballet lessons. Rita took gymnastics, I took gymnastics. Rita went to White Gloves & Party Manners classes, and I went to White Gloves and Party Manners classes. She got a gold signet ring. I got a gold signet ring. We both took baton twirling lessons from a former Miss North Carolina. Rita was reading *Seventeen* magazine and I started reading it, too. When Rita got her long hair cut into a bob, shorter in back, longer in front, I went to the hair salon to get my hair cut the same way. (It didn't matter that her hair was stick-straight, perfect for a blunt cut, while my curly hair wasn't suited a'tall for that style.) Rita took horseback riding lessons, so I had to take lessons, too, and learned that English was cool, Western, crass. She wanted to be a large animal veterinarian and I… didn't want to do that. And then Rita scored a modeling contract. End game. There was no way I could match that. They didn't much have models for the wearers of Belk Department Store's Chubettes line back then.

Reminiscing, Rita and I realized something, as she sipped her chardonnay, and I knocked back a couple cans of Diet Cherry Dr. Pepper. I was a child of divorce and loved going to her house where there were two parents and a wonderful predictability. When he wasn't playing golf at the country club or gardening, my uncle would be in his contemporary leather reclining chair reading or watching golf. My aunt, when she wasn't volunteering at the art museum, would be sewing or cross-stitching by a side table with a good light and a cup of hot tea. Even with three children in the house, it was quiet and cozy.

Rita told me she loved to come to my house for the opposite reason. You never knew what my mother, younger brothers and I would be doing: Going to the drive-in movies, a day trip to the mountains or roller skating in our basement, it was always exciting precisely because it was so unpredictable.

We could easily have talked all night, but bedtime came early, in anticipation of an early wake-up call. As requested, Mike had reveille at eight, and I threw on some clothes and went directly to the kitchen while our guests showered and dressed. Breakfast was plentiful and everyone seemed happy with cereal and fruit. I realized we didn't need to make a big impression with fresh vegetable frittatas or homemade waffles and whipped cream. This was our routine for five mornings, except one day, I couldn't get to my hanging blouses because the closet was temporarily too full of bins and cartons of scarves. Mike was in the shower, so I decided to go back to bed and let him host breakfast. *And that was okay, too.*

There's no denying that it was stressful packing up our business each evening and entertaining three guests in such close quarters, but we had a great time, and the thank you email I got from Rita when they got home made it all worthwhile: "*We all enjoyed the trip, especially Leah, who said she had the best time ever.*" It brought tears to my eyes, but none more than when I read further down the note: "*Leah wants to know if we can come back next summer....*"

* 11 *

HANGING WITH THE COOL GIRLS

"There cannot be a crisis next week. My schedule is already full." --
Henry Kissinger

Business was booming. Our social media specialist, Elle, had just started. Recommended by several people, Elle was young and cute and bubbly, just as you might expect a social media person to be. We first met over pumpkin spice lattes at Starbucks. She had a full-time job handling social media and public relations for a local business and was excited to tackle this freelance job where she could be more creative. We felt Elle could help increase sales in short order.

This was a move we should have made a few years ago. I had a wake-up call when I read a business article online that gave reasons why a small business must utilize social media. I was committed after the first entry of the line-up: Expect the average business to increase sales by at least 10% or more in just a few weeks. If we met this one "promise," Elle's fee would more than pay for itself.

We made a modest Facebook advertising budget of $50 - $100 per month and in the first week doubled our "likes" and acquired several new customers. Business was good. Business was exciting. Mike and I were happily content working long hours keeping up with the orders and logging and photographing new scarves so Suzanne could list them. Some evenings, Mike even gave up his ritual of watching the midnight *Perry Mason* so we could finish our work before going to bed.

At some point during the mayhem, I found myself at a doctor's visit about a recurring infection in my leg. I thought I was having a flare-up; my calf was sore and I had a spot that was oozing a little bit. I assumed I would be given a prescription for an antibiotic like I had in the past and hobbled into Dr. March's office. Our plan was to go out for a quick lunch after the appointment, pick up the prescription I was bound to get, and then go back home and finish packing the orders. We needed to get them out quickly to maintain our high ratings and fee discounts.

My mind was wondering how many additional orders we would have when we got home.

Dr. March pressed and poked my leg while measuring the infected area at the same time. After just a few minutes of hemming and hawing, she said I needed to go to the Emergency Room right then. The infection was too deep to respond to oral meds and I needed IV Antibiotics Therapy.

Before I absorbed the information, she had excused herself and called for my husband to join us in the tiny exam room. She and Mike were talking in the hallway, and I saw Mike's eyes well up when she mentioned the word "hospital." He sniffed a couple of times and the tears were gone. He gave me a loving but worried expression. Mike was scared.

"Go right now," she said. "Do not go home first, just go straight to the ER." She told me she would call ahead so they would be expecting me. Mike told me later that my jaw dropped when I heard 'ER,' and I said, "Huh?" but I don't remember it. I hadn't felt sick – Dr. March asked me several times if I had fever or general malaise - and I said I had not. I was tired, sure, but we had been working like lunatics taking care of our business. She said she could tell from my blood work that the infection was widespread and we didn't have time to dilly-dally.

My husband started with an avalanche of questions while I sat on the exam table, sticking to the plastic and listening as though I were a child overhearing the adults.

"What happened?" he asked, though he knew darn well it was another flare-up, perhaps more serious than the flare-up I had in the past. Dr. March was very patient, surely realizing Mike was shaken. She answered every question in a calm and sensitive fashion, but Mike's constant interruption was, "Is she going to be alright?"

Yes, I would be alright. But I needed the antibiotics that had to be fed through a vein in my arm.

"Go straight to the ER, they'll be waiting for you. Don't go home first, don't have lunch first, just go straight there."

We drove straight home. I needed to pack a bag with my expensive face cream, a familiar nightshirt, underwear and toothbrush. After all, we had to pass right by our apartment to get to the hospital. As we pulled into the parking lot, I inadvertently looked behind our car to make sure Dr. March wasn't watching us; I felt like an escaped convict on the lam.

After a mercifully uncrowded ER wait, I was admitted to the hospital and told I would be there for five to seven days.

Almost immediately, I was given some strong pain medicine in my IV, and I couldn't wait to get out of the ER and up to a quiet room where I could sleep the afternoon away. I had been assuring Mike he didn't have to stay with me, but he said he wasn't leaving until I was settled into a regular room. There was no rest – or quiet - in the ER cubicle.

We debated whether we should wait until I got home to ship orders, but he insisted could do it himself, no problem. Mike was quite competent with his responsibilities such as packing and shipping, but there were some things he didn't know how to do, particularly computer work like packing lists and inventory updates. Likewise, I didn't have any idea how to work the postage scale and meter connected to his laptop. I resolved we would learn each other's jobs as soon as I got out of the hospital.

I gave him detailed instructions on how to get the orders out the door without me. I knew there was a good possibility we would be in trouble when I saw he wasn't taking notes. "Call Suzanne," I suggested. "Maybe she can at least help you pull the orders."

"No, I'll be okay alone. We can be in touch by phone," he said. "If I have a problem, you can talk me through it."

"Okay," I said, but I was already exasperated.

We were waiting for a room. The nurse brought drinks, then a turkey sandwich as she buzzed through every now and again. "It won't be much longer," she assured us.

Finally, about mid-afternoon, a room was ready, but we had to detour along the way to radiology where I got a chest X-ray and a sonogram of my infected leg. An aide wheeled me around on a stretcher when we were on the move, but wait, wait, wait was the watchword. About the time I would doze off, the aide swung the stretcher around and we barreled down the hallway to the next stopping point. I was afraid she was going to knock off a few people in her haste, but I decided to close my eyes and hope we didn't collide with another stretcher or pedestrian.

The procedures went smoothly with no problems, but I was sulking because I was wasting good sleeping time, and I knew Mike was waiting for me in the new room. All rooms at the hospital were private, and after we pulled in the door, I moved from the stretcher to the bed. It had been a long day, and I finally convinced Mike to go home. It was rest time for me.

I sighed when Mike left, but then my nurse came in briefly to introduce herself. I was just beginning to doze when her "tech" (aide) dropped by to bring the classic pitcher of ice water with the bendable straw.

"My name is Nefertitti," she said. "But if that's too difficult for you to pronounce, just call me T.T." No problems pronouncing her name, I thought, as she explained to me the room service procedure.

Room service? Last time I had room service it was at the Four Seasons Hotel in Toronto. Mike and I ordered a fruit plate, an artisanal bread basket and Diet Cokes. I was thinking room service at the hospital might not be quite as delicious. (Or quite as expensive.)

"The food's not *that* bad," Nefertitti told me. I was to call "room service" an hour or so before each meal to put in my order. The menu was somewhat limited, and each item was designated "low salt," "low cholesterol," "low-fat," or "low carb." Maybe this would be like a spa after all, I thought.

Mike called frequently to keep me posted. Our sales continued to increase, and we were way over the projected 10% increase. Call One: Our good customer in Westchester ordered. Call Two: We got our first order from Israel. Call Three: Someone from Chile inquired about shipping charges. Call Four: A new customer bought nine scarves in a shopping cart. Call Five: Suzanne needs more work....

Suzanne needs more work? I had been working on a log and pictures for her and was almost finished when I left to go to the doctor, thinking I would be home in an hour. But now, she had nothing to do, and there wasn't anything I could do about it. Mike was adamant he didn't need to ask for her help with the orders.

Mike came back to visit that night and at my direction brought a comb, bodywash and shampoo. At my insistence, he also brought my laptop computer. I was going to try record-keeping from my hospital bed. I would be the business woman at that exclusive (and tres expensive!) spa, who couldn't stay away from her computer.

It didn't take long to abandon that idea. I had forgotten to ask Mike to bring my reading glasses, and I couldn't see the screen very well. (Wasn't it just recently that I did my computer work without glasses?) It was also a tad on the darkish side in the room. I was not used to doing actual work on the laptop, and it was just awkward. I also worried that it would be stolen while I was sleeping or in the bathroom, so I finally told Mike to take the computer home, and he would be on his own with the scarves.

Before he left for the night, I pointed out the heat was going full blast and I was lying on top of plastic (with just a thin sheet covering the plastic liner), which made my back damp. Mike tried to adjust the heat, but it wouldn't budge. I called for the nurse, who said we couldn't adjust the heat; we were in the old wing, with heat and air controlled centrally. She apologized as she left the room, shaking her head and saying it was always too hot when the heat was on.

Mike raised the blinds and discovered the window opened a little bit and some cool, fresh air poured in. It wasn't terribly cold out, so this was perfect. Every time a nurse or an aide came into the room, they marveled that the window opened (most had been sealed shut, we were told) and commented how glorious it felt to escape the heat.

"Sit awhile," Mike said to the throngs in and out of my room. "Whenever you get hot, come in here and take a break, no problem." Then I think he had second thoughts (perhaps remembering it was not his party), so he said, "Terri? That's okay with you, isn't it?"

"Yeah, sure." What else could I say?

By the second day, word had gotten around that my room had some cool air and staff seemed to make excuses to come in for some reason or other so they could cool off. During his mid-day visit, Mike again offered hospitality and encouraged people to come on in, take a break and keep me company. *But I didn't want company.* After all the years we had been together, didn't he know this? Mike is the life of any party and loves to schmooze. I crave alone-time.

When all the guests left, I turned on the TV. There were only about a half dozen channels, including CNN, so I kept it tuned to news. I was listening to Anderson Cooper talking about returning veterans when an aide, Lisa, came into the room to see if I needed anything.

"Your husband is a character," she said, standing by the window fanning her scrubs top to get maximum air.

"Yup."

"Bet you have a lot of fun together. How many kids do you have?"

For some reason, I wanted to say six, but I didn't. "We don't have any children."

"You didn't want kids?" Lisa sounded perplexed.

"We did, but we couldn't have any. We tried everything."

"Oh, that's too bad. Your husband would make a great father." *What about me?*

"Yup."

Lisa continued to tell me about her family. Though she didn't look much over 30 to me, she had a couple of grown children, a daughter in high school and was also raising her 14-year-old niece.

By then, Lisa had made herself at home in the guest chair by my bed.

"It's hard," Lisa explained, "even though I feel blessed to have her." She went on to say, "I live in a neighborhood in the city where people get shot at."

I didn't know what to say, and Lisa continued, "My niece is in her awful teens, and she thinks she's *all that*. She even has a boyfriend, and he's 25 years old! I don't like that one bit."

Speaking like an expert family dynamics counselor, I just agreed with her that the boyfriend was way too old to date a teenage girl.

"I'm worried about her," Lisa told me. She said she had fought with her older children for years, making sure they went to school and was very proud to tell me they had all graduated high school. "But this girl… I don't know. What should I do about her?"

I suggested a hobby or other activities. Was there an after-school community center where her niece might go? Perhaps someone was there to help with homework?

"Lord, no. There's no place like that near where I stay."

I tried to think of another brilliant suggestion, since I reckoned I was in it for the long-haul at that point. I could see that Lisa needed someone to talk with. Unfortunately Mike was at home, probably asleep. He's always good with advice.

"Would she want to get involved with some fun classes or clubs to help occupy her time?" I asked.

"I don't know where she would find that."

I guess Lisa sensed I didn't have anything else to offer on that topic, so she asked if I work. Next thing I knew, I had told her about my V-Cart scarf business. Lisa rebounded from her lethargy and sat up straight. "Did you wear one of your scarves when you were admitted?" If so, she said she wanted to see it. I didn't have the energy to show and tell, so I told her I didn't have one with me, even though I knew the scarf I wore was in the top drawer of the bedside table.

The door opened and the nurse called for Lisa to help with another patient. Within a few seconds, it was just me and CNN. Maybe I had needed someone to talk with, too.

As anyone who has been hospitalized knows, it is not a time for renewal and relaxation. I was vexed the nurses barged in during the night to take blood or adjust the IV. One night, a nurse came in with her rolling computer cart to get a family history. Another night, a nurse came in around 4 AM to say she needed to do a routine search for moles and other skin problems. The most irritating thing was that when the nurses left the room, most of the time they didn't turn the lights off or shut the door. I had just about fallen asleep when someone came in to draw blood. This produced just one more large bruise on my arm, which was already a black, purple, pink and yellow tie-dye-looking specimen. The latest look in "all natural" tattoos.

Room visits seemed endless: Put the meds in the IV... take the meds out. Check on pain levels: "On a scale of one to ten..." A large beep startled me, then I heard the voice over the speaker, "What can we do for you?" I realized my CALL NURSE button had accidentally been pressed when I was maneuvering in bed, trying to get comfortable.

I had to go to the bathroom, so I called for the aide. Lisa was still on duty. She came in and pulled the plug, putting the IV on battery pack so I could wheel the IV pole into the bathroom with me. That was all I needed, but she plopped down on the chair, waiting for me to get back to bed. "You don't need to wait for me," I said, but she assured me she didn't mind waiting. She watched a segment on CNN and cooled off.

After I was safe in bed, she said she wanted to buy some of my scarves. I explained again how to find my line on V-Cart. I don't know if she even had a computer, but I would've bet my bottom dollar that each of her kids had smart phones, and probably a tablet or laptop, so maybe she could ask one of them.... Lisa asked, "Do you think your husband could bring some scarves tomorrow night?"

"Down here?" I asked incredulously, sensing a flea market in the works.

"Yeah, I know several other girls would be interested in buying some, too."

"Well, I don't know. We might get in trouble."

"I'll take care of you hon'," she said. "Nothing will happen." I thought that was amusing because when I said *we* might get in trouble, I really meant *she* might get in trouble.

"I'll have to talk with Mike about it."

"Well, you know I'll be here by 6:30. Things settle down around 8:30, so I'll have time to look." Lisa seemed to become aware of the time and jumped out of the chair. "See you later, hon', just call if you need me," and she put the call button next to my pillow and exited, leaving the lights on and the door open.

I was about to nod off when the night nurse, Sinead, came in with a list of routine questions. I would say she was beautiful, except I couldn't get beyond the small silver nose ring she was wearing. "Are you having any difficulty breathing? Shortness of breath? Any headaches?" The list seemed to go on and on, and then the last question: Any difficulty urinating or any constipation? I answered my usual, "No."

Sinead asked, "So everything's cool 'downtown'?"

Everything's cool downtown. I was chuckling as she left the room to inquire about the next patient's "downtown" business.

A meal at the hospital was an adventure, because what one ordered was not necessarily what one was served. Every morning, I ordered yogurt with a fruit cup and asked room service to leave off the granola on top of the yogurt. Every morning, I was served yogurt with granola on top. One dinner, I ordered the Homemade Yankee Pot Roast and received the Crustless Chicken Pot Pie. I really didn't mind, I just ate what I was served. I had been told correctly, the food wasn't that bad.

Now the beverages – that was another story (my sodas are important to me). I didn't expect my Diet Cherry Dr. Pepper, but they didn't even have Diet Coke. All sodas were Pepsi, Shasta or Schweppes products only. I ordered Diet Pepsi and every time, without fail, I was brought two short six ounce cans of regular Pepsi. I pointed this out and the server would call for someone to bring up the Diet Pepsi, and she would leave the cans of regular on my tray. When Mike visited, he would line up the non-diet sodas on the top of the small chest of drawers, amassing quite a collection.

During every visit, Mike gave me a very detailed account of what orders had gone out. I had tried to get Mike to wait until I got home before sending out orders, but he said we needed to maintain our great shipping record, so he was up until all hours of the night finding the scarves -- matching the computer listing photo to scarves in our numbered baggies. This is not an easy task for a man who is color-blind and still doesn't know silk from burlap.

He fessed up to a few things: He was using the tissue paper for wrapping, but he wasn't putting ribbons on the packages. "I can't tie a bow, and you know that!" I also learned that no newsletter was going out with the packages. He ran out of them and didn't know how to find the computer file to print more. "Besides, I don't know how to print front and back," he reminded me.

But most worrisome, Mike thought he may have sent the wrong order to a new customer, but he wasn't sure. I gave him some suggestions on how to figure it out, but it was above his head and above my head, too, as I was reeling from Oxycodone and Dilaudid. I finally told him to do the best he could, "but just don't tell me about it until I get home."

I laughed as I told Mike about the request from Lisa to bring in some scarves, but he didn't think it was funny. He thought it was a great idea. "I'll get some together tomorrow," he said.

"Mike!" I said with a touch of horror at the gills. "She'll probably forget all about it. Please don't bring it up!"

"Why not? We could make a few sales."

"Mike! This is not a flea market!"

"Okay, okay, I won't bring it up."

Dinner arrived. This time, I got the Yankee Pot Roast, but I ordered broccoli and there were green beans on the plate. And on my tray, there were two short cans of regular Pepsi. Mike had ordered a guest tray and was served the same substitution. When we pointed out the usual problem with the Pepsi, the server again called room service to ask for 4 cans of Diet Pepsi. The sugared Pepsis went into our collection.

At about 6:45, Lisa and her nurse came in to see me during rounds. Their business included writing their names on the dry erase board, routine with each shift. Thank goodness Lisa didn't mention anything about scarves, I was thinking as they were walking out the door. But she ducked her head back in and said, "I'll be back as soon as we finish our rounds."

Caught!

"Oh, I'm so sorry, I forgot to tell Mike about it," I said later when Lisa and two other aides dropped in, apparently expecting to see a boutique display of vintage scarves draped around the room, hanging from the IV pole and stacked on the rolling tray table. The ladies were clearly disappointed as they stood by the window holding up their arms and twirling around to capture the cool air.

"I'll be back tomorrow night," Mike said. But Lisa said she was off the next night, so it would have to be the following night. She had spoken, and Mike seemed to think we had to obey.

Talking about how much she loved scarves, Lisa said, "I don't always wear these scrubs, you know." One of her friends wanted a big silk scarf with some flowers on it. "Do you have anything like that?"

"I like bright colors," Lisa chimed in and went on to say she knew of several more people who were interested in scarves, and she would tell them they had to wait two more nights. She was saying something to the other aide, wondering how she could get her older daughter up there to buy some scarves, as I whispered to Mike, "You are in sooooo much trouble!!"

The very next morning, an aide I had not seen before – Keesha was her name, according to the board -- told me she was looking forward to seeing my scarves. Her shift would be over, but she would come and take a gander before she went home, she assured me.

"How did you hear about the scarves?"

"There's a notice on the bulletin board over at the nurses' station."

I was a celebrity, and apparently this spa didn't protect the privacy of its VIPs.

Day Five and the big scarf fete was scheduled for that evening "after seven thirty." It was the first thing I thought about when I woke up and ordered from room service. This is another fine mess my husband got us into. Was there a gracious way out? Maybe. When my doctor came by early afternoon, I started the spiel. I was better. I could go home, I insisted. I'll have less stress at home, I could tend to my business, and maybe the oral medication would work at this point. I would faithfully go to the wound center the next morning. Or, if you'd rather, I could come in for an outpatient IV therapy for a couple of hours a day. Or....

Am I on trial here? I realized I was talking and talking without letting the doctor get a word in. I stopped abruptly and let her talk.

And talk, she did. Lecture might be a more appropriate word. She told me I should put my health first. "Without your health, there is no business," she said. "There's plenty of time for that later." I needed a few more days, she insisted. I cowed like a scolded child and to each of her points said, "Okay. Okay. Okay."

I was too embarrassed to tell her about the evening scarf bazaar, though it did occur to me later that she didn't always wear that white lab coat. Perhaps the doctor could use a nice silk scarf in jewel tones to accentuate her exotic complexion.

Mike wandered in about 6:30, an hour before the show. He had a small suitcase with about fifty scarves he had grabbed off the stack we hadn't yet listed. He also had a handful of flyers to pass out to browsers. We artfully arranged the folded scarves, not thinking that within minutes, the display would be a mess from the frenzy. When the nurse popped in to adjust the IV, I thought we were busted, and she might even confiscate the scarves.

"Oh, these are beautiful, you'll sell a lot," she said while unfolding a light blue floral silk Oscar de la Renta long scarf. "Can you save this one for me? I don't want it gettin' gone before I can come back in here."

Mike jumped up and wrote her name on a flyer, tucked it into the fold of the scarf and set it on the closet shelf. One down. As the nurse left the room, I realized I missed the battle-axe nurses from *Marcus Welby, M.D.* and *The Doctors* with their starched dresses, white stockings and caps. They would never have allowed this kind of shenanigans in a hospital room.

Lisa came by and said she just wanted to make sure we were ready. She also needed a break to cool off, she said, even though she had only been at work a half hour or so. Mike asked her how many people to expect later on, and Lisa said she didn't know if word had traveled beyond the third floor. Further, her daughter would not be able to come at all. "There may be a few people." She proceeded to count off names of co-workers and rate the probability of their coming to the party.

When there was an opening in the conversation, I asked Lisa if there was a hair salon in the hospital. I didn't care about styling, but I felt desperate to get my hair washed. No salon, she said, "but I'll wash your hair for you." She explained how she did it with two wash tubs of water and a few towels. "You won't get wet at all… 'cept your hair."

"Oh, no, I can't take up your time like that."

"It's okay, I do this sometimes for people," said Lisa. "We'll do it later on tonight." It didn't take much to placate me. Clean hair, room service, and a shot of Dilaudid in the IV can work wonders.

"Come on in, we're giving the hospital discount tonight," Mike said as he greeted people.

"You forgot to bring the balloons for the door," I said dripping with sarcasm, but Mike offered to go down to the gift shop and get a few.

At one point, we had seven people in the tiny room, not counting Mike and me. I was sitting up in bed, with the IV still in the back of my hand, and we had scarves draped over the side safety rails. I don't know what was more popular – the scarves or the open window. Mike was giving deep discounts while I was shushing people, as it seemed to get louder and louder. (Don't they know there's a sick person here?)

Mike pointed to our stash of regular Pepsi, asking who wanted a drink. One of the aides left briefly to get some cups and a pitcher of ice, and Mike was passing out the drinks with one hand and taking in the cash with another.

"Are you sure it's okay with you that we drink your Pepsi's?" asked one of the aides. "We're not really supposed to eat or drink anything from a patient's room." I thought this was slightly ironic in the midst of the full-blown swap meet stall, still going strong. Both nurses and aides participated equally, in and out of the room, and even a male nurse from another other wing bought a scarf for his mother.

With this good turnout, I thought it was a shame that we didn't have some Tupperware to sell. I thought I saw a spot where it could be displayed.

My sister-in-law called during the pandemonium, but I told her I couldn't talk. She asked if there was a doctor in the room with me, and I quickly said, "No, we're hosting a scarf party, I'll call you later." As I hung up, I heard her laughing and telling my brother about our little fun fest.

Cool air and a free small cup of Pepsi on ice were effective sales tools. We sold thirty-something scarves and had over $150 in the till.

Except for an occasional straggler coming in to cool off, the party was over. Mike cleaned up the cups and cans and put everything back in place, packing up the leftover scarves. A nurse came in, and I asked for my pain medicine. I was ready to wind down and try to sleep, relieved Lisa had gotten busy or forgotten about washing my hair.

Anderson Cooper was back on CNN chatting with a panel of experts when Lisa and another aide came in the door, turned the lights on and said, "I'm going to do your hair now."

"Are you sure you're not too tired?" I asked, hoping she would take the "out" and maybe we could do it the next night.

"No, I'm on duty until 6:30 in the morning - might as well keep myself busy." Indeed.

Lisa took full command of the room, directing her buddy, LaTonya, to put warm water in both wash tubs. I pulled out my own shampoo from my tote bag and Lisa examined the bottle, front and back, for some time and said, "I guess we can use this." I feared I might have upset her routine. "You come and sit in this chair," directing me to the guest chair under which she had placed several towels. She wrapped a towel around my neck and began. LaTonya had made herself comfortable in the recliner, moving it closer to the window. She was watching TV, fanning herself with a newspaper and repeating "aaaahhhhhh."

I've never had such a head scrubbing, probably since I was about 10, when I cooked up a purple Kool-Aid hair "dye", which did indeed turn my hair a reddish purple. I loved it. I was all about peace, love and tie-dyed shirts, but my mother wasn't impressed and scrubbed the daylights out of my hair. The dye faded a bit, but I remember it did not come out for some time.

Lisa artfully used the washtubs to rinse and repeat, even though I told her once was really enough. She said she always does it twice, just like the salons do. As promised, I didn't get wet at all, and neither did the floor. I don't know how she managed that. All the soap was out of my hair, too, so clean it squeaked, as Lisa proudly demonstrated.

"Ow!"

"Am I hurting you?" Lisa asked as she used a comb to tackle a few tangles.

"Well, no, I guess not," I mumbled, wondering if I had lost a hunk of hair. I thought I best not complain.

"You'd look pretty with blonde hair," she said, thoughtfully. "You'd look younger."

"You think so?" I asked, amused, as I'd never once entertained the idea of going blonde.

"Um-Hmm. LaTonya, wouldn't she look good with blonde hair?" Without even waiting for an answer, Lisa said, "I could do it for you, too. I have a lot of experience with hair, and I'm good with styling."

"Oh, did you go to beauty school?"

"No, but I've read a lot of books about it."

"Oh wow!" was all I could think of to say, contemplating how one gets hair styling experience from reading books. At that moment Pam, my nurse, came in to check my IV. I thought sure someone would be in hot water over the little pajama party we had going on.

"Pam, don't you think Ms. Kane would look pretty as a blonde?"

Pam stood back and gave me the once-over, and said "I think it would complement your complexion to go a little lighter."

Oh dear. There were three of them who could gang up on me and whip out the bleach. "No, I'd really have to give it a lot of thought first." Pam's job was done, and she left the room.

"Why don't we cut it just a little bit?" Lisa suggested. "It would be so pretty chin-length." I wondered just which chin she meant.

"Lisa can cut it, she's real good," LaTonya said, suddenly interested and breaking away from the TV. I thought the pink foam rollers were going to roll out any time now, and we could all jump on the bed and make crank calls to boys, just like Doris Day at a slumber party.

After a brief pause, acting as though I was considering Lisa's cut, the best I could come up with was "I appreciate your offering, but I am trying to grow it out."

"Hon', you need it shorter," Lisa said again.

I didn't know how I was going to get out of this. "That's a good idea, Lisa, but let me think about it, okay?"

"Okay," she agreed, obviously disappointed. I felt like a heel.

Earlier, when I had foraged for my shampoo, I put a $10 dollar bill in my pocket so I could tip Lisa. She was sitting on the bed, resting, helping herself to a cup of ice water and I gave her the money, discreetly, feeling awkward with LaTonya nearby.

Lisa stood up, abruptly, and said "What's this?"

"Just a little something to thank you."

Lisa handed the money back to me and said, "I take my payment in blessings." As she picked up the towels and put them in the laundry bin, she expounded on the subject and said she was truly blessed to be able to help people and make them feel better. I didn't know what to say, except "thank you." Lisa and LaTonya left my room, leaving the lights on, the door open and the remote control across the room on the windowsill.

On Day Seven, my doctor came to visit while I was picking the brown and wilted pieces of iceburg lettuce out of my salad. I could go home that afternoon, she announced, with a big smile. I was pleased, but at the same time apprehensive about leaving the cocoon. I even suggested it might be better for me to stay one more day. "You've been so anxious to go home," she said, "I already put in the paperwork."

"Oh, okay, thanks."

While she proceeded to discuss my post-hospital plan, it dawned on me that going home meant cleaning and updating the mess I feared my husband had made with the business. Sure, Mike shipped out orders, and was very proud of it. But he saved a copy of each packing slip so I could back-pedal on record-keeping.

It did feel good to be home, and Mike was an attentive nurse-maid, smothering me with instructions and "doctor's orders." It took about a week to catch up our business, on top of keeping current with the new orders flowing in. We did the best we could to reconstruct the sales, but nothing much balanced out for that big week when I was absent.

I learned what *did* add up after my first week home when I went to the Wound Center for my first post-hospital appointment: My leg was swollen and oozing because I hadn't spent enough time elevating my legs, as instructed. I got a lecture from the nurse and then from the doctor, too. ("The infection could come back! Is that what you want?") It's hard to elevate the legs when one is in front of a 24" computer monitor eighteen hours a day, but I was scared straight, vowing to take regular breaks to take care of my health business. I recalled from my childhood that my grandmother was always fretting over the need to elevate her legs. And here I was.

* 12 *

I Have Broad Shoulders (But The Life Jacket Fit)

"You're braver than you believe, and stronger than you seem, and smarter than you think." – A. A. Milne

I was weary and my shoulders ached. Mike and I had been packing orders all day without much of a break, and I had just ironed a basketful of scarves. I wanted to ask Mike to rub my shoulders with Ben Gay, but I heard him on the phone in the bedroom. I surmised he was talking with our niece when I heard him grilling her about a new boyfriend. Mike's obsession is talking on the phone – no, let's just make that talking, period.

It was only about eight, but since Mike was temporarily unavailable, I declared myself finished for the evening. I moved the ironing board to the side of the chair and pushed away several plastic bins of silk squares I had sorted earlier. I felt what I called a "good tired." It had been a great day to stay indoors, avoiding the January weather, and I was grateful our business allowed us to work at home. These scarves were a particularly fortunate "get," and I knew I could flip them quickly. In just the small batch I ironed, I came across scarves with names like Anne Klein, Adrienne Vittadini, Pierre Balmain, Elsa Schiaparelli, and Vera.

Surveying the living room, which we often called the adjunct office and holding room, I realized what a wreck it was. UPS came earlier bringing several cartons filled with another large lot of scarves we had won at auction. We would take them to our warehouse when we sorted and re-packed everything into bins. As usual, Trash was the largest pile, and it would go to the dumpster in the morning. I recalled Bette Davis' famous movie line: "What a dump!"

I pulled over the ottoman, slumped down in the chair and propped up my legs, as I was still under strict doctor's orders to keep my legs elevated as much as possible. Ahhhh. I was ready to watch some TV.

Fiddling with the remote control, trying to decide which program to watch was the biggest problem I had at the moment. We had a pot of fresh green beans with onions, red potatoes and fresh dill slow-cooking on the stove. The aroma reminded me it was suppertime.

"Mike!" I hollered, concerned the beans might run out of liquid and burn. "Mike!"

"I'm on the phone!"

Debating whether I should get up and check the pot or keep yelling for Mike, I heard a sudden torrent of rain outside our patio door. Odd, I thought, we never get rain on our patio.

"Mike!" It sounded like a tsunami heading our way.

"Coming!"

And at that exact moment, three things happened: I turned the TV to the Weather Channel to check the radar; the fire alarms in the hallways of the building started their ear-piercing screeches; and it began to rain in the living room.

I took my feet off the ottoman, stood up and noticed Mike had wandered in. "What happened?" he asked, as though I had suddenly decided to clean the apartment.

Water was pouring in through the sprinkler outlets, the chandelier, and the baseboards. "Get a trash can!" I yelled, not yet realizing this was beyond the occasional drip that prompts a collection bucket. It occurred to me that grabbing a trash can was akin to saying "boil some water" when a woman goes into labor. Mike brought over the trash can and several plastic garbage bags, but it was ridiculous to try and capture the torrents. By that point, we had about three inches of water on the floor, and counting.

The scarves I just ironed were on the floor, wet and soggy with all-new wrinkles. They would have to be re-ironed, I mused, and then I realized all the cartons of scarves were saturated. The walls were wet…. the furniture was wet… the ceiling fan spewed water with every rotation. I noticed my books and knick-knacks were ruined. It was raining all over the photo albums of our wedding, our families and our travels. The force of the water had knocked our silver candlesticks from Mike's grandmother to the floor, the top broken off one. I picked up the little piece and put it in the pocket of my nightshirt.

"Should we call the fire department?" I asked. Maybe it was time to take some action.

While Mike called 911 ("it's raining in our apartment") and then our apartment maintenance emergency number (getting voice mail), I got dressed and urged Mike to do the same. My clothes from the day were draped over the back of a dining room chair, and I put my blouse on over my nightshirt and pulled on the pants that were already half-soaked. I grabbed my pocketbook and my Keds and headed to the hallway bare-footed. Mike put his jeans on over his sweatpants and quickly looked into the office and the bedroom. "Oh, God, it's really bad!"

"Come on!" I was worried about electrical shocks, as the power was still on even as the torrential "rain" continued. Mike was looking around the bedroom and I yelled, "Grab the jewelry drawer from the armoire!"

"Should I turn off the beans?" Mike asked as we walked toward the front door. Bet there was plenty of liquid in the pot now. Was he thinking we would take a break shortly and eat some string beans?

We left the apartment with the (dirty) clothes on our backs and wet shoes. I had my wet pocketbook slung over my shoulder, and I carried the velvet-lined antique drawer holding my jewelry. I berated myself for not storing more of my "valuables" in our safe deposit box. For some reason, Mike grabbed a laundry basket of clean underwear and pajamas from the counter as we passed by. "Might as well," he said. (I realized later what a convenient decision it was.) And as we passed the hall closet, he grabbed both our coats (not yet wet). We were out. We were safe.

People from our building had already congregated on the steps to the second floor. It looked like the circus came to town and they were sitting on the bleachers, waiting for the elephant walk. The carpet in the first floor hallway was wet and tenants from all four floors said their carpet was soaked, though no one else had experienced flooding from above. We were all waiting -- for the fire truck and the maintenance crew to arrive, for the flooding to stop, and just to see how things played out, I suspect.

Even though the hallway was inside the building, it was very cold. I found a space on the bottom step and sat down, putting the drawer with the family jewels close by my side. I put my pocketbook on top of the drawer to try and hide the loot from prying eyes, but I saw that water was seeping from the pebbled leather and I quickly moved it. There was no way to hide a whole drawer of sparkly diamonds, emeralds and

pearls. Well, maybe one diamond, one emerald and one or two pearls --
and lots and lots of semi-precious and fashion jewelry.

I had a tough decision to make: *Should I put on wet shoes or stay
barefoot?* Heck, it was about 10 degrees outside, my pants were soaked
almost to my knees and my blouse was damp. I accepted the fact that
I would get a bad cold, then possibly pneumonia, in short order. Mike
definitely would, too, I was sure. I put on my shoes.

My husband was holding court, describing the chain of events in
our little home to the audience. I noticed he omitted the part where he
was in the other room when the action began.

Our neighbors, who were no more than acquaintances, were very
friendly. While concerned about wet floors in their own apartments,
they offered us hot coffee and a blanket. One woman asked if we
would like some macaroni and cheese she had made for dinner. At one
point, I noticed my reflection in the window. My wet hair was curled
and matted to my head. I was wearing the leopard print blouse but the
knee-length aqua nightshirt with the butterfly print was showing in the
neckline and sticking out below the blouse. *This is sooo not me.* I didn't
even care. I rested my head against the wall, made an effort to breathe
deeply while the fire alarm was blaring, surely damaging my hearing,
and waited.

Several people asked Mike if he wanted help getting some things out
of the apartment. I was nearly hysterical hearing this, and I reminded
Mike about the possibility of shocks. Don't go back in there, I insisted.
The stairway crowd seemed to have mixed (unsolicited) opinions, some
siding with me and some with Mike. I wondered if we should call for
a vote. A few minutes later, I looked around and noticed Mike was not
in the hallway, and the apartment door was open. I got up and hobbled
into the apartment with my drawer, my pocketbook and my cane -
squish, squish – the water was above my ankles. My feet felt frozen. I
called for Mike and the guys to please come out. The water was still
pouring in, while the TV was blasting a recipe for low carb oven-fried
chicken. I was relieved my husband finally listened to me. He came back
out to the hallway with an armful of file folders, and his entourage of
four was empty-handed.

After forty minutes, the brigade arrived. There were two fully-
decked-out fire trucks, a car and an ambulance on our cul-de-sac. It
would've been easy to just escape, slip into denial mode, and ask to be

taken to the hospital. I was seriously considering it, but I couldn't leave Mike there to deal with the crisis alone. He needed me.

"Is everybody out of their apartments?" one fireman asked, scanning the hallway, while another turned off the alarms. A third asked if anyone knew where to find the water valve shut-off. No one had an answer for either question, so while a fireman went door-to-door to the sixteen apartments in the building asking everyone to get out, a couple others joined the hunt for the water source.

A few minutes after the fire department arrived, our maintenance manager, Candee, ran in the door. She had driven from her home across town and was out of breath after running from the other side of the parking lot to our unit. She directed the firemen to the rear of the building and after a while, they came back in and Candee announced the water was cut off. Everyone started whooping and gave them a round of applause. Apparently a pipe had burst in the unit above ours, we were told. We would later learn that more than five pipes broke from the frigid weather, as did pipes in many other apartment and condo buildings around freezing Baltimore.

Mike asked the fireman in charge if we could go into the apartment to get a few things and was abruptly told it wasn't safe. (I thought about offering my "I told you so" dance to Mike, but I was way too tired.) The fireman was very kind and offered to go in himself and get one armload of things if Mike could tell him specifically what to get. I remembered a beloved painting on the wall of the living room, but I knew it was soaked, so I didn't see the point.

Mike started a list, first asking for his cell phone, which was charging on the kitchen counter and his laptop on the dining room table. "Could you look in the armoire and get the red sweater on the middle shelf?" Mike requested. I had to snicker; that red "Mr. Rogers" sweater was his favorite, a hand-knit bulky cotton cardigan with a shawl collar, tie belt and pockets. It was a very expensive sweater we had bought at a deep discount at Bergdorf's on one of our jewelry show trips.

There was one more thing Mike asked the fireman to bring out to the hallway, and that was a large carton with over a hundred boxes of Kleenex we had in a corner of the office. Bought with coupons – doubled – so that it was less than a dime per box, Mike had stocked up and was proud of his stockpile.

"What did you say was in this box?" said the fireman.

"Kleenex!"

"Well, you don't want it. It's soaking wet. Just leave it be."

Mike looked like someone took away his retirement fund, as he turned to me and said, "Terri, we lost the Kleenex."

I wasn't nice. "Who cares! That's the least of our problems right now. Forget it!" I regretted my comment as soon as it came out of my mouth. Again, I leaned my head against the wall and closed my eyes.

A plan. We needed a plan. Plan A, Plan B… I always had a plan. But that night, I didn't have a clue what would happen next, as we all waited for the authorities to say or do something. It was a rare time when I would welcome being told what to do. Right then, during the lull, the manager and assistant manager of the apartments came in the door together, their jaws dramatically agape, seeing and hearing about the damage. Both had on knee-high boots with high heels, and it was entertaining watching the ladies uncomfortably step through the water, ruining the footwear.

"Don't worry," Scotia, the manager, told us in her best Superwoman voice after she had toured our apartment. "You can stay in the model apartment as long as you need to." This was a relief, as it had crossed my mind we should check around for a hotel reservation. One decision made for us. While she was talking, Scotia was wiping off her boots with a Kleenex, but that made it worse because the shreds of the tissue embedded into the suede. Then she stepped back into the water anyway. What was she thinking?

Mike was on the phone calling our insurance company. On his farewell spin through the apartment, he had retrieved the policy from the file cabinet. It was damp, but fully readable. Fortunately, we knew we had ample coverage with our tenant policy, as Mike learned from his father that good insurance coverage is never a waste of money. Mike was pacing the hallway, yelling at someone on the phone while I sat motionless on the steps, feeling like I was in a daze. My mind went from worrying if we would be out of business for a while and, if so, what would be our financial plan. Then, suddenly hungry, I wondered what we might have for supper.

On hold, Mike walked over and said he got a recording on the claims number that only emergency calls were accepted after 9 PM, Eastern Time. It was a little after eight, Eastern Time, but he had to punch certain buttons regarding the nature of the call and then was put on hold for a live person. After twenty minutes, a (sort of) "live" person told him he would get a call back from an adjuster within 24 hours, and the call was over.

Someone from the stairway congregation heard Mike giving me the update and said we had been snookered: "You should call back and demand an adjuster *tonight*. Everything you own is ruined!" Others echoed, "Yeah! Go for it," "Get 'em!" and "Give 'em hell!" The troops were ready to fight for us.

Mike felt empowered now, and re-dialed the claims number, once again pacing the wet hallway—squish, squish. Although I knew Mike was really quite worried, at least he was occupied and had probably forgotten about the tragic Kleenex incident.

After touring the building and primping along the way, Scotia announced the water had started to drain from apartments on the upper floors. The carpet was wet, but most tenants were cleared to go back home, with the promise that fans were on the way to help dry out each apartment.

"I thought they'd put us up in a hotel," one man from the fourth floor complained, as he started the long haul back up to his apartment. "I can't believe they expect me to sleep in a wet apartment tonight."

After about twenty minutes, Mike hung up rather than continue holding. With help from some of the stairway lingerers, we put our meager saved items in the car and drove to the model apartment where Scotia met us.

"Terri, aren't you glad we have sodas in the car?" Mike asked. "Otherwise, I'd have to go to the store and get some." Truthfully, I was glad, but somehow felt it was wrong feeling grateful for a 12-pack of half-frozen cans of Diet Cherry Dr. Pepper and Diet Mountain Dew. Scotia helped Mike carry the drinks and our laundry basket into the small model apartment while I waited in the car. I would be Mike's second "load."

The sidewalk was icy, my legs were throbbing, and my feet were numb. I was afraid I would slip and fall, really needing the ambulance. Thankfully the model apartment was on the first floor, but there were several outside stone steps to navigate and then once inside the building there were more steps to get to the model. Holding onto Mike with one hand and my cane with the other, I made it inside the building only to slide, but not fall, on the wood floors. When I finally hobbled over the threshold to the model, I collapsed on the seat closest to the door, an uncomfortable little dinette chair. But I was so relieved to be safely inside a dry room and feel the glorious heat, I thought I might stay in that chair forever.

"Do you need anything?" Scotia asked. I considered the irony of the question, but answered that we were fine. Yes ma'am, Terri and Mike were just fine. We had everything we needed. Shortly after Scotia closed the door behind her, reality started to settle in. This would now and forever be the night of the Great Flood of '14.

The apartment was nicely decorated. Or, *over*-decorated, as though the designer had just left the premises. The draperies matched the throw pillows and lampshades, and the furniture was a matchy-matchy living room "suite." There was artwork on the wall that picked up the aqua and navy colors of the room, and a large aqua and navy glass bowl was on the coffee table. I suggested to Mike that we not touch anything.

I took off my shoes and Mike brought me a nightshirt and underwear from the clean laundry basket. I changed on the spot, still in the chair. He put on his PJs and immediately put our wet clothes in the washer. I hadn't realized Mike, ever resourceful, had also rescued a box of laundry detergent from the flood.

Mike sat down in the large armchair (which tastefully matched the sofa, drapes, wall art and glass bowl). He sighed and said, "We're safe." We sat in silence for a while, both still stunned. I moved over to the sofa and asked if he'd seen the remote control for the TV. He looked around and then pointed out that it was a plastic façade fake "TV" sitting in the entertainment armoire. I thought we might not get cable, but it never occurred to me we wouldn't even get a TV.

We were too tired to put the sheets on the bed. Mike sprawled out on top of the bedspread and was out cold in sixty seconds. I feared the spread might be dirty, which was really funny because I felt absolutely filthy myself at that point. (We decided to take showers in the morning since we still felt partially frozen.) I spread out the borrowed sheet on the sofa, leaned back, and tried to relax.

It was hard to fall asleep without the racket of cable news, a rerun of *Everybody Loves Raymond* or even an infomercial for miracle face cream in the background. But I dozed off at some point, and woke up when I heard Mike screaming on the phone at someone I gathered was from our insurance company.

"I need an adjuster to meet me over here at 9 AM, *today!*" Mike said. "All our possessions are rotting, and we don't have time to wait another day." I checked my watch and saw it was a few minutes after eight.

Mike raised his voice even more: "I don't care if you're busy! I need some help, and your company is contracted to help me."

"Put your boss on!" Mike demanded. I didn't need to hear the other end of the conversation to know what was going on.

"What do you mean, you don't have a boss? Do you own the company?"

"I didn't think so. Just put on the person who supervises you."

"Well, go interrupt the meeting and tell them it's time to get to work!" Mike's voice was getting louder and louder.

"No, I'll hold…. No… No, I won't wait for a call back. Go get someone *now!*"

I was about to burst into tears seeing my husband acting like a crazy person. "Mike, be nice," I pleaded. "Please calm down."

"I will wait on hold for three minutes and if your boss doesn't come on the line, I will hang up and call right back. THREE MINUTES, I'm telling you! Do you understand?"

"*Mike!*"

And then he was on hold. Mike was watching the clock on the oven.

"Please just calm down…" I was worried.

"Terri, this is important! They have two more minutes…"

"Mike…," I said, but he held up his hand indicating his phone adversary had come back on the line. (And with time to spare.)

"Okay… okay… okay…" said my husband, almost nicely. "Well, exactly what time do you mean by 'the end of the day'"?

"And what's your boss' name and number in case we don't hear from anybody by five?" Mike scribbled the info on a napkin, and then the call was over.

"We are supposed to hear from the adjuster by five," he told me, "but if we don't hear by four, I am going to call. I can't wait until tomorrow."

I was just relieved he was off the phone.

Insurance companies sure aren't like you see on TV. We didn't have a friendly agent bringing a breakfast of bagels and cream cheese to us this morning after a disaster and reassuring us about the company's commitment to help. Agent? We didn't even have an agent – friendly or otherwise. This was an over-the-phone kind of policy, Mike told me. Still, it was a comprehensive policy from a major company that included flood damage, unlike many tenant policies. Mike had done a good job selecting the coverage and avoiding shortcuts to save money. I was grateful.

"Let's get going," Mike said.

"Where? I was going to try to go back to sleep."

"We have orders to ship."

I couldn't take a shower. There were towels in the bathroom closet, but they were navy blue (which matched the living room décor) and they didn't seem clean. They were props for display purposes only in the model apartment. Meanwhile, Mike walked around with one of the towels around his waist, shaving himself while he unloaded his jeans and shirt from the dryer. He dressed and carried our belongings out to the car in Hefty Bags found under the sink. We owned two sets of nice luggage, but here we were, shuffling our few remaining possessions in disposable plastic bags.

I put on my freshly washed pants, blouse and Keds (minus the nightshirt underneath) and we were out the door. It was frigid, about 18 degrees and I didn't have my scarf, gloves or lambswool hat I had bought at least a decade earlier. I only wore it a few times a year, on the coldest days, and I missed it now. I recalled seeing it the previous night, totally soaked, sitting on my coffee table.

We went to the bagel shop around the corner and got our own breakfast. We had been too preoccupied to feel hungry; we hadn't eaten dinner the night before and didn't even miss it.

"What's the plan?" I asked Mike.

"We are going to get out orders, same as always."

"We can't go back in the apartment!" I was mortified.

"Why not? We'll stop by maintenance and see if it's safe to go in. By the time we get the orders packed up and go to the post office, it will be time to start hounding the insurance company again."

The details unfurled: We would ask the ladies in the apartment office if we could print our packing lists from Mike's laptop. We would take the lists to the apartment and pull the scarves on order. Our working inventory of V-Cart-listed scarves was in zip-lock bags filed in uncovered bins, and should have survived the flood. But just in case, we remembered we had sealed rolls of paper towels in the apartment and could wipe off any residual floodwater.

I knew it would be a long day, as I blindly followed my husband to the apartment clubhouse and office. Mike talked with Scotia, explaining about the printing. We had eighteen orders and would print two packing lists per page – a quick nine page run. I fixed myself a cup of cappuccino at the coffee bar in the clubhouse and settled at a small table.

"I can't let you plug your computer into our system," I heard Scotia saying.

"Well, your printer doesn't have Wi-Fi, so it would have to be plugged in."

"I think you should try Staples," Scotia said coldly, like it was the final word.

What had happened to her since last night when she was so affable, wanting to help us "in any way possible"? I really didn't think we were asking too much. Matter of fact, on second thought, it occurred to me that Scotia should have brought that breakfast to us earlier.

Never one to let another have the last word, Mike asked her what she *was* willing to do to help us. She finally said we could work in the clubhouse all day if we needed to. Oh, and before she walked back into the office, she casually announced, "You'll need to make other arrangements because I can't let you stay in the model apartment another night."

Boom! It was a short route from "you can stay there as long as you need to," to "I can't let you stay there another night." We found out later in the day that someone from our insurance company had called to remind her of the apartment owner's liability, and it wasn't a pleasant conversation.

Before Mike even came over to join me, he was on the phone again with the same insurance person he intimidated earlier. He told her we needed to move to a hotel immediately and couldn't wait until the end of the day when the adjuster would (possibly) call us.

After several stints on hold and talking to various people, he was told someone from the accommodations service would call and secure a hotel for us "by the end of the day." We were homeless.

We talked with Candee, the bedraggled maintenance manager, and she said it was safe to go back into the apartment briefly. The electricity was still on. They had wet-vac'd the floors during the night, Candee told us, and there were a couple of large fans blowing.

Walking back in the front door was heartbreaking. There was still standing water everywhere, and it was starting to stink. Almost everything we owned was soaked. We went into our spare bedroom, our office, which surprisingly had the least damage. We later learned that the sprinklers had not worked in the office so the water came down the walls and onto the floor only – not from "above." Everything lining the walls was ruined, but my desktop computer was safe. My printer was safe. We were still in business.

Mike's plan unfurled. I took my damp seat at the desk, my feet firmly planted on the wet carpet, and got to work. We took care of our paperwork, and the scarves in the plastic bags were fine. Our packing supplies were ruined, so after a trip to Staples to get paper and envelopes, we packed the scarves and got all the parcels ready to take to the post office. Each order was packed without a newsletter (soaked), without being wrapped in tissue paper (soaked) and without a ribbon (soaked). But the important thing was to ship on time. We couldn't let our customers down.

The next morning I awoke from a deep sleep and saw that I was in a hotel room, with Mike nowhere to be found. It took a minute or so to remember who I was, where I was, and what was going on. I vaguely recalled the night before, when Mike and a couple of his friends moved our salvageable essentials, setting up a temporary office/warehouse/living space. The insurance was paying for our lodging while the apartment was being repaired. We were offered a large suite, but that option was only available at a hotel across town by the casinos. Considering our world was enough of a crapshoot right then, and knowing Baltimore's legendary traffic problems, we chose a closer location. We needed to be near our PO Box, mini-warehouse and our apartment. The hotel we settled on was nice and new, two towns over, in the sub-suburbs, yet only seven miles from our apartment. There were no suites, but we had a handicapped-accessible room near the elevator which was larger than the standard room. The bins were already lined up in the extra wide hallway and a makeshift folding table for my computer, large monitor and printer was set up at the foot of the bed. Mike stationed his laptop and label printer on the hotel's desk in a dark corner. We would need a few extra lamps, but we were ready for business.

In my groggy haze, I answered our messages. I still didn't know where Mike was. I was going to call his cell, but I didn't have my reading glasses and couldn't see the directions on the room phone for outgoing calls. While I was on hold for the front desk, Mike came in the door with a breakfast tray.

"You're awake!" he said, as though it was usual for me to sleep this late.

"What time is it?"

"It's 10 AM. I just got up, too, but rushed downstairs before they ended breakfast service." I noticed Mike had on sweatpants, a sweatshirt and bedroom slippers. Apparently he was already too comfortable in our new diggs.

That first week, our daily routine included getting orders out the door and a trip to the apartment. It was still upsetting to see our belongings rotting away. The fans weren't "drying" anything, and the stench from the mold was so strong it made me gag. I don't know how anyone in our building managed to stay in their apartment with wet carpet. There was a sign requesting the outside door be left open to let in fresh air despite the record cold. Not surprisingly, the door was always shut when we dropped over.

Four days after the flood, we got a call from a woman who introduced herself as our insurance adjuster. Hallelujah! Things would get moving soon, we thought. "Here's what's going to happen," the adjuster told us on speakerphone. "The apartment management is responsible for draining out the standing water and drying out the floor. Then our recovery team comes in to evaluate and move everything from the apartment to their warehouses."

"Does the apartment management know they are supposed to do this?" Mike asked.

"Yes, but don't worry about it," the adjuster assured us, "We can make them do it."

I bet.

The adjuster and the recovery team captain would meet with us to discuss the process. The first available appointment was four days later – eight full days and nights since the flood. At least our case was finally getting some attention.

Apparently, the message to the apartment management wasn't clear. We continued our daily visits, and we took photos with the time and date stamp on the camera to show the lack of progress. I took pictures of the closets and our clothes, our shoes and my pocketbooks, still wet with mold starting to sprout, and our soggy and buckling wedding photo album. Mike's pictures were more practical; he got many shots of the large hole in the ceiling of the bedroom walk-in closet where the pipes initially broke through. He showed the drapes in the living room that got so heavy from being saturated that the rod fell off the wall. Mike also shot the mold growing on top of the baseboards and on the furniture, above the waterline.

Included in his photography portfolio were plenty of pictures of the inside of both the pantry and the refrigerator, so we could claim the loss of food. The camera's preview pane showed artful photos of a dozen tins of imported sardines and two dozen cans of tuna in the pantry (my husband's double coupon deals). The cans were wet, but I thought sure they would eventually be salvaged. We had recently received a web order of gourmet herbs and spices, still in a padded envelope on a pantry shelf and now a moldy mess. Gone was the garam masala, harissa powder and pink sea salt. Staples like flour, sugar, Splenda, cartons of chicken stock and assorted tea and coffee pods were ruined. We lost all the regular refrigerator items… but we had great pictures! Mike even managed to take a couple of the pot of beans, rotting and moldy on the stovetop. We laughed at the time, at the beans and because I made Mike re-shoot several photos when I saw that his fingers were in the way of the lens. But it wasn't so funny when we got back to the hotel and I transferred the pictures to the computer. I filed them quickly, not wanting to look too carefully, or I might cry.

Every time we went in the door of our sad little home, it was clear nothing had changed. We would stop by the apartment office and ask the property manager when we could expect to see some action, but the answer was always the same: "Give me some time. I'm working on it." And then ultimately, "Next week."

After several visits, I refused to go into the apartment and sat in the car while Mike made the pilgrimage. When he came out, he was shaking his head indicating things were still the same.

With the exception of the property manager, people were happy to see us. We had neighbors come out to see us and ask questions, both in the parking lot and in the clubhouse. Candee would see our car parked by the office, and she'd stop in to say hello. We ran into a woman at

Staples who recognized us and asked about the flood. A neighbor called on our cell phone one evening to say we had received several packages from UPS and they were left outside our door in the damp, rancid hallway. We couldn't imagine how the neighbor got our names and phone number, but we were glad for the tip. Mike drove over and got the packages right away. This neighbor caught Mike in the hall and said she wanted us to come over for dinner soon, and just let her know when would be a good time. We were *disasterlebrities*.

Most days, we would sit in the clubhouse for a while and make some calls. The first would be to the insurance adjuster to tell her nothing had changed regarding our wet, moldy mess. She repeatedly told us she would call the management to see where in line we were.

We finally had our meeting with the recovery "team captain" and the adjuster. We all sat on the same hallway steps where we had waited the night of the flood. The adjuster explained the claims process, and defined terms such as "replacement value" and "depreciation." She grilled us with a long questionnaire, asking where we bought our clothes, what brands we favored in clothes and furniture, how old each piece of furniture was, and how long we typically kept clothes. She had a separate list of questions for our home business. And then she asked to verify our income.

"Do we really need to answer all of this?" Mike asked.

"You don't have to," she said, "but it will make it much harder for us to process your claim if we don't have this information."

We complied, primarily because we were too broken down to argue.

Again, the adjuster said Mike and I should not worry about the apartment management's lack of cooperation: "We'll handle that."

The recovery team captain said we could step into the apartment for just a few minutes if we needed to retrieve anything, but there was nothing further we wanted. A team of four arrived wearing gas masks, and we saw that a dumpster had been pulled up near our patio door for the express purpose of trashing our things.

I couldn't take the stench, so I went out and got in the car, put my head back and breathed deeply. Mike came out shortly, and we felt the gravity of the situation. Furniture was being tossed into the dumpster like it was chicken bones from last night's supper. Everything was going. When I saw the slant-top desk hurled out the patio and upended, I stopped watching the expo. We had been playing the "glad game" but it was harder now. It took some concentration; I was glad we had good insurance, glad we had each other, glad we had good friends, and glad it wasn't worse. We were truly grateful.

On the drive back to the hotel, Mike was uncharacteristically quiet until we pulled into the loading zone by the front door. I was in a wheelchair, because I hadn't been mindful about keeping my legs elevated since the flood and my left leg was sore and painful. Mike set up the folding wheelchair and pushed me to our room. I felt bad he had to tend to me when I knew he was worn out, so I suggested we take a rest and watch a little *Judge Judy*. Typically, whenever I suggested a little daytime rest, Mike would argue he didn't have time to rest, or he wasn't tired at all. This day, however, he said, "Okay."

We turned off the lights, turned on the TV and got underneath the covers. I watched Judy preside over the case of a pit bull biting a neighbor, and Mike slept. It felt good to be in a clean, dry room. I was sure we could tolerate the cramped quarters for another week or so.

It would be nine weeks later before we checked out. Mike and I felt closer than ever (literally). Our old apartment was empty and we were still waiting for the management to clean it, remove the carpet and the mold, which was considerable. We did our work and often went shopping in the late afternoons, starting to slowly replace items we lost in the flood. We bought clothes, shoes and underwear. I ordered a couple new handbags and bought a fresh round of my skincare, bath products and cosmetics. We had some time yet before we had to replace practical items like a can opener and a ceramic container of herbs de Provence.

There were some good things about getting all-new chattel, courtesy of our insurance company. But we mourned the loss of our beautiful armoire and a large oil painting my in-laws passed down to us. Other losses were not due to the flood directly; the restoration team fessed up about "misplacing" our Kitchen Aid Mixer (with four attachments), an antique sterling and glass pansy flower ring, and my mother's Joan of Arc sterling silverware service from her hope chest when she and my father married in 1952. I was sick over it, though I tried not to dwell on our losses. My sister-in-law commented she "couldn't believe" I hadn't fallen apart. *Was I supposed to take to my bed for a few months?* When friends and acquaintances offered their condolences, I would say, "Oh, it's okay! Really, it is," uncomfortable with the sympathy. I didn't consider our plight a real tragedy. I don't know why, but I never shed one tear.

One morning, Mike was in the laundry room of the hotel and I was typing a log of new scarves to be listed. Mike came in the door with a laundry basket, holding up something in his hand. "What's this?" It was the broken piece from the silver candlestick I had picked up the night of the Great Flood. It was in the pocket of my nightshirt and had survived a round in the washing machine. I smiled. We would get our candlesticks fixed and our lives repaired. Eventually.

Our days and nights weren't all gloom and doom by any means, and we had some fun with the living arrangement. We joked about living out of town, outside of the beltway for the first time. We referred to our hotel as our country home and our apartment as our city home. Friends came to see us in the country, where we met with them in the spacious lounge area adjacent to the lobby with complimentary coffee and hot chocolate. The lounge was decorated like a British Hunt Club with plenty of burgundy, gold and plaid. (Or at least, that's how all the British Hunt Clubs I have been to are adorned.) One morning, I held a committee meeting for a women's group in our lounge where we discussed plans for an upcoming fundraising dinner. The ladies enjoyed coffee with French Vanilla creamer and mini cinnamon rolls leftover from breakfast as we discussed the menu, centerpieces and speaker arrangements for our event. The day before, Mike had asked the desk clerk if we could get some goodies for the ladies to take home, like you might find in a swag bag: Small soaps, individual sizes of hand lotion, shampoos and conditioners and maybe a dozen tiny sewing kits, providing they still made those things. But the desk clerk had been too busy, she said, to gather the parting gifts.

The following week, on a cold, snowy night, I hosted my writer's group. We critiqued our pieces as we sat in the Hunt Club on comfy, overstuffed chairs, a roaring fire in the background and CNN softly playing on the wide-screen with no one watching.

Every day, Mike would take longer and longer to fetch our breakfast. He told me he met some guys at the buffet (many of whom were also bringing food back to their wives). They were at the hotel indefinitely due to a situation similar to ours. The pipes burst from the freezing cold in their apartment or condo, and their insurance company put them in the hotel until everything was fixed. The men sat around, commiserated, talked insurance strategies and ate waffles. When the guys had to leave for work, or to take their children to school, Mike would go through the buffet again and bring back some scrambled eggs and wheat toast for me – oh, and some hard-boiled eggs and a bagel or two with peanut butter for his mid-morning snack. (Mike insists when the food is free, the calories don't count.)

I never met these men from the Breakfast Club, but I heard all their stories. Mike told me the other married men said their wives were bitching and complaining about being stuck in a cramped hotel room. With pride, Mike said he pointed out how *his* wife was handling things just fine, never complained about anything, and was "cheerful." Oh, my! I didn't recognize myself. *Cheerful?* I wouldn't ever use words like cheerful, chipper or perky to describe myself, but I understood the gist of what Mike meant. I stood a little taller for a while.

Living and working in one room presented many challenges. With my erratic sleep patterns, I was up at all hours, usually sitting at the computer in the dark working, reading news, or playing jigsaw puzzles. Mike slept soundly most of the time, but occasionally he would get up and we would pack some orders or answer messages. I spent many evenings in the bathroom reading. It was the only room with enough light, and we had a comfortable chair at the spacious vanity table. This was my escape – until Mike would knock on the door and say he needed to use the toilet.

Maid service in the country home was tricky. Mike became friendly with Sandrine, the woman who covered our end of the hallway. He got fresh towels from her every morning and told her we only needed room cleaning every other day. When she came in to vacuum and tidy up, I sat at my desk in my nightshirt and continued working, as there was nowhere I could move to be out of the way. Everything in the room was "in the way" of something. Sandrine told us she recently immigrated from Cameroon, and we couldn't tell how much she understood, but we sure couldn't understand much of what *she* said in her Cameroon-French. Forget cleaning the desk area, Mike told her, and no need to change the bed sheets more than once a week (we handed back the bedspread and blanket to her the very first day – we've read how even nice hotels seldom clean those things). Vacuuming once a week would be sufficient, and the most important thing we asked her was not to spray her heavily scented room freshener. Apparently, this was one of the things that didn't translate, because she managed to get that spray in every visit on her way out the door. We would start gagging and Mike would open the window for a few minutes and let the clean, freezing air take a spin in our room.

There was something else that Sandrine understood only too well. Though we never handled the scarves when she was around, she somehow – perhaps by osmosis - knew there were scarves in the bins and cartons. One day, she asked if she could buy one. I said she could look in the top carton, where there were probably a hundred scarves waiting to be sorted, and pick out a few she liked, and there would be no charge. She was so happy, she immediately opened the carton flaps and started humming while she foraged for "a few" scarves, which turned out to be at least eight or ten, I think. I wasn't sure, but when she left, she carried an armful. I asked her to please not tell anyone about the scarves, as I didn't want a repeat performance of the hospital flea market opening up in our tiny temporary home.

Despite the crowded quarters, it wasn't altogether unpleasant working from the hotel. My desk was by the window where I had a good view of a big intersection and could offer traffic and weather reports. During the snowstorms, we didn't go out. As Mike said to everyone, "We're from the South," and we didn't cotton to ice and snow and northern drivers. When we tired of watching cable news, "Perry" or "L & O," we entertained ourselves by watching cars slide around when they were going way too fast for conditions. If it looked like they were going slow and still managed to slide, we empathized. We saw a tow truck rescue cars on the side of the road at least a dozen times during the storms, and we saw so many fender-benders we lost count. One afternoon, the snow was coming down and there was nearly a white-out. We heard a loud crash and then watched while two ambulances and two police cruisers came to the scene. We couldn't get a clear view of what happened, and we watched local news hoping to see a story about the accident outside our window. But there were so many car crashes around town that this one didn't make the cut.

There wasn't a comfortable chair in the room (other than in the bathroom), so when we weren't at our desks, we sat on the bed. With the large table desk at the end of the bed, I had a narrow sightline to the television. Unless I wanted to sit up, I had to lie on my side at a certain angle, with my head at the foot of the bed and watch through an opening between the computer tower and the printer. If I had stashed some papers in that cubbyhole earlier, I couldn't see the TV at all.

The hardest task to perform in the hotel room was ironing scarves and taking photos. The hotel provided an iron and mini-ironing board, but after the frustration of trying to use those, we bought a full-size board and a good iron... just two more things "in the way."

There was so much hotel-style artwork screwed to the walls, we were limited in finding a photo background. I suggested the inside of the shower, with a large, clean white wall of tile, but Mike didn't like that idea. We used the back of the room door. We didn't have great lighting in the hallway, so I had to kick up the colors with my photo software. On pictures of the sheerest scarves, you could make out the occupancy/rate card that hangs on the inside of every hotel room door.

We didn't have a full kitchenette in our room, only a tiny refrigerator and the smallest microwave I had seen. Every evening, we either went out to eat or brought dinner into our room. We didn't feel like traveling two towns over to pick up dinner at our usual dining spots in the city when there must have been a hundred restaurants within a one-mile radius of the hotel. We scouted the neighborhood for casual restaurants, preferably with healthy foods. We found our country Chinese carry-out, our country Italian restaurant that delivered, and our country sub and salad shop. Mike felt we were not being loyal to his buddies at the city places, but he tried to make new relationships with our temporary picks.

The Chinese restaurant lady wasn't friendly at all, Mike reported. She charged fifty cents for soup noodles (not noted on the menu) and argued every visit over his request for plastic forks and napkins. He explained about the flooding and living at the hotel, but she wasn't interested. At least the food was good there, as it was at the Italian joint. Tony, the owner, took Mike under his wing after hearing our story. Mike was given a discount on the first order, and Tony insisted we take two real knives, forks and spoons to the hotel to use until we settled back into our apartment. "You can't use plastic for good Italian food," Tony said.

We noticed the differences in our new country cuisine and our "usual" city fare. I reminded Mike that ours is a large country with diverse customs, tastes and recipes. It's what makes our nation great. So maybe the dumplings were made differently in the country than they were in the city. They were still very good! The lunch special paired chicken lo mein with fried rice – what a combination! Rice and noodles in the same Styrofoam container. And there were mushrooms in the lo mein; not so at our regular take-out place. We realized that perhaps country people have more of a hankering for woody-tasting wonders than do quasi-city folks. We had to respect their traditions, I told Mike. (Of course, that respect waivered the first time I ordered "no mushrooms" in the lo mein, and when I opened it at home, it was *mostly* mushrooms.)

Our city sub shop made meatballs without cheese in them (good for Mike's allergies), while the country sub shop not only added cheese, but also mixed in pork. Mike learned to live with a steak sub instead of meatballs.

Turns out, the sub shop owner was a cousin to the owner of our city sub shop around the corner from our apartment. While Mike waited for the order to be made, they discussed how busy the cousin's city shop was, and who's steak sub or Greek salad was better (Mike never committed). We discovered that sometimes a big salad with grilled chicken from a fast food place could be very good. The next time, though, the mixed salad greens would be half-wilted, or they would erroneously give me the salad with the canned mandarin oranges and slivered almonds.

Sometimes, we just couldn't decide between Szechuan Chicken and a turkey sub with cucumbers and tomatoes, hold the oil. Sometimes we just wanted a good ol' frozen dinner we could home-cook in our microwave. Mike would study the aisles of frozen foods at the grocery store, and I'd be on the phone with him from the hotel room.

"Turkey Pot Pie?" he asked.

"No."

"Hot Pockets?"

"No!" I'd never had a Hot Pocket and wasn't about to start down that road.

"Mrs. Paul's fish?"

"Mike…"

"How about a Stouffer's dinner?"

"Great. Surprise me."

Problem was, the meal he picked out came in a container that didn't fit into our microwave. But with our borrowed metal utensils, we scooped out the frozen portions of Salisbury steak onto paper plates pilfered from the breakfast buffet and nuked them individually. That worked! We had a delicious sort-of-homemade dinner, and we laughed about it all night.

It wasn't a bad life, but it wasn't *our* life. We still stopped by the apartment a few times a week to check on its progress. Nothing was happening, and Candee repeatedly told us they were having problems finding a contractor to do the work. She ended every conversation optimistically saying hopefully "next week" construction would commence.

Residing and working in one room (even with maid service, access to the spacious Hunt Club and Mike's Breakfast Club) began to wear on Mike and me. We made an appointment with a lawyer and learned that since no repairs had started within a reasonable amount of time and management could not provide us with a comparable apartment, we could give notice that we were terminating our lease. (Yes, as we expected, several months later they sued us. We won the case – without a lawyer - and they won a lecture from the judge on responsibility and the law.)

On Day 58 post-G.F., we signed a lease for a new apartment about a mile away from our old one. It was outside the beltway, which presented an altered view of our community, but we knew we could adjust. It was a much larger place with an open floor plan, huge walk-in closets and an attached garage. Concierge service was included and best of all, there were no steps for me to navigate with my leg problems. We didn't move in for another couple of weeks, until we could at least buy a few pieces of furniture, but things were starting to look up.

We bought two desks and a table, two good desk chairs and an entertainment and storage armoire for the guest room, also known as our new office. We found tall shelf units to hold the bins of scarves, had it all delivered in a few days. Mike and his friend moved over our computers and printers and set everything up. It was both convenient and functional, and before we actually moved in, we visited daily to do our work.

We didn't spend extra time at the new apartment because other than the office chairs, there was no place to sit. After an exhausting furniture hunt, we bought a swanky medium brown leather sectional sofa, a rustic dining room table hand-made from reclaimed wood and six "soft pumpkin" chairs. This was a departure from our old style, but it seemed to fit our new lives. We ordered a bed and linens online, and a large abstract print wool rug for the living room. Most everything was purchased at different stores, so delivery was erratic with a piece or two coming at a time. I was just hoping everything would coordinate.

We made it clear with the insurance adjuster that we couldn't move out of the hotel until we had our bed and sofa. We had anticipated an argument, but she said it was fine, just let her know when we were ready to move. It was a little bit of a relief to stay snugly in the hotel room for just a little longer. As the furniture came in, it looked good. But it was unfamiliar and – frankly -- not very welcoming.

The worst thing about the move was changing cable TV companies, but we didn't have a choice as the apartment complex had an exclusive contract. We got all the same channels, but they had different numbers. How could I learn all these new channels? It had taken me years to master them with the other service. The technician who installed our system left a laminated card chart for us, but the writing was so small, I couldn't even see the darn thing.

As luck would have it, our bed and sofa were the last two pieces of furniture to arrive because they came from a warehouse in the middle of the country. We couldn't stall any further; we were ready to move into our new lives.

When we checked out of the hotel, we were given a small party, complete with blueberry muffins and juice leftover from the breakfast buffet. All our new friends were there: The daytime desk clerk, the evening desk clerk (who was a computer student by day), the maintenance man, the groundskeeper, the breakfast ladies and Sandrine, wearing a bright, floral print silk scarf with her uniform. They were sorry to see us (and our generous tips) leave.

The first night in our new place, Mike asked, "Why am I so tired?" I was incredulous he would wonder about that.

"Shall I draw up a list of reasons for you?"

Neither of us said a word for the next few minutes. We both settled in nicely like bookends on the new sofa—Mike in the recliner and me in the chaise.

"Feels so good to just relax," Mike said as he fiddled with the remote control for our new, 42" flat-screen TV (with the new cable station numbers), mounted on the wall above the fireplace mantel. Mike was also holding (hoarding) a second remote control for the gas logs and soon had them burning at full blast. I could see we would have one more thing over which we could bicker. The fireplace was a pretty picture, but the air felt hot and heavy, and I had to start: "Mike, please turn down the logs. It's way too hot in here!"

"But isn't it nice that we have the fire going?"

"Fire? You mean the *remote control* fire?" I had resorted to sarcasm, as I realized my face was red and I had a few hives on my arms. (When I was a child and we enjoyed a rip-roaring fire in our real fireplace, I never imagined I would be able to operate a fake fire from a remote control.)

"Terri, do you know it's snowing outside?" Mike was adamant. "Besides, we need the extra heat because we don't have any throws to bundle up in."

"Maybe that remote control has a button that will move the fireplace to the patio, and then you can sit out there in the evenings," I suggested, making a mental note to add a couple of wooly-bully throws to my shopping list for the next day.

Mike found what he wanted to watch, right off. His learning curve for numbers was much faster than mine, so he already knew where to find all his programs. He tuned in during the middle of *Law & Order*. It was one of the earliest episodes, I could tell, because the stars looked so young. I had a moment of nostalgia thinking we had moved to Baltimore about the time that episode first aired. Phase Two of our married lives began with that gutsy gamble. Odds were probably about 2:1 we'd find success in Baltimo', but I'd say we broke the bank with our good fortune in business and the friends we made along the way.

And now, after the Great Flood of '14, we were starting Phase Three, and I don't think anyone would've bet against us. We had a new apartment and new furniture. We had new clothes and shoes and everything fit comfortably in the closets with room to spare. But we didn't have any pictures on the walls, we didn't have a glass in the cabinet for iced tea, and we didn't have a coffee table to sit the glasses on anyway. We had a tidy sum of insurance money in the bank so we could buy everything else we needed, but as much as I loved shopping, it was a real job buying all-new-everything. We had been to Big Lots where we spent $180 on necessities like shower curtain hooks, trashcans, a broom, a toilet plunger, a can opener and Febreze "Linen & Sky" air freshener ("the fresh clean scent of breeze-dried laundry touched with hints of sweet honeysuckle"... alright, whatever). Our shopping cart overfloweth.

Mike had begun re-stocking his cache of toilet paper and Kleenex while we were still at the hotel. I ordered new herbs and spices and had made a grocery run for some pantry staples: Soy sauce, Worcestershire sauce, flour in a shaker canister, K-cups, egg noodles, balsamic vinegar, couscous, Italian-flavored Panko breadcrumbs, and bulgur wheat. I had made tabouli with the bulgur years before, and I thought I might like to make it again soon. (But first, of course, I needed to get a bowl, a wooden spoon and a colander.) The larder wasn't bare.

———✺———

Sometimes things happen that make you realize how strong and resilient (and tired) you are. I don't know if we have another phase with major changes coming to us, but whatever happens, hopefully we'll have the grace and strength to see it through. Of our recent transition, Mike said we each deserved a pat on the back. We made it!

ABOUT THE AUTHOR

Terri Kane is an entrepreneur who runs her successful online sales venture from home. She has worked as a newspaper and magazine writer, owned two accessories companies, and has extensive experience in sales and marketing for the candy business. Her husband, Mike, is her partner in business and in life. They live in a suburb of Baltimore.